THE

GEOGRAPHIC

REVOLUTION IN

EARLY AMERICA

THE *Geographic* REVOLUTION IN EARLY *America* MAPS, LITERACY, AND NATIONAL IDENTITY

Martin Brückner

Published for the

OMOHUNDRO INSTITUTE OF

EARLY AMERICAN HISTORY AND CULTURE,

Williamsburg, Virginia,

by the UNIVERSITY OF NORTH CAROLINA

PRESS, *Chapel Hill*

The Omohundro

Institute of

Early American

History and Culture

is sponsored jointly by

the College of William

and Mary and the

Colonial Williamsburg

Foundation. On

November 15, 1996,

the Institute adopted

its present name

in honor of a bequest

from Malvern H.

Omohundro, Jr.

Set in Arnhem and Snell types
by Keystone Typesetting, Inc.
Manufactured in the United States of America

Library of Congress
Cataloging-in-Publication Data
Brückner, Martin, 1963–
The geographic revolution in early America : maps,
literacy, and national identity / Martin Brückner
    p. cm.
Includes bibliographical references and index.
ISBN-13: 978-0-8078-3000-0 (cloth: alk. paper)
ISBN-10: 0-8078-3000-3 (cloth: alk. paper)
ISBN-13: 978-0-8078-5672-7 (pbk.: alk. paper)
ISBN-10: 0-8078-5672-X (pbk.: alk. paper)
1. Historical geography—United States—Maps. I. Omohundro
Institute of Early American History & Culture. II. Title.
G1201.S1 B8 2006
911'.73—dc22   2005051412

cloth   10 09 08 07 06   5 4 3 2 1
paper   10 09 08 07 06   5 4 3 2 1

This volume received indirect support from an
unrestricted book publications grant awarded to the
Institute by the L. J. Skaggs and Mary C. Skaggs
Foundation of Oakland, California.

To Kristen

ACKNOWLEDGMENTS

Once, while working as a land surveyor in the German army corps of engineers, I was chased through a field by a bull. At the time, I little expected that my experience working with the land would set me on the path to this book.

Many people inspired, advised, and sustained me on the way. The faculty in geography and Americanistics at the Johannes Gutenberg Universität in Mainz, Germany, fostered my interest in cultural geography and literature. I am deeply grateful to my teachers at Brandeis University. Since the beginning of the project, Michael T. Gilmore has been a mentor and a friend; his attentive readings and unflagging enthusiasm for all things geographical provided encouragement as well as focus. Wai Chee Dimock watched the project evolve from an idea into a dissertation argument. Steven J. Harris introduced me to the history of science. At my dissertation defense, Leo Marx offered comments that still resonate now many years later.

In the course of writing the book I received help from many, providing everything from bibliographic tips to thoughtful comments to an exciting intellectual community governed by interdisciplinary curiosity and debate. I want to thank Tom Augst, Susan Courtney, James Curtis, Matthew Edney, Joseph Fichtelberg, Fritz Fleischmann, Ezra Greenspan, Bob Gross, Udo Hebel, Winfried Herget, Alfred Hornung, Mary Kelley, Ed Larkin, Leo Lemay, Robert Levine, Paul Mapp, Barbara McCorkle, Ben Mutschler, Joel Myerson, Dana Nelson, Vincent Pecora, Dan Richter, Klaus Schmitt, David Shields, Shirley Wajda, Doug Winiarski, and Julian Yates. I wish to acknowledge with great gratitude Patricia Crain, who took the time to read and talk about the manuscript; her comments made it a better book. I also want to thank the readers for the Omohundro Institute book series, in particular David Waldstreicher in history, and the two anonymous readers in geography and literature. Their comments and questions helped shape the book at a critical stage.

Research libraries, public and private, and their remarkable staffs have been the book's mainstay. I wish to thank particularly Georgia Barnhill, Joanne Chaison, John Hench, Tom Knowles, Marie Lamoureux, and Caroline Sloat at the American Antiquarian Society, and Roy Goodman at the American Philosophical Society. Iris Snyder and her staff at the Morris Library of the University of Delaware cheerfully hauled cartfuls of atlases and geography books. I am also grateful for comments by Jim Green at the Library Company of Philadelphia. Linda Eaton and Patricia Halfpenny at the Winterthur Museum and Library opened doors and drawers to rare objects and fabrics. Margaret Beck Pritchard, Laura Barry, and Catherine H. Grosfils provided invaluable access to rare prints and maps at Colonial Williamsburg. There are many more curators who helped me search for early American signs of geographic literacy, and I wish to thank summarily the staffs of the Bodleian Library at Oxford University, the Boston Public Library, the Folger Library, the Houghton Library at Harvard University, the Huntington Library, the Library of Congress (especially its Map Division), the Massachusetts State Archive, the Virginia Historical Society, and the Thomas Cooper Library at the University of South Carolina.

I benefited greatly from the feedback I received when presenting aspects of the book at the periodic meetings of the American Studies Association, the Society of Early Americanists, the Society of Authorship, Reading, and Publishing, and the International Conference of the History of Cartography. My argument was honed after presenting chapters at special seminars offered by the Humanities Consortium at UCLA, the McNeil Center for Early American Studies in Philadelphia, the Omohundro Institute of Early American History and Culture, and the Delaware Seminar in the History of Culture at the University of Delaware.

The book was made possible by the generous assistance of the following institutions and their fellowship programs: the American Antiquarian Society, the American Philosophical Society, the Dibner Institute, the Mellon Foundation, and the General University Research Program of the University of Delaware.

I am most grateful for receiving the Andrew W. Mellon Postdoctoral Research Fellowship at the Omohundro Institute of Early American History and Culture, and the esprit de corps that was afforded by its director, Ronald Hoffman. In particular I wish to thank Fredrika J. Teute for her continuing and spirited enthusiasm for this project. She read and critiqued the manuscript in its various incarnations, and at the Institute provided the kind of convivial setting that fostered conversation between the disciplines. Gil Kelly and Ellen Adams were the copy editors; their careful readings made all the difference as they prepared the manuscript for publication. I appreciate having the permission to use materials from earlier versions of chapters 3, 6, and 7, which appeared in "Lessons in Geography: Maps, Spellers, and Other Grammars of Nationalism in the Early Republic," *American Quarterly,* LI (1999), 311–343; "Contested Sources of the Self: The Geographies of Lewis, Clark, and Native Americans," in Udo Hebel, ed., *The Construction and Contestation of American Cultures and Identities in the Early National Period* (Heidelberg, 1999), 25–46; and "Literacy for Empire: The ABCs of Geography and the Rule of Territoriality in Early-Nineteenth-Century America," in Helena Michie and Ronald R. Thomas, eds., *Nineteenth-Century Geographies: The Transformation of Space from the Victorian Age to the American Century* (New Brunswick, N.J., 2002), 172–190.

My deepest thanks are for my family. I thank my parents, Hannelore and Siegfried Brückner, for continuing to travel between two continents and cultures. I thank my daughters, Corinna and Juliana, for being so full of life. Most of all, I thank Kristen Poole. She has read every word many times, listened to my ideas and edited my prose, and always made time while working on her own book projects on Renaissance literature. When all is told, words still cannot describe my admiration and gratitude for her companionship and love. I dedicate this book to her.

CONTENTS

LIST OF ILLUSTRATIONS

THE

GEOGRAPHIC

REVOLUTION IN

EARLY AMERICA

introduction

THE GEOGRAPHIC
REVOLUTION IN
THE WILDERNESS

Let us consider two family portraits in order to glimpse how geography shaped Anglo-American identities during the long eighteenth century. In a 1667 portrait celebrating the second Lord Baltimore, Cecil Calvert holds out a manuscript map of Maryland boldly inscribed *Nova Terrae-Mariae Tabula;* standing before the lord is his grandson, playfully pawing at the same map under the watchful gaze of an African servant (Figure 1). Shown in the hand of a British statesman, the map—emblazoned with the family crest—represents the Calverts' possessions in the British American colonies. Handed down to the American-born boy, the map also signals the patrilineal exchange of landed property from fathers to sons, imperial landowners to future colonists. Linking three generations, the map becomes the symbolic text and literary key to British American self-representation.

A century and a half later, in the newly formed United States, a painter marshals a much larger array of geographical texts to limn the members of an emerging middle class (Figure 2). In an 1810 group portrait, the Reverend Jedidiah Morse—a conservative Federalist and successful author of geography schoolbooks—has gathered his wife Elizabeth Breese and their three sons around a table, upon which are placed a globe, a geography book, and a foldout map. This portrait still celebrates the patriarch, possessions, and the ritual display of modern identity, but in a new and different way. Instead of a single map representing landed property as the basis of identity, diverse geographical texts have now become the prized possessions defining the early American subjects.

What is fascinating about these portraits is that American identities are not predicated on the visual display of maps or geography books as such. Rather, what appears to prop up the self-image of the imperial,

Figure 1. Cecil Calvert, Second Lord Baltimore. *By Gerard Soest. 1667.*
Photo Courtesy of Maryland Department, Enoch Pratt Free Library

Figure 2. Morse Family. *By Samuel F. B. Morse. 1810.* Permission of National Museum of American History, Smithsonian Institution, Behring Center

colonial, and early national subject is the demonstration of geographical literacy: the basic competence to read maps and to read and write about the world in modern geographic terms. In the portrait of Lord Baltimore, the map is visible only to the viewers and thus assumes an audience that is trained in map reading. In the Morse family portrait, the textual tools of geography are highlighted as essential to the education of Anglo-American citizens, adults and children. Both portraits illustrate how geographical literacy served a symbolic, cognitive, and pedagogic role in the representation of early Anglo-American identity.

This study explores the geographic revolution in early America from the 1680s to the 1820s. Concentrating on Anglo-American culture in North America, it brings to light the interaction between geography and literary education and examines how this relationship influenced the textual practices surrounding the process of identity formation. The aim of this study is thus twofold. First, it tells the story of the rapid rise of geography, from a scarce and symbolic text that symbolized privileged lives inside an imperial culture, to a form of everyday discourse widely used by a socially diverse population of English-speakers living in colonial British America and the early United States. To better understand how fundamental geographical literacy was to the overall literary experience in early America, I examine the circulation and sociology of geographical texts, recovering geography as a broadly defined genre consisting of many vibrant textual forms: property plats and surveying manuals, decorative wall maps and magazine maps, atlases and geography textbooks, flash cards and playing cards, paintings and needlework samplers.

Second, in order to show how geographical literacy affected eighteenth-century conceptions of American identity, this study examines the discourse of geography in relation to early American literary productions, paying close attention to genres that treated issues of self-representation. The various forms of geographical writing (for example, maps and textbooks) profoundly informed early American literary documents—such as poems and natural histories, diaries and novels—because their conception and production were deeply linked to the cognitive, pedagogic, and material practices derived from the study of geography. The study's more specific aim, then, is to show how lessons in geographic modes of reading and writing intersected with the more familiar practices that we commonly associate with literary competence, from the first ciphering of the alphabet to performing speeches to writing narrative compositions in the English language.

Geography has traditionally been viewed as one of the crucial "contexts" defining Anglo-American identities. Calling upon the material realities of the North American continent—its abundance of space, availability of landed property, or distinct topography—influential studies have discussed geography as a constructive background in order to explain the Americanness of social, aesthetic, or psychological models of identity. In those accounts, the discussion of geography tended to foster exceptionalist narratives in which the collective identity of American colonists or United States citizens was tied to the experience of physical geography. These sometimes exuberantly patriotic studies have been complicated by cultural historians who continue to emphasize the contextual function of geography as the physical, and hence quantifiable, background for explaining early ideas of community and identity. Their studies show how the perceived surplus of geographic space spurred the early commodification of American lands and how the meshing of economic practices and political decisions provided fuel for the double fantasy of an Anglo-American empire and nation-state.[1]

Similarly, as literary scholars have shown, the description of physical geography provided a highly productive metaphor through which American identities were imagined in opposition to European modes of self-definition. Seminal discussions commenting on the relationship between language and identity—examining, for example, Mary Rowlandson's New England, Thomas Jefferson's Virginia, or Henry David Thoreau's Massachusetts—have pointed out how, in the hands of Anglo-American authors, the real geographical landscape became the foundational topos through which authors imagined a variety of American selves. In forging links between the land, the heart, and the home, early American writers expanded references to physical geography into strategic settings, including the "American wilderness," the "American garden," and "American nature." Cast in these terms, the descriptions of American geography have served as deterministic, symbolic, or ontological metasettings in which authors turned the continent's physicality into a dynamic literary trope that could be used to explain social changes and at the same time ground individual characters. Thus, depending on the various interpreters' ideological convictions, descriptions of physical geography

1. According to H. Roy Merrens, the old-school approach to geography falls into three lines of inquiry, beginning with the "man-land tradition" and its environmental deterministic stance, the "spatial tradition" and its penchant for demographic charts and land use analysis, and the "area studies tradition" and its desire to create a holistic snapshot of any given location. See "Historical Geography and Early American History," *William and Mary Quarterly,* 3d Ser., XXII (1965), 529–548.

Representative authors of these approaches are, for example, Frederick Jackson Turner, *The Frontier in American History* (1920; rpt. New York, 1996); Percy Wells Bidwell and John I. Falconer, *History of Agriculture in the Northern United States, 1620–1860* (Washington, D.C., 1925); Roderick Nash, *Wilderness and the American Mind* (New Haven, Conn., 1967); James T. Lemon, *The Best Poor Man's Country: A Geographical Study of Early Southeastern Pennsylvania* (Baltimore, 1972); Douglas R. McManis, *Colonial New England: Historical Geography* (New York, 1975).

For examples of modern cultural studies of geography, see William Cronon, *Changes in the Land: Indians, Colonists, and the Ecology of New England* (New York, 1983); D. W. Meinig, *The Shaping of America: A Geographical Perspective on Five Hundred Years of History,* I, *Atlantic America, 1492–1800* (New Haven, Conn., 1986); T. H. Breen, "An Empire of Goods: The Anglicization of Colonial America, 1690–1776," *Journal of British Studies,* XXV (1986), 467–499; Timothy Sweet, *American Georgics: Economy and Environment in Early American Literature* (Philadelphia, 2002).

have provided the imaginary setting into which writers inserted distinctly American identities such as the heroic colonist farmer, the patriotic anarchist-revolutionary, the feudal patriarch as new man, the fierce regionalist, and the capitalist imperial self.[2]

By privileging the contextual approach to geography, academic and popular discussions of identity have invariably established geography as a material history and symbolic structure of early American feeling. In this interpretation, early Anglo-American encounters with real mountains stir up real emotions (William Byrd and the Blue Mountains), geological formations are objects of wonder (Thomas Jefferson and the Natural Bridge of Virginia), and the view of unfamiliar water systems creates lasting memories of reverie (William Bartram and coastal Florida). Whether enlisted for patriotic, Marxist, or feminist purposes, in critical examinations of American literature geography has one recurring plot line: the realities of the land overwhelm the individual author or fictional character to the point of reconfiguring his or her sense of identity. Personal meditations on geography are seen as evidentiary tales of how geography invariably transforms personal experiences into heartfelt characterizations of selfhood.[3]

In contrast to these contextual evaluations of American geographical identities, this book proposes an alternative source of geographic affect, the text of geography itself. It takes as its starting point the observation that in theory and practice the construction of the American subject was grounded in the textual experience of geography. During the period of this study, from the late seventeenth to the early nineteenth century, Anglo-Americans consistently defined and applied the terms of *geography* according to the literal signification of the Greek word, as "to record, draw, and write the earth." This was the meaning of the word repeatedly invoked by professional geographers and students throughout the seventeenth

2. Studies discussing geography in its material form—and there are many—include Perry Miller, *Errand into the Wilderness* (Cambridge, Mass., 1956), and *Nature's Nation* (Cambridge, Mass., 1967); Leo Marx, *The Machine in the Garden: Technology and the Pastoral Ideal in America* (London, 1964); Sacvan Bercovitch, *The American Jeremiad* (Madison, Wis., 1978); Myra Jehlen, *American Incarnation: The Individual, the Nation, and the Continent* (Cambridge, Mass., 1986); Lawrence Buell, *The Environmental Imagination: Thoreau, Nature Writing, and the Formation of American Culture* (Cambridge, Mass., 1995).

3. I think, for example, of the geographical-literary surveys of Cape Cod (William Bradford), of the Dismal Swamp between Virginia and North Carolina (William Byrd), or of the forests of upstate New York (James Fenimore Cooper).

and eighteenth centuries. By drawing upon this definition, this study locates geography not only at the intersection of the verbal and the visual (to record and to draw) but also recovers geography as a material form and stylistic device of literary production (to write).[4]

As the discourse of geography has become second nature, we rarely notice the extent to which geography as text and form of literacy permeates the modern mass media, from the magazine *National Geographic* to the nightly news to online map services. We easily forget how place-names and coordinates, borders and topographic symbols are continually providing a writing system and thus a quasi-linguistic code through which we structure our daily perception of and relation to land, variously calling it country, place, or space. For eighteenth-century Anglo-Americans, however, the very forms of geographic writing—in particular the map and geography book—were new tools of communication taking hold of the literary practices of new audiences. While today the term "geography" is associated with spectacles of adventure or the tedium of memorizing facts and figures, becoming geographically literate provided many ordinary people with a vehicle for describing and defining their personal place in both the local and global community. Indeed, for many British Americans, geography was the gateway to literacy itself, as learning to read was linked to geographic instruction.

As they arrived in North America, British colonists left behind a culture of letters that included a rich and complex tradition of mapping and geographic literature. Starting in the late sixteenth century, the coincidence of overseas colonization, domestic enclosure acts with their ensuing land surveying projects, and the extensive production of geographical books worked far-reaching changes in the everyday habits and literary life of English men and women. Cartographic and geographic discourses

---

4. Scholars of geography regularly gesture to the literary qualities of geography. See, for example, Svetlana Alpers, *The Art of Describing: Dutch Art in the Seventeenth Century* (Chicago, 1983), 135–139; Margarita Bowen, *Empiricism and Geographical Thought: From Francis Bacon to Alexander von Humboldt* (Cambridge, 1981), 28; David N. Livingstone, *The Geographical Tradition: Episodes in the History of a Contested Enterprise* (Oxford, 1992), 99–100. These authors, however, move on to apply the analysis of the term's literal translation not directly to the practice of writing but to the early modern debate over the disciplinary value of the subject of geography (locating it among the classical genres of cosmography and chorography or, in the context of the scientific revolution, differentiating between mathematical and civic geography). Though important, these distinctions are not central to the argument of my study.

helped to propel and articulate the emergence of English nationalism. Artists and craftsmen worked the nation's geographic outline into symbolic and literary expressions of a national community: in paintings, the body of Queen Elizabeth was projected on the outline map of England, and playwrights like William Shakespeare developed narratives of national power by deploying geographical texts, such as maps in a theater called the Globe; between the literary hack and the aesthetic theorist, a variety of geographic writing practices became the focus for popular discussions addressing everything from the Englishness of literary forms to political stability.[5]

As geography fostered a sense of national identity at home, it also paved the way for imperialism abroad. The same media and technology that had propagated the idea of geographic cohesion as fundamental to the nation's self-image also provided government agents and trading companies with the kind of textual blueprint that invited and legitimized international expansion. Following the English Revolution in the mid-seventeenth century, British subjects living on both sides of the Atlantic consumed geographic texts that envisioned America as an unclaimed part of the world upon which a centralized state apparatus or an individual entrepreneur could impress the mechanisms of colonization and enact personal narratives of an emerging British imperial identity.[6]

A closer examination of the representational strategies surrounding

5. Richard Helgerson, *Forms of Nationhood: The Elizabethan Writing of England* (Chicago, 1992); Jeffrey Knapp, *An Empire Nowhere: England, America, and Literature from "Utopia" to "The Tempest"* (Berkeley, Calif., 1992); Lesley B. Cormack, " 'Good Fences Make Good Neighbors': Geography as Self-Definition in Early Modern England," *Isis*, LXXXII (1991), 639–661; John Gillies, *Shakespeare and the Geography of Difference* (Cambridge, 1994); Garrett A. Sullivan, Jr., *The Drama of Landscape: Land, Property, and Social Relations on the Early Modern Stage* (Stanford, Calif., 1998); Kristen Poole and Martin Brückner, "The Plot Thickens: Surveying Manuals, Drama, and the Materiality of Narrative Form in Early Modern England," *English Literary History*, LXIX (2002), 617–648.

6. The cartographic image of geography in elite and common cultures of Renaissance Europe is a central aspect of studies such as Immanuel Wallerstein, *The Modern World-System*, I, *Capitalist Agriculture and the Origins of the European World-Economy in the Sixteenth Century* (New York, 1974); Chandra Mukerji, *From Graven Images: Patterns of Modern Materialism* (New York, 1983); Fernand Braudel, *Civilization and Capitalism, Fifteenth to Eighteenth Century*, III, *The Perspective of the World* (London, 1984). On the institutionalization of geographic writing before 1700, see James C. Scott, *Seeing Like a State: How Certain Schemes to Improve the Human Condition Have Failed* (New Haven, Conn., 1998); Anthony Giddens, *A Contemporary Critique of Historical Materialism*, II, *The Nation-State and Violence* (Berkeley, Calif., 1985).

national and imperial writings reveals that the lessons for internalizing geographical knowledge were intimately linked to the methods and practices surrounding the earliest steps of literacy acquisition. There was considerable practical as well as conceptual cross-fertilization between geographical texts and alphabetic literacy. For example, geography's most elementary graphic form, the grid, impinged upon the traditional technologies of writing. As a simple script consisting of longitudinal and latitudinal lines, the grid elegantly enclosed and organized the earth on paper in modern map images and textbook tables. At the same time, the grid also affected the graphic design of the letter alphabet, writing instructions, and the design of print fonts. As early as 1529 the French printer Geoffrey Tory demonstrated a protocartographic sensibility. By drawing letters using the Euclidian grid, Tory introduced a mapping habit into the design of early modern letters. At about the same time, the work of Gerard Mercator illustrates the practical overlap between alphabetic literacy and geographic writing. A sixteenth-century writing instructor turned mapmaker, Mercator not only popularized the now-familiar cartographic image of the earth's geography but codified the use of alphabetic text on maps and in geography books. For some writers, like the seventeenth-century philosopher René Descartes, the very practice of cartographic writing became indelibly tied to narrative meditations on the state of modern selfhood.[7]

By the end of the century, pedagogues embraced geographical writings as the practical context through which to test literacy skills such as reading and writing and even, as John Locke suggested, the exercise of foreign languages. Indeed, throughout the seventeenth century, geographical instruction supplemented the first years of education. Geography provided

7. On the cartographic grid, see William Boelhower, "Inventing America: A Model of Cartographic Semiosis," *Word and Image,* IV (1988), 475–497. Longitudinal lines were at the time much more easily come by in geographical writing than in the actual navigation. For the history of calculating longitude, see Dava Sobel, *Longitude: The True Story of a Lone Genius Who Solved the Greatest Scientific Problem of His Time* (New York, 1995). For the history of letter design, see Johanna Drucker, *The Alphabetic Labyrinth: The Letters in History and Imagination* (London, 1995). For a discussion of Tory's *Champ Fleury,* see Tom Conley, *The Self-Made Map: Cartographic Writing in Early Modern France* (Minneapolis, Minn., 1996), 86, and, on Descartes, 279–301. On Mercator, see Eileen Reeves, "Reading Maps," *Word and Image,* IX (1993), 51–65; David Woodward, "The Manuscript, Engraved, and Typographic Traditions of Map Lettering," in Woodward, ed., *Art and Cartography: Six Historical Essays* (Chicago, 1987), 174–212; A. S. Osley, *Mercator: A Monograph on the Lettering of Maps . . .* (London, 1969).

a cornerstone for Locke's theory of the modern curriculum. According to *Some Thoughts concerning Education* (1693), the ideal modern child, having been taught by his mother, "could readily point . . . to any Country upon the Globe, or any County in the Map of *England,* knew all the great Rivers, Promontories, Straits, and Bays in the World, and could find the Longitude and Latitude of any Place, before he was six Years old."[8]

Replete with its own vocabulary, writing system, and publishing industry, by the end of the seventeenth century the "spatial discipline" of geographical literacy had begun to substantively supplement the alphabetic order of the English-speaking and -writing world. Through its persistent application in classrooms and widespread dissemination in popular handbooks, the genre of geography was shaping the English literary consciousness and the way in which individuals and institutions explored the relationship between alphabetic literacy and the modern subject. Thus, by the late seventeenth century, as English men and women were simultaneously charted as national and imperial subjects, the textual venues of geography engendered a new literary consciousness. Restoration writers from Aphra Behn to Thomas Southerne, soon to be followed by authors from Daniel Defoe to Jonathan Swift, frequently commented on the new geographical order, as their novels, plays, and essays explored (or lampooned) the effect of maps and cartographic writings upon the emergence of a modern identity.[9]

8. "At the same time that he is learning *French* and *Latin,* a Child . . . may also be enter'd in *Arithmetick, Geography, Chronology, History, and Geometry* too. For if these be taught him in French or Latin, when he begins once to understand either of these Tongues, he will get a knowledge in these Sciences, and the Language to boot. *Geography,* I think, should be begun with." John Locke, *Some Thoughts concerning Education,* ed. John W. Yolton and Jean S. Yolton (Oxford, 1989), sect. 178. A century earlier, Thomas Blundeville, teacher of the sons of English aristocrats and merchants, was one of the first textbook authors to incorporate geography lessons into his schoolbook: Blundeville, *His Exercises: Containing Eight Treatises* (London, 1597). On the history of geography in English Renaissance education, see Bowen, *Empiricism,* 67–122; Livingstone, *Geographical Tradition,* 63–101.

9. See the pathbreaking work of J. B. Harley, especially "Maps, Knowledge, and Power," in Denis Cosgrove and Stephen Daniels, eds., *The Iconography of Landscape: Essays on the Symbolic Representation, Design, and Use of Past Environments* (Cambridge, 1988), 277–312. Also of interest are his essays "Deconstructing the Map," *Cartographica,* XXVI, no. 2 (Summer 1989), 1–20, and "Cartography, Ethics, and Social Theory," *Cartographica,* XXVII, no. 2 (Summer 1990), 1–23. These essays are now collected in Paul Laxton, ed., *The New Nature of Maps: Essays in the History of Cartography* (Baltimore, 2001). On eighteenth-century literary adaptations of cartographic writings, see Barbara Maria Stafford, *Voyage into Substance: Art, Science, Nature, and the Illustrated Travel Account, 1760–1840* (Cambridge,

At the turn of the eighteenth century, British American colonists enthusiastically participated in this culture of geographic letters. Geographic print materials, including maps and textbooks, became staple goods in the American literary marketplace. Those with financial means ordered lavishly illustrated atlases and folio geographies. Those of lesser means encountered descriptions of the latest geographic theories, expeditions, or territorial conquests in almanacs and magazine maps.[10] Moreover, growing numbers of British colonists studied the science of geography in day and evening schools. Men and women practiced reading the globe and maps, they memorized the differences between mathematical and civil geography, and they proudly swapped their sons' and daughters' school assignments in geography. Indeed, as the colonial and early national records suggest, British Americans effectively included geography

Mass., 1984); Mary Louise Pratt, *Imperial Eyes: Travel Writing and Transculturation* (London, 1992).

10. See, for example, the records of *The Library of the Late . . . Mr. Samuel Lee* (Boston, 1693); Samuel Gerrish, *A Catalogue of Curious and Valuable Books . . .* (Boston, 1718); Joshua Moodey and Daniel Gookin, *A Catalogue of Rare and Valuable Books* (Boston, 1718); B[enjamin] Franklin, *A Catalogue of Choice and Valuable Books . . .* [Philadelphia, 1744]; Elizabeth Reilly's transcription of Jeremiah Condy, "A Bookseller's Account Book, 1759–1770" (Boston, 1978), at the American Antiquarian Society. These catalogs give a sense of the range of geographical texts owned by colonial readers. They included Peter Heylyn's *Cosmographie* (1st ed. 1652; date of copy is 1669) as a folio edition, and a quarto edition of his *Description of the World* (n.d.); Philip Clüver's *Introduction into Geography* (1st English ed., 1657; n.d.); a folio edition of Herman Moll's atlas, *A Compleat System of Geography* (1701; here 1709) and his textbook *The Compleat Geographer . . .* (London, 1723); Patrick Gordon's school geography, *Geography Anatomiz'd* (1693; here 1704); Isaac Watts, *Principles of Astronomy and Geography* (n.d.); Thomas Salmon, *The Geographical and Historical Grammar,* now appearing under the new title, *Present State of All Nations* (London, 1738); a French two-volume edition, *Geographie par M. Robbe* (n.d.), and a two-volume edition entitled *World in Miniature* (n.d.). Probate records detailing the libraries of the colonial elite in New England (the Mather family) and the southern colonies (the Byrd and Custis families) generally record a similar range of cartographic and geographic writings.

For geographic instructions in almanacs, see "Geographical Paradox: Answers and Questions," in *The Ladies Diary; or, The Woman's Almanack, for 1711,* owned by Benjamin Franklin; or Franklin's *Poor Richard Improved, for 1755.* American newspapers began occasionally printing maps in the 1710s; see David C. Jolly, comp. and ed., *Maps of America in Periodicals before 1800* (Brookline, Mass., 1989). British magazines like the *Gentleman's Magazine* or the *London Magazine* included maps beginning in the 1730s. For a detailed account of the history of magazine maps, see E. A. Reitan, "Expanding Horizons: Maps in the *Gentleman's Magazine,* 1731–1754," *Imago Mundi,* XXXVII (1985), 54–62; and Christopher M. Klein, *Maps in Eighteenth-Century British Magazines: A Checklist* (Chicago, 1989).

and related subjects such as geodesy and cartography into the basic educational curriculum; taught next to the *New England Primer* and the Bible, maps and geography books informed basic literacy, even as geographical literacy was shaping secular and sacred knowledge.[11]

In view of the nexus between geography and conventional literacy, this study ultimately expands from a proposition made by Ludwig Wittgenstein: "The limits of my language mean the limits of my world." Applying this dictum to the American experience of the geographic revolution, I explore the textual frontier along which individual, social, and institutional practices integrated geographic instruction with literary education. How did the discourse of geography change the limits of language in British America and the early United States? How do the signs and symbols on the map or the rhetoric and narrative structures of geography books affect the practices surrounding the production of literature? Finally, how does the internalization of geography as a kind of language shape the literary construction of the modern American subject?[12]

My argument builds upon three developments in early American studies. First, the more general argument, namely that geography is a highly diversified genre, has been substantively shaped by historical studies of cartographic and geographical writings. While these histories have relieved me from having to present a comprehensive history of geographic texts, they also leave unanswered questions about the cognitive, peda-

---

11. Diaries and letters from the mid-eighteenth century reveal the personal and generational interest in geographic instruction. For an example, see the diaries of Joseph Shippen, Jr., "Letter Book, 1763–73" (American Philosophical Society MSS guide, 1124). Similarly, the anonymous diary of a South Carolina teacher shows the entry for April 1: "to Mr Bal . . . Esq. Begd me to give Son some lesson in Latin Geography which I begun to do Today," in "Diary" (South Carolina, 1760), American Antiquarian Society, MSS Coll. 1, box 20. Students keeping notebooks included extensive quotations from geography textbooks or listed the textbook titles: see Nathan Fiske's "Notebook, 1752" (AAS Mss. Coll.).

On the history of geography in colonial education, see William Warntz, *Geography Now and Then: Some Notes on the History of Academic Geography in the United States* (New York, 1964); John A. Nietz, *Old Textbooks* . . . (Pittsburgh, Pa., 1961); Lawrence C. Wroth, *An American Bookshelf, 1755* (Philadelphia, 1934); Kevin J. Hayes, *A Colonial Woman's Bookshelf* (Knoxville, Tenn., 1996); Robert Seyboldt, "Source Studies in American Colonial Education: The Private School," *University of Illinois Bulletin,* XXIII, no. 4 (September 1925), 35–53. Colonial newspapers, such as the *Pennsylvania Gazette* and the *South-Carolina Gazette,* frequently carried advertisements for lessons in geography.

12. Ludwig Wittgenstein, *Tractatus Logico-Philosophicus,* trans. D. F. Pears and B. F. McGuinness (London, 1961), sect. 5.6.

gogic, aesthetic, and social function of geographical literacy. Second, my argument is informed by critical work in literary and cultural studies, in which a few early Americanists have quietly repositioned geography away from being a purely metaphoric or extraliterary ("natural") context, understanding it instead as a concrete literary practice though not quite as an aspect of popular literacy.[13]

But, above all, my argument has been made possible by those innovative studies in the fields of media, book, and reading history that have constructively challenged the primacy of the "Word" as the dominant building block out of which Anglo-Americans simultaneously invented and transmitted ideas of individual and communal identity. To be sure, the fabrication of early American identity relied heavily upon the creative interplay between English rhetoric, writing, and print. Yet, the critical base of analysis was inherently logocentric and has thus obscured the way in which the identity work of Anglo-Americans depended also on extraverbal vehicles of popular mediation, including music, theatrical performance, and visual images. I join these revisionist explorations into broader conceptions of Anglo-American literacy by turning to geography and suggest that over the course of the eighteenth century its signs, symbols, and rhetoric became an everyday language by which men and women

13. Important surveys of the Anglo-American geographical literatures are Margaret Beck Pritchard and Henry G. Taliaferro, *Degrees of Latitude: Mapping Colonial America* (New York, 2002); Barbara Backus McCorkle, comp., *New England in Early Printed Maps, 1513–1800: An Illustrated Carto-Bibliography* (Providence, R.I., 2001); Alex Krieger and David Cobb, eds., *Mapping Boston* (Cambridge, Mass., 2001); Thomas F. McIlwraith and Edward K. Muller, eds., *North America: The Historical Geography of a Changing Continent* (Lanham, Md., 2001); John Rennie Short, *Representing the Republic: Mapping the United States, 1600–1900* (London, 2001); J. B. Harley, "Power and Legitimation in the English Geographical Atlases of the Eighteenth Century," in John A. Wolter and Ronald A. Grim, eds., *Images of the World: The Atlas through History* (Washington, D.C., 1997); Harley, "The Map User in the Revolution," in Harley, Barbara Bartz Petchenik, and Lawrence W. Towner, eds., *Mapping the American Revolutionary War* (Chicago, 1978), 79–110; David Buisseret, ed., *From Sea Charts to Satellite Images: Interpreting North American History through Maps* (Chicago, 1990); Peter Benes, *New England Prospect: A Loan Exhibition of Maps at the Currier Gallery of Art* (Boston, 1981).

For studies exploring geography as a literary practice, see Wayne Franklin, *Discoverers, Explorers, Settlers: The Diligent Writers of Early America* (Chicago, 1979); William Boelhower, *Through a Glass Darkly: Ethnic Semiosis in American Literature* (Venice, 1984); Robert Lawson-Peebles, *Landscape and Written Expression in Revolutionary America: The World Turned Upside Down* (Cambridge, 1988); Walter D. Mignolo, *The Darker Side of the Renaissance: Literacy, Territoriality, and Colonization* (Ann Arbor, Mich., 1995).

not only spoke and wrote about each other but came to symbolically represent themselves.[14]

In pursuing this study, I had expected to find that the textualities of geography would convey the stories of others, but I had not anticipated that geographic literacy would have its own tale to tell. Studying geography's symbolic, pedagogic, and literary role in North America from the late seventeenth to the early nineteenth centuries, I discovered that the story of geographic literacy assumed its own dramatic arc. From its beginning in surveying manuals and property maps, geographic literacy enabled British Americans to quite literally get their feet on the ground, granting them a sense of place and entitlement, engendering a process that led to the Revolution. In the early Republic, geography helped the country to come together and mature, providing the vehicle that new citizens used, usually deliberately and self-consciously, to emerge from an ideologically complicated relationship with the mother nation, imperial England. However, in the context of western expansion geography became a language for instilling, expressing, and enacting the new imperial dynamic of the eastern states. What had enabled a people to find and define themselves as a republican nation was transformed into expressions of imperial self-identification and actions of territorial annexation.

For the most part, this study moves in chronological order, beginning with the crown's revocation of British land charters in 1690 and ending on the verge of the Indian removal policy in 1825. Within this chronological movement, I have organized the chapters thematically around different

14. On the role of the written and spoken word in colonial and early national culture, see Michael Warner, *The Letters of the Republic: Publication and the Public Sphere in Eighteenth-Century America* (Cambridge, Mass., 1990); Larzer Ziff, *Writing in the New Nation: Prose, Print, and Politics in the Early United States* (New Haven, Conn., 1991); Jay Fliegelman, *Declaring Independence: Jefferson, Natural Language, and the Culture of Performance* (Stanford, Calif., 1993); Christopher Looby, *Voicing America: Language, Literary Form, and the Origins of the United States* (Chicago, 1996); Sandra M. Gustafson, *Eloquence Is Power: Oratory and Performance in Early America* (Chapel Hill, N.C., 2000).

For studies that argue directly or indirectly for a more inclusive definition of literacy in early America (though without considering geography), see David D. Hall, "The Uses of Literacy in New England, 1600–1850," in William L. Joyce et al., eds., *Printing and Society in Early America* (Worcester, Mass., 1983), 1–47; Patricia Crain, *The Story of A: The Alphabetization of America from "The New England Primer" to "The Scarlet Letter"* (Stanford, Calif., 2000); David Waldstreicher, *In the Midst of Perpetual Fetes: The Making of American Nationalism, 1776–1820* (Chapel Hill, N.C., 1997); Robert Blair St. George, *Conversing by Signs: Poetics of Implication in Colonial New England Culture* (Chapel Hill, N.C., 1998).

media, social aspects, and aesthetics of geographic literacy in order to test how various geographic texts impinged upon or conformed to the conventions of alphabetic literacy, classical rhetoric, the visual arts, print culture, and public education.

Chapter 1 explores colonial writing habits, how a geodetic consciousness and a proliferation of surveying manuals created an early American culture in which writing and surveying became conceptually, practically, and ideologically intertwined; how geodetic writing practices created a literary mode that privileged the individual surveyor-writer, at once upholding and opposing the central authority of English imperial mapping projects. The second chapter takes up the role of geography in colonial notions of political rhetoric and speech; in a move that at once appropriated and diverged from classical modes of oratory, colonial speakers crafted the figure of the "continent" as a discursive vehicle that allowed for the individual and collective expression of a different, American selfhood. Chapter 3 shows how linguistic reformers promoted the semiotics of cartography, in particular the logo of the national map, as an answer to the quest for a universal, revolutionary, non-English language that would distinguish the early Republic from its former imperial ruler.

Chapters 4 and 5 demonstrate the reciprocity of early national geographies and the novel. Geography textbooks, among the most widely published and circulated genres in the late eighteenth and early nineteenth centuries, set out to shape ideal republican citizens through the teaching of geography. Geographic literacy in turn shaped the strategies and sentiments of the picaresque and sentimental novel, as in the case of Charles Brockden Brown, in which the dominance of geography as a literary and affective mode overwhelms the integrity of the novel form. Chapter 6 traces this failure of geographic discourse into its practical, political application in the journals of Meriwether Lewis and William Clark, who encountered the epistemological limits of Western geographical discourse. The book's concluding chapter discusses how an emotionally charged aesthetics of geography taught by nineteenth-century schoolbooks and atlases primed a geoliterate population for the seemingly natural necessity of westward expansion and the elimination of the indigenous inhabitants.

chapter one

THE SURVEYED SELF

GEODESY, WRITING, AND COLONIAL

IDENTITY IN EIGHTEENTH-CENTURY

BRITISH AMERICA

The early American land survey is part of a much-overlooked literary movement, one set in motion by the English nation-state and subsequently adopted by British American colonists living up and down the Atlantic seaboard. The land survey became a mass phenomenon when, as part of policy changes designed to consolidate imperial claims in North America, the British Parliament revoked the New England land charters in 1690.[1] This act nullified existing land grants, titles, and deeds and demanded the survey (or in many cases the resurvey) of publicly and privately owned land in New England, the mid-Atlantic, and the southern colonies. The results of the surveying activities—marked trees, clear-cuts in forests, and ultimately the creation of geometrically shaped lots—quite literally changed the early Anglo-American landscape.[2]

1. See Jack P. Greene, *Peripheries and Center: Constitutional Development in the Extended Polities of the British Empire and the United States, 1607–1788* (Athens, Ga., 1986), 7–39; second Massachusetts charter, in Greene, ed., *Great Britain and the American Colonies, 1606–1763* (Columbia, S.C., 1970), 116–145.

2. On the impact of the revocation of land charters, see Richard R. Johnson, *Adjustment to Empire: The New England Colonies, 1675–1715* (New Brunswick, N.J., 1981); Philip S. Haffenden, *New England in the English Nation, 1689–1713* (Oxford, 1974), 1–36; Richard L. Bushman, *From Puritan to Yankee: Character and the Social Order in Connecticut, 1690–1765* (Cambridge, Mass., 1967), 41–106. That a call for resurveys was the by-product of these policies is rarely noted. For the northern colonies, see Peter Benes, *New England Prospect: A Loan Exhibition of Maps at the Currier Gallery of Art* (Boston, 1981), 76–77; for Virginia, see Sarah S. Hughes, *Surveyors and Statesmen: Land Measuring in Colonial Virginia* (Richmond, Va., 1979), 17–19.

On the relationship between surveying, private property, and land use patterns, see the wonderful study by Edward T. Price, *Dividing the Land: Early American Beginnings of Our Private Property Mosaic* (Chicago, 1995). Regional studies include James L. Garvin, "The Range Township in Eighteenth-Century New Hampshire," in Peter Benes, ed., *New En-*

This profusion of new surveying activities also transformed the early Anglo-American literary landscape. Although this latter transformation has gone largely unnoticed, the impact of surveying practices on the late-seventeenth- and early-eighteenth-century writing culture was far-reaching. After 1690 and throughout the first half of the eighteenth century, as individual landowners or landowning institutions complied with the state's demand to survey property, individuals took up pen, compass, and paper in unprecedented numbers. Surveying, which comprised both mathematical measurement and descriptive writing, became a common practice and the subject of numerous publications. Colonists thus became both writers and readers of the survey. Surveying, an art that is highly conscious of its own instrumentation and technical implementation, presented itself as a new form of popular literacy. Ultimately, the survey—a text consisting of both written word and graphic figure—became an important literary site that opened new and creative ways for Anglo-Americans to represent their sense of community and identity.

The advent of the land survey worked its way into the British colonial canon of belles lettres as geodesy ("the art of land surveying or the measuring of land") became both a trope and narrative structure. Poems such as Richard Steere's "Earth's Felicities, Heaven's Allowances" (1713) exploit the visual and figurative possibilities offered by the idea of the survey. Steere's poem is a religious meditation on human happiness, exposing the limits of worldly pleasures while praising the rewards to be gained by the virtuous in the afterlife. And yet, at the climactic spiritual turning point, as the poem prepares the reader for the transition from "Earth's Felicities" to "Heaven's Allowances," Steere looks back at a life lived well, a life he imagined in strongly geodetic terms:

Having thus Transciently, in brief *Survey'd,*
Wherein all Earthly Happiness consists;

gland Prospect: Maps, Place Names, and the Historical Landscape (Boston, 1980), 47–68; Carville V. Earle, *The Evolution of a Tidewater Settlement System: All Hallow's Parish, Maryland, 1650–1783,* Department of Geography, Research Paper No. 170 (Chicago, 1975); James T. Lemon, *The Best Poor Man's Country: A Geographical Study of Early Southeastern Pennsylvania* (Baltimore, 1972); Lemon, "Spatial Order: Households in Local Communities and Regions," in Jack P. Greene and J. R. Pole, eds., *Colonial British America: Essays in the New History of the Early Modern Era* (Baltimore, 1984), 86–122; John Barry Love, "The Colonial Surveyor in Pennsylvania" (Ph.D. diss., University of Pennsylvania, 1970); Anthony N. B. Garvan, *Architecture and Town Planning in Colonial Connecticut* (New Haven, Conn., 1951).

To the intent we may therein be safe,
We with *Content* must fortify our minds,
That in all *Stations, Accidents, Conditions,*
We may Enjoy this worlds felicities,
Abstracted from the Ills that do accrue.

Steere draws on the technical lexicon commonly found in popular surveying manuals. In the parlance of the land surveyor, "Content" signified the
area of land surveyed and depicted by the surveyor's record, the field book
and the plat. The "Station" was the surveyor's position, from which the
land was measured and transcribed. "Accidents" referred to irregular
topographic features, which, after the survey had been completed, would
become "Abstracted," that is, drawn up on a plat. And the term "Conditions" encompassed the economic as well as legal terms describing everything from the surveyor's pay to the landlord's proof of ownership to the
tenant's rent scale.[3]

In a more secular vein, William Chandler uses the idea of geodesy to
frame his poem, *A Journal of the Survey of the Narragansett Bay, and Parts
Adjacent, Taken in the Month's of May and June, A.D. 1741 by Order of the
Honourable Court of Commissioners Appointed by His Majesty King George
the Second* (1741). As the title suggests, the poem's primary objective is
public accountability. Printed as a broadside, it is a belletristic report
justifying to the imperial sponsor and fellow colonial taxpayer the ex-
pense required to conduct the survey. Following the introductory stanza
in which Chandler states the poem's purpose ("These Lines below, describe a just Survey / Of all the Coasts, along the 'Gansett Baye"), the poem
recounts the survey's progress in anecdotal form, mixing satirical and
sentimental styles that were characteristic of travel stories in the English
literatures of the transatlantic world. What holds the anecdotes together,
however, is not the diarist's calendar or the heroic figure of the traveling
surveyor but the survey's diction and textual form. Phrases such as "the

3. The poem is part of R[ichard] S[teere], *The Daniel Catcher: The Life of the Prophet
Daniel: In a Poem, to Which Is Added Earth's Felicities, Heaven's Allowances, a Blank Poem*
([Boston], 1713), 58 (emphasis added).

The *Oxford English Dictionary* cites these geodetic connotations for the late seventeenth
and early eighteenth century. Several of them were developed by the mid-seventeenth
century in manuals such as William Leybourn, *The Compleat Surveyour: Containing the
Whole Art of Surveying of Land* . . . (London, 1653); John Eyre, *The Exact Surveyor* . . . (London,
1654); George Atwell, *The Faithfull Surveyor* . . . (Cambridge, 1658); Vincent Wing, *The
Geodaetes Practicus; or, The Art of Surveying* . . . (London, 1664).

next Lines" and "We next survey'd," or "Turning more points" and "And turn'd about new Courses," conspicuously mark the surveyor's passage through time and space. Of equal importance, these words refer to the surveyor's actual writing efforts. The poem ends by presenting the reader with the survey's paper trail: "Here we left off (and did it with a Jirk) / And then retired, our Field Book for to scan, / And of this large Survey to make a Plan." That these poems are saturated with the technological vocabulary of surveying suggests the degree to which geodetic practices were considered widespread knowledge.[4]

While the structural and conceptual merits of the survey might have delighted poetically minded audiences, the topic of this chapter is more prosaic: less the impact of the survey on the world of the imagination (although in many ways the survey is an inherently imaginative exercise) than on its ramifications for the nuts-and-bolts daily practices of putting pen to paper. The imperial decrees to resurvey all property forced large numbers of individuals to take up this particular form of writing, to educate themselves in its practices, and to become invested, consciously or not, in its sociopolitical implications. This writing phenomenon, however pragmatic its initial impulse, would profoundly affect colonial literary appetites. This chapter examines the everyday survey's aesthetic as it emerged in theory and practice through colonial surveying instructions, and the advent of a culture that was preoccupied with the conditions and mechanics of geodetic writing. The individual surveying records by Joshua Hempstead of Connecticut and William Byrd and George Washington of Virginia illuminate how geodetic writing became a creative art. As the common plat restructured the geographic representation of colonial land as property, its textual form provided a visual and narrative framework enabling Anglo-American landowners to reimagine the relationship between property and identity, colony and empire.

4. I discovered William Chandler's *Journal* in the broadside collection of the American Antiquarian Society. On the narrative conventions of travel writing, see Charles L. Batten, Jr., *Pleasurable Instruction: Form and Convention in Eighteenth-Century Travel Literature* (Berkeley, Calif., 1978); Percy G. Adams, *Travelers and Travel Liars, 1660–1800* (1962; rpt. New York, 1980); Mary Louise Pratt, *Imperial Eyes: Travel Writing and Transculturation* (London, 1992).

The British American application of geodesy and its representation of landed property emerged from the transatlantic context of English nationalism and nascent practices of imperial consolidation. The rhetoric surrounding the survey in America must be seen as a continuation of the early modern emergence of what Richard Helgerson has called "a cartographically and chorographically shaped consciousness of national power." In the late 1570s, "for the first time [Englishmen] took effective visual and conceptual possession of the physical kingdom in which they lived." The new print genres of county maps, chorographies, and cosmographies provided uniquely visual as well as textual access to the land. At the same time, English men and women also witnessed the increased circulation of surveying records, such as estate plans and cadastral survey maps introducing the rectangular grid survey to local landowners and tenants. In particular, the plat, a document containing both a map and a verbal account of the land, became widespread as a means of determining taxes and rents as well as the more ethereal values of social hierarchy. By the seventeenth century, the plat had become more than a standard feature of English land economics; it permeated popular discourse, as surveyors performed dialogues in print and on stage.[5]

The political changes in postrevolutionary England set the stage for a significant revaluation of the function and textual nature of British plats. Coinciding with England's 1690 demand of colonists to resurvey their land was the advent of "an imperial or hegemonic planning mentality."

5. Richard Helgerson, "The Land Speaks: Cartography, Chorography, and Subversion in Renaissance England," *Representations,* no. 16 (Fall 1986), 51–52. For a comprehensive history of the form and function of cadastral surveys, including their late-seventeenth- and early-eighteenth-century British American forms, see Roger J. P. Kain and Elizabeth Baigent, *The Cadastral Map in the Service of the State: A History of Property Mapping* (Chicago, 1992), 236–289. On the English history of land surveys, see David H. Fletcher, *The Emergence of Estate Maps: Christ Church, Oxford, 1600 to 1840* (Oxford, 1995); P. D. A. Harvey, "English Estate Maps: Their Early History and Their Use as Historical Evidence," in David Buisseret, ed., *Rural Images: Estate Maps in the Old and New Worlds* (Chicago, 1996), 27–61. The shift of estate maps from rarity to popular form is noted by Maurice Beresford, *History on the Ground: Six Studies in Maps and Landscapes* (London, 1957). For materials on the popular and artistic response to the survey, see Garrett A. Sullivan, Jr., *The Drama of Landscape: Land, Property, and Social Relations on the Early Modern Stage* (Stanford, Calif., 1998); Kristen Poole and Martin Brückner, "The Plot Thickens: Surveying Manuals, Drama, and the Materiality of Narrative Form in Early Modern England," *English Literary History,* LXIX (2002), 617–648.

Many Western European governments endeavored to render society as legible, predictable, and hence governable as possible. Thus they created state agents such as the royal surveyor, the hydrographer, and the geographer, officials who were advised to measure populations, landholdings, harvests, wealth, and the like. In order to manage this onslaught of new information, there was a need for new ways in which to record, analyze, and store information. For the purpose of measuring and regulating the land, bureaucratic agencies began to implement the cadastral land survey; the cadastral survey was also promoted by parliamentary acts that demanded the enclosure, inventory, evaluation, and redistribution of landed properties. Derived from the Greek word *katastichon,* meaning "line by line," the cadastral survey represented the land through a grid. Gone were the church spires from city maps and pictures of manor homes from estate maps, as territorial boundaries were now represented through the abstractions of geometry.[6]

In British America, the power to document and survey the imperial markets of landed property fell to the Plantations Office, better known as the Board of Trade. One of the newly centralized bureaucracies—replete with office buildings, letterhead, and an emergent class of civil servants— it became the clearinghouse for all kinds of statistical and geographical information. This institution was responsible for devising new methods that would codify, represent, and ultimately forecast economic and social conditions in the colonies. These new methods were in heightened demand following the crown's 1670 directive for the board "to procure exact

6. James C. Scott, *Seeing Like A State: How Certain Schemes to Improve the Human Condition Have Failed* (New Haven, Conn., 1998), 6, 24. Scott here departs from the standard discussion of landed property, directing our attention to issues of land management and the relationship of landowners to imperial institutions (as opposed to the prominent acts of conquest and dispossession). See also David Buisseret, ed., *Monarchs, Ministers, and Maps: The Emergence of Cartography as a Tool of Government in Early Modern Europe* (Chicago, 1992). By the end of the seventeenth century, the transition from a previously communal form of land tenure to individual freehold tenure among the propertied classes was complete in England. See Peter Eden, "Three Elizabethan Estate Surveyors: Peter Kempe, Thomas Clerke and Thomas Langdon," in Sarah Tyacke, ed., *English Map-Making, 1500–1600* (London, 1983), 68–84; J. A. Bennett, *The Divided Circle: A History of Instruments for Astronomy, Navigation, and Surveying* (Oxford, 1987); A. W. Richeson, *English Land Measuring to 1800: Instruments and Practices* (Cambridge, Mass., 1966); and the pioneering work of E. G. R. Taylor, *The Mathematical Practitioners of Tudor and Stuart England* (Cambridge, 1954), and Taylor, "The Surveyor," *Economic History Review,* XVII (1947), 121–133.

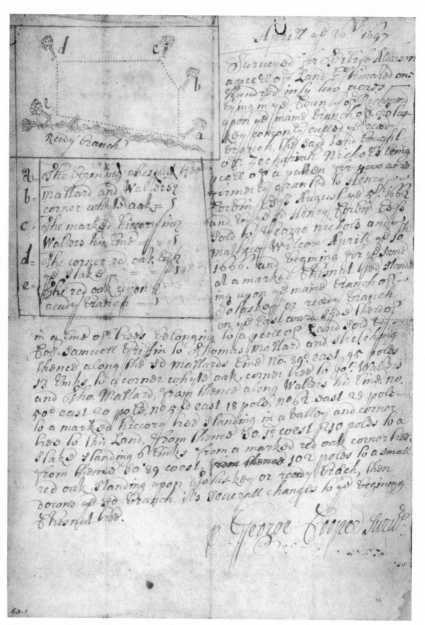

Figure 3. Northern Neck Survey for Teleife Alverson. By George Cooper. 1697.
Courtesy, The Library of Virginia

Mapps, Platts or Charts of all and Every [of] our Said Plantations abroad, togeather with the Mapps and Descriptions of their respective Ports, Harbours, Forts, Bayes, Rivers with the Depth of their respective Channells," all of which they "are carefully to Register and Keepe."[7]

In British America, the colonists followed the crown's mapping instructions with gusto. They dutifully documented harbors, coastlines, and city plans. But the primary concern of most colonists was the survey of their own property. Seeking to keep stride with the social and legal customs of the mother country, community leaders and individual proprietors living in the New England provinces and Virginia, and later in South Carolina and Georgia, commissioned plats of their land. Previously, when colonists had first arrived to inhabit the cartographic tabula rasa of the continent, boundaries between property were defined according to natural landmarks (such as clusters of trees, boulders, streams). With the coming of the plat at the end of the seventeenth century, geodetic description superseded popular custom in records of the land. As William Cronon has observed, "Whereas the earliest deeds tended to describe land in terms of its topography and use—for instance, as the mowing field between a certain two creeks—later deeds described land in terms of lots held by adjacent owners, and marked territories using the surveyor's abstractions of points of the compass and metes and bounds." The surveyor's plat was a central component of such land deeds. Handwritten and drawn to scale on parchment or paper, the plat included the geometric shape of surveying lines, the proprietor's name, verbal descriptions of boundary markers, and other landmarks necessary for establishing the land's area, value, and ownership (Figure 3).[8]

---

7. See Charles M. Andrews, *British Committees, Commissions, and Councils of Trade and Plantations, 1622–1675* (Baltimore, 1908), 122.

8. William Cronon, *Changes in the Land: Indians, Colonists, and the Ecology of New England* (New York, 1983), 74. Colonial property maps were mostly stark and functional, compared to their English counterparts. Peter Benes observes that the "English-style 'estate map' . . . did not become an accepted mapping form in New England where small holdings were the rule and tenancies on large properties the exception" (*New England Prospect: A Loan Exhibition,* 81). Similarly, Sarah Hughes states, "No evidence remains of . . . [ornate estate maps] made in the first two periods of surveying in Virginia," noting that whereas "Virginians at an early date were exceptionally conscious of the insignia of rank and property . . . it is curious that the first extant Virginia plat is not especially decorative" (*Surveyors and Statesmen,* 48).

The sources showing colonial maps are numerous; see, for example, Barbara McCorkle, *New England in Early Printed Maps, 1513 to 1800* (Providence, R.I., 2001); Richard

In response to the imperial imperative to chart the land, between the 1690s and the 1720s Virginians quadrupled the amount of land that had been surveyed. The communal archives witnessed a proportional on-slaught of plats that had to be entered, modified, or moved from town and county records. Farther to the north, in Maryland, "surveyed" and "resur-veyed" lands are the dominant feature in probate records. In New En-gland, plats were attached in increasing numbers to legal documents such as bills of sale, land deeds, personal wills, and auction records.[9]

A driving force behind the increase of plats was a runaway real estate market. From New England to Georgia, speculative transactions in landed property (mostly property that was yet to be occupied by the English) soared by the mid-eighteenth century. As an indication of how pervasive plats had become in communal life, between 1738 and 1760 the small town of Kent, Connecticut, witnessed more than six thousand land trans-actions—and this in a community where the male population at its peak was only 872. This meant that the citizens of Kent were exchanging plats to seal the sale of land at an average of more than seven trades per head. In Pennsylvania, the traffic in documents pertaining to land transactions prompted Benjamin Franklin to create the neologism *"Coined Land,"* de-fining deeds and plats as a form of paper currency.[10]

Stephenson and Marianne McKee, *Virginia in Maps: Four Centuries of Settlement, Growth, and Development* (Richmond, Va., 2000); William P. Cumming, *British Maps of Colonial America* (Chicago, 1974). For examples of early American plats and other surveying rec-ords, see David Buisseret, "The Estate Map in the New World," in Buisseret, ed., *Rural Images,* 91–112.

9. On Virginia, see Kain and Baigent, *Cadastral Map,* 273; Price, *Dividing the Land,* 101; Hughes, *Surveyors and Statesmen,* 106, 118–119. On Maryland, see Jane Baldwin, ed., *The Maryland Calendar of Wills* (Westminster, Md., 1988–1994), I–XIV. For example, see IX (1744–1749), 166, 186, or XIII (1764–1767), 3, 15, 28, 59, 147, 163. On New England, see *State of New Hampshire Town Charters* (Concord, N.H., 1867–1947), XXVI–XXIX; *Mas-sachusetts Archives,* 3d Ser., "Ancient Plans, Grants, etc.," IV, 139 (microfilm); also see Benes, *New England Prospect: A Loan Exhibition,* 75–88.

10. On Kent, see Charles S. Grant, "Land Speculation and the Settlement of Kent, 1738–1760," *New England Quarterly,* XXVIII (1955), 54–55. Grant elaborates in *Democracy in the Connecticut Frontier Town of Kent* (New York, 1961). On the pervasiveness of land specula-tion in eighteenth-century British America, see Marc Egnal, *A Mighty Empire: The Origins of the American Revolution* (Ithaca, N.Y., 1988); Woody Holton, *Forced Founders: Indians, Debtors, Slaves, and the Making of the American Revolution in Virginia* (Chapel Hill, N.C., 1999), 1–13; on land companies, see Charles Royster, *The Fabulous History of the Dismal Swamp Company: A Story of George Washington's Times* (New York, 1999).

On deeds and plats as currency, see Benjamin Franklin, "A Modest Enquiry into the

Manuscript plats, initiated by imperial demands and rapidly circulated by speculation mania, were being drawn up in tremendous numbers and passing through many hands, from long-established landowners to newly propertied commoners who had recently migrated to the English colonies. For many, even most, of these immigrants, the experience of landownership was new and profound. In their native lands, property was held by a privileged few, and landownership was directly connected to social prestige and political clout. For the vast majority of those living in Europe, landownership was unthinkable. The purchase of American land was a highly charged act, emotionally and socially. We might imagine that the plat which signaled that ownership thus carried the frisson of the experience. Not only was the plat infused with emotional and social energy due to its signification, but it was also a unique document because its construction was often the responsibility of the individual landowner. This all-important document—one carrying deep personal, economic, and political weight—was often written by the property owner himself. Even when this was not the case, individuals needed to know the principles and techniques of composing a plat. We thus see the emergence of a population that was well versed in the art of writing the survey.

GEODAESIA, OR THE ART OF GEODETIC WRITING

Embracing the new experience of widespread private landownership, colonial culture became preoccupied with the terms, concepts, and processes of surveying. The colonial archive reveals how the fascination with all things geodetic extended across geographical and class lines. A range of journals written by New Englanders and southerners—including

Nature and Necessity of a Paper-Currency" (1729), in Leonard W. Labaree et al., eds., *The Papers of Benjamin Franklin* (New Haven, Conn., 1959–), I, 151. The colonists' preoccupation with geodesy coincided with the formation of the provincial land banks, the first being founded in South Carolina in 1680. Following further inceptions of "land banks" (credit institutions using land as collateral) in Maryland and Massachusetts, in 1715 a Boston bank began to trade paper notes based on land securities by accepting land deeds and subsequently plats as promissory notes and debtor's bills. Writing in response to the inflation of land prices, Franklin proposed that such a land standard would hinge on the representation of land: "For as Bills issued upon Money Security are Money, so Bills issued upon Land, are in Effect *Coined Land.*" On the relationship between land and paper money, see Alexander Del Mar, *The History of Money in America: From the Earliest Times to the Establishment of the Constitution* (New York, 1968), 117. I wish to thank J. A. Leo Lemay for the Franklin reference.

the Massachusetts journeyman Richard Hazzen, the Connecticut farmer Joshua Hempstead, the Pennsylvania merchant Joseph Shippen, the Virginia planter Colonel Landon Carter, and the secretary to the trustees of Georgia William Stephens—demonstrate that colonial subjects of different ranks and occupations had a working knowledge of geodesy. This knowledge consisted of surveying terms and basic mathematical skills, map reading and abstract spatial thinking, and the writing skills necessary for constructing a plat. This knowledge was often earned by experience, as well-read gentlemen and semiliterate farmers alike took to the fields and then took up their pens.[11]

Given the lack of professional surveyors, the burden of surveying fell in large part on the layperson and individual landowner. Colonists thus pursued geodetic instruction in droves. Enterprising individuals were quick to capitalize on this growing demand for geodetic knowledge. Advertisements for personalized surveying instruction mushroomed throughout colonial towns. In a March 1709 issue of the *Boston News-Letter,* for example, one Owen Harris ran an advertisement offering evening instructions to gentlemen in "Geometry, Trigonometry, Plain and Sphaerical, Surveying." At the southern end of the colonies, the *South-Carolina Gazette* advertised on May 19, 1733, that "at the House of Mrs. Dalamare in Broad Street, is taught these Sciences, viz., Arithmetick, Algebra, Geometry, Trigonometry, Surveying, Dialling, Navigation, Astronomy, Gauging, Fortification." While many of these students might have been landowners themselves, many others might have been young, landless men seeking to make their way in the world. After bookkeeping, surveying was the most popular subject of vocational training in eighteenth-century America. As a supplement to or surrogate for personal instruction, surveying manuals offered an education for the autodidactic colonist. Readers engaged with handbooks such as John Wing's *Geodaetus Practicus Redivivus: The Art of Surveying* (circa 1700), Adam Martindale's *Country Survey-Book; or, Land-*

11. See "The Boundary Line of New Hampshire and Massachusetts: Journal of Richard Hazzen, Surveyor, 1741," *New England Historical and Genealogical Register,* XXXIII (Boston, 1879), 323–333; *The Diary of Joshua Hempstead of New London, Connecticut, 1711–1758* (New London, Conn., 1901), 2, 12, 84, 96, 142, 196, 248, 275; Joseph Shippen, Jr., "Letter Book, 1763–73" (American Philosophical Society MSS guide, 1124), letters of July 24, 1753, Feb. 15, 1754. Also see E. Merton Coulter, ed., *The Journal of William Stephens, 1741–1745* (Athens, Ga., 1958–1959), I, 48, 98, 177, II, 43, 47–48; Jack P. Greene, ed., *The Diary of Colonel Landon Carter of Sabine Hall, 1752–1778* (Richmond, Va., 1987), I, 149.

Meters Vade-Mecum (circa 1682, 1711), or Samuel Wyld's *Practical Surveyor; or, The Art of Land-Measuring Made Easy* (1730).[12]

Such manuals were exclusively English imports. Not surprisingly, given their origins, they tended to teach the principles of surveying through an imperial lens. Take, for instance, John Love's *Geodaesia; or, The Art of Surveying and Measuring of Land, Made Easie.* Published for the first time in 1688 and in a sixth edition in 1753, this handbook was one of the few specifically addressing British American surveying practices. Moreover, gauging by book sales and probate records, Love's *Geodaesia* was by far the most available surveying manual teaching British colonists the theorems of geometry and trigonometry, the methods of surveying land by compass and chain, and the art of writing the plat.[13]

12. Similar ads for surveying instruction were placed by Joseph Kent in the *Boston News-Letter,* Oct. 6–9, 1735, or anonymously in the Dec. 31, 1744, issue of the *South-Carolina Gazette.* These examples appear in American newspapers throughout the eighteenth century. Surveying was taught throughout British America; it was advertised in the *Independent Advertiser* (Boston) between 1724 and 1749 and was a regular subject in the *American Weekly Mercury* and *Pennsylvania Gazette* (both Philadelphia). See Robert Seyboldt, "Source Studies in American Colonial Education: The Private School," *University of Illinois Bulletin,* XXIII, no. 4 (September 1925), 35–53.

On the history of surveying manuals, see E. G. R. Taylor, "The Surveyor," *Econ. Hist. Rev.,* XVII (1947), 130–131; Taylor, *The Mathematical Practitioners of Hanoverian England, 1714–1840* (Cambridge, 1966); Richeson, *English Land Measuring,* 104–129, 142–157; Edmond R. Kiely, *Surveying Instruments: Their History and Classroom Use* (New York, 1947). On the application of these surveying handbooks in British America, see Hughes, *Surveyors and Statesmen,* 28–37.

13. Eighteenth-century book catalogs and auctions document the popularity of Love's *Geodaesia* as late as 1761, when Jeremiah Condy sold at least five copies; see Elizabeth Reilly's transcription "A Bookseller's Account Book, 1759–1770" (Boston, 1978), 4, at the American Antiquarian Society. Also see a 1766 book sale advertised by a Boston broadside, offering "a valuable Collection of Books, a Variety of Maps and Prints, with several Optical and Philosophical Instruments," listed under the header "Natural Philosophy and Mathematicks . . . Love's *Surveyin[g]*" ("Boston, September 30, 1766: On Monday . . ."). A century after its first publication, Love's surveying manual was still deemed one of the crucial textbooks among American surveyors. In 1793, Samuel Campbell of New York reprinted Love's manual as "the twelfth edition, adapted to American surveyors." The only other early modern surveying manual including American concerns, though only nominally, was William Folkingham's *Feudigraphia: The Synopsis or Epitome of Surveying Methodized* (London, 1610), dedicated to "all Under-takers in the Plantation of Ireland or Virginia."

Because of their English origins, seventeenth- and eighteenth-century surveying man-

In the preface, Love develops his title's advertisement ("How to Lay-out New Lands in America, or elsewhere") within a context of imperial interest. He refers specifically to the British American reader and surveyor's apprentice:

> I have seen Young men, in *America,* often nonplus'd so, that their Books would not help them forward, particularly in *Carolina,* about Laying out Lands, when a certain quantity of Acres has been given to be laid out five or six times as broad as long. This I know is to be laught at by a Mathematician; yet to such as have no more of this Learning, than to know how to Measure a Field, it seems a Difficult Question: And to what Book already Printed of Surveying shall they repair to, to be resolved?

Love's self-promotional caution raises the specter of practical incompetence and bad surveying manuals (that is, the books of his competitors). But while Love's preface is meant to scare students and boost his book sales, his preface states a more serious concern: that without proper surveying instructions "Young men, in *America*"—that is, the sons of England—threatened to wreak havoc in the imperial mapping archive.[14]

Underlying much of the manual's preface (and the ensuing narrative of instruction) is the author's unalleviated fear that, because of the perceived failure of books to offer appropriate textual solutions to surveying problems, the "nonplus'd" readers of manuals were likely to spurn the principles of geodesy and stray from the imperial code regarding land surveys. The preface thus warns both British and American audiences: without the proper textbook the British surveyor could easily subvert the empire's mapping enterprise. Inherent in this warning seems to be the suggestion that in America a new generation of landowners could emerge who, having received inadequate surveying instructions, would cease to

---

uals have eluded American scholarly attention. They are briefly mentioned in Hugh Amory and David D. Hall, eds., *A History of the Book in America,* I, *The Colonial Book in the Atlantic World* (Cambridge, 2000); also in Louis C. Karpinski, *Bibliography of Mathematical Works Printed in America through 1850* (Ann Arbor, Mich., 1940). This omission is understandable, since probate records like the *Maryland Calendar of Wills* log references to surveying handbooks in this fashion: "To Richard, my mill, desk, and surveyor's books" (IX, 160) or "Surveying instruments and mathematick books to son Theophilus" (XIII, 113), thus leaving it unclear whether the books are actual surveying manuals or records of finished surveys.

14. James Love, *Geodaesia; or, The Art of Surveying and Measuring of Land, Made Easie* (London, 1688), vi.

be influenced by British surveying rules and imperial land regulations. Or, to put it otherwise, without proper textual training in geodesy, the colonists, left to their own devices, could repudiate the empire's cartographic dominance by inventing their own local schemes for representing land.

In an effort to control the habits of the surveyor, manuals like Love's *Geodaesia* conceptualized the art of surveying in textual terms, as a process that included the production of a book and a plat through the survey's adaptation of the alphabet and unique writing system. Commenting on the fallibility of surveying instruments in the thick woods of the American wilderness, Love emphasizes that for an American audience the "Field-Book" is the best technology for performing the survey in a controlled (and controllable) fashion. In the chapter "Of the Field-Book," Love explains:

> You must always have in readiness in the Field, a little Book, in which fairly to insert your Angles and Lines; which Book you may divide by Lines into Columns, as you shall think convenient in your Practice; leaving always a large Column to the right hand, to put down what remarkable things you meet with in your way, as Ponds, Brooks, Mills, Trees, or the like.

The colonial geodetic writing lesson begins, not by measuring the actual field, but by producing a written ledger. The field book provides a textual space in which the surveyor recounts particular observations ("remarkable things") in narrative form. Surviving examples of such a field book illustrate how the descriptive, verbal element nearly overwhelms the graphic component of the survey. Not only does the field book assume a discursive function, but it acts as a scrivener's writing manual, leaving ample space for the surveyor's penmanship. Notes Love: "You may chuse whether you will have any Lines or not, if you can write streight, and in good order, the Figures directly one under another. For this I leave you chiefly to your own fancy; for I believe there are not two Surveyors in *England,* that have exactly the same Method for their Field-Notes." In Love's directives, then, the construction of the plat becomes primarily an exercise in writing, rather than measurement, as much a matter of good penmanship as mathematical accuracy.[15]

---

15. Ibid., 61–62. Love's manual acknowledges that geodetic theories and surveying instruments were problematic in America. The English measuring "Chain" was inconvenient: "If you find the chain too long . . . especially in *America,* you may then take the half of

Indeed, Love's very description of measuring the land depicts the surveyor as the author at the center of the overlapping fields of dirt and alphabetic text. In Love's exercise called "How to take the Plot of a Field at one Station in any place thereof" he instructs:

> Admit ABCDEF to be a Field, of which you are to take the Plot: First set your Semicircle upon the Staff in any convenient place thereof, as at ☉, and cause Marks to be set up in every Angle: Direct your Instrument . . . for Example, to A and espying the Mark at A through the fixed Sights . . . then turn the moveable Index about . . . 'till through the Sights thereof you espy the Mark at B. . . . Write that down in your Field-Book, so turn the Index round to every one of the other Angles, putting down in your Field-Book what Degrees the Index points to, as for Example, at C 107 Degrees, at D 185 . . . at F 315 Degrees. [Figure 4]

In subtle ways, these instructions placed the surveyor at the center of a field that is not only chthonic but alphabetic. The system of identifying points on a geometric figure with the letters of the alphabet was, of course, pragmatic and widely accepted—but it was, nonetheless, an exercise in arranging the alphabet. The command "Admit ABCDEF to be a Field" translates the imaginary field into an alphabetic construct in which the written letters function as the substitute for the actual land. Although I do not wish to overread the significance of using letters to label geometric

---

the Chain." The "Plain Table" (a draft board for plotting an area in one station) and the theodolite (which relied on a clear field of vision) were both useless when surveying densely wooded areas. And, although Love concedes, "We must sometimes make use of the Needle, without exceeding great trouble, as in the thick Woods of *Jamaica, Carolina,* etc.," the magnetic compass attached to the "Circumferentor" (a full or half circle marking off degrees) provided dubious technological support ("if there be no Iron Mines") for any of the colonial mapping ventures. Ibid., 55, 57, 59.

Half a century later, the American cartographer Lewis Evans echoes Love's reservations. In his *Geographical, Historical, Political, Philosophical, and Mechanical Essays: The First, Containing an Analysis of a General Map of the Middle British Colonies in America* . . . (Philadelphia, 1755), Evans writes: "An European may be at a Loss to know, why there is a Necessity for these Sorts of Helps in making a Map of a Country; for that Reason it must be observed, that all America, East of Missisippi, low Lands, Hills and Mountains, is every where covered with Woods, except some interval Spots of no great Extent, cleared by the European Colonist. Here are no Churches, Towers, Houses or peaked Mountains to be seen from afar, no Means of obtaining the Bearings or Distances of Places, but by the Compass, and actual Mensuration with the Chain" (5).

For examples of field books, see Hughes, *Surveyors and Statesmen,* 118–124.

C H A P. VI.

How to take the Plot of a Field at one Station in any place thereof, from whence you may see all the Angles by the Semicircle.

ADmit A B C D E F to be a Field, of which you are to take the Plot: Firſt ſet your Semicircle upon the Staff in any convenient place thereof, as at ☉, and cauſe Marks to be ſet up in every Angle : Direct your Inſtrument, the *Flower de Luce* from you to any one Angle: As for Example, to A, and eſpying the Mark at A through the fixed Sights, there ſcrew faſt the Inſtrument ; then turn the move-

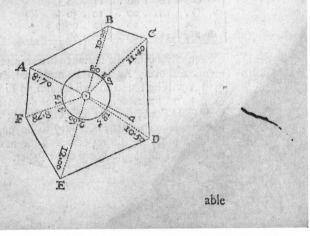

able

Figure 4. "How to Take the Plot of a Field. . . ." From Geodaesia; or, The Art of Surveying and Measuring of Land, Made Easie, *by John Love. 1688.* By Permission of the Houghton Library, Harvard University

points, the ramifications of this long-standing practice as it was carried out by self-trained surveyors are interesting. The surveyor, to whom this system might well have been new and thus still fresh in its connotations, found himself in a mode of land representation that is saturated with textual associations. At its most basic element, the alphabetic component to the process of recording a geometrical survey required that the surveyor write down letters and think about their spatial relationships. Fundamentally—on a level that is, quite literally, literal—the composition of the plat is about describing letters.[16]

Moreover, the letters of the survey are predicated upon the presence of the author at the center of the field. While geodetic writing exercises like this serve to reify land as a written text, they also engender a set of self-emplacing principles by which the geodetic text hinges on the bodily figure of the surveyor. By asking the reader to perform the labor of surveying, the textbook invites the surveyor's body to enter into the geodetic writing process. As the instructions call directly on the reader to "set your Semicircle upon the Staff" and mark the place "as at ⊙," *Geodaesia* acknowledges that the geodetic record and the plat turn upon the surveyor's body, sensory perception, and creative translation. While the reader is to imagine "ABCDEF to be a Field," the exercise depends on the surveyor's ability to "espy" and "see" the alphabetic markers in order to write them down. For the duration of these activities, the symbolic center of the station (the "⊙") collapses the individual surveyor's bodily position with that of the instrument and the land he is standing on. The surveyor is conflated with, even becomes, the ⊙—he is, we might say, the point, or the eye, or the I, of the exercise. As ⊙, he becomes the perspective dominating and constructing the figure, yet in the end he also becomes enmeshed in the alphabetic order, at home in a lineup of ABC⊙DEF.

The phenomenon of the surveyor's being integrated into the geometric-graphic form of the survey finds an interesting parallel in the construction of alphabetic letters. The modern printed alphabet was derived from geometric figures. Since the sixteenth century, scriveners and printers had designed the alphabet using the ordinate lines of the Euclidian grid. Through a series of step-by-step instructions, writing handbooks used "points" and "lines" (as would surveyors) to assemble the graphic figure of a letter. Two eighteenth-century handbooks illustrate this almost-forgotten structural link connecting literacy and geodesy. Looking at the tables side by side—one is taken from Michael Baurenfeind's *Schreib-Kunst* [The Art of Writing] (1716) and the other from John Hammond's *Practical Surveyor* (1731)—it becomes apparent that designing alphabetic letters and surveying land were conceived as similar exercises (Figures 5, 6). This conceptual homology between designing letters and writing about

16. Love, *Geodaesia*, 71–72.

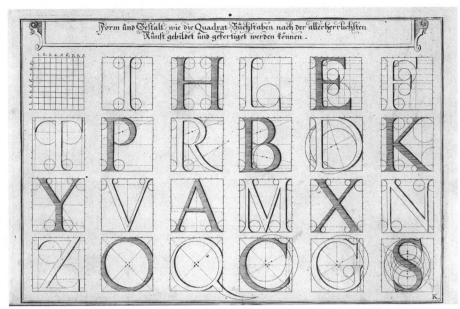

Figure 5. "Form und Gestalt wie die Quadrat Buchstaben nach der allerherrlichsten Kunst gebildet und gefertiget werden können" [Form and shape for designing and crafting square letters . . .]. From Vollkommene Wieder-Herstellung . . . , *by Michael Baurenfeind. 1716?* By Permission of the Houghton Library, Harvard University

geography dates back to the sixteenth century, when the graphic design of the letter alphabet was the result of pragmatic and often aesthetically inspired collaborations between writing instructors, printers, and cartographers. Not only do alphabetic letters have a historical connection with surveying; they also carry a homological association with the human body. Early modern treatises on letter form, script, and type used the figure of the body as a structural device for writing the alphabet (Figure 7). Depicting letters with faces, heads, necks, and bodies, the treatises not only fantasized about an innate congruity between the human and the letter shape but, by rendering both into squares and circles, also presumed them to be the products of the structural logic of the geometric grid.[17]

17. For discussions on this overlap between writing, cartography, and surveying, see Tom Conley, *The Self-Made Map: Cartographic Writing in Early Modern France* (Minneapolis, Minn., 1996); Eileen Reeves, "Reading Maps," *Word and Image,* IX (1993), 51–65; David Woodward, "The Manuscript, Engraved, and Typographic Traditions of Map Lettering," in Woodward, ed., *Art and Cartography: Six Historical Essays* (Chicago, 1987), 174–212. The history of the human alphabet is sketched out by Johanna Drucker, *The Alphabetic Labyrinth: The Letters in History and Imagination* (London, 1995), 162–166. See also Tamara

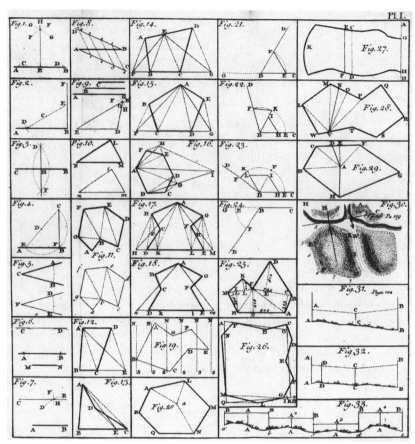

Figure 6. Foldout Chart Containing Practice Surveys. From The Practical Surveyor . . . , *by John Hammond. 1750.* From the Goldsmiths' Library of Economic Literature, University of London Library

It is doubtful that Love was consciously considering these homologies when he directed the surveyor to become a ⊙. But Love's text is situated inside a wider cultural discourse that was sensitive to the structural and conceptual overlay of alphabet, survey, and human form, all of which were mapped onto a Euclidian grid. What was the effect of this overlay on the surveyor, on the ⊙? There are a few working principles that I would like to draw together thus far: (1) The legal imperative to survey all property

Plakins Thornton, *Handwriting in America: A Cultural History* (New Haven, Conn., 1996), 27–29. Tom Conley theorizes the relationship of the geodetic grid and the letter form in *The Self-Made Map,* 62–87, esp. 71.

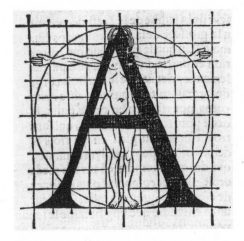

resulted in an outpouring of newly produced plats. (2) These plats were produced by newly trained (often self-trained) surveyors, sometimes the (new) landowners themselves, who had a deep personal investment in the plat. (3) The plat was largely a textual rather than a graphic document; its construction revolved around plotting alphabetic points and writing prose. (4) The implied or imaginative center of the plat was the body of the surveyor himself; it was his perspective, judgment, and prose that shaped the plat. Thus, while I would not argue for the plat as a literary form in the sense of belonging with the belles lettres, I would maintain that the plat is a pointedly textual (or alphabetical) writing practice, one that entailed the strong presence of a first-person author. While surveyors might not have perceived their work as poetic in the way of Steere and Chandler, many did experience the writing of the survey as a type of literary production, even as one adhering to narrative principles.

The Surveyor's Diary of Joshua Hempstead

The diary of the Connecticut farmer Joshua Hempstead exemplifies how the practical labor of land surveying and geodetic writing engendered a self-conscious writing style among American colonists. Between 1711 and 1758, Hempstead recorded the daily weather and weekly sermon topics, carefully monitored advertisements and other genres of popular print culture, and remarked upon the ways in which he kept up his correspondence and cut letters into tombstones. Throughout the diary, his language was generally plain and matter-of-fact: "Tuesd 16 [April 1728] fair. I was at home most of the day writing and other things. Ad Carted out Some dung and fetcht Mulch into the yard and Hay for Capt Buttolph. Wednsd 17 fair. a Genll Fast. Mr Adams pr[ayed]. al. day. Thursd 18 fair. In the foren I was in Town to and Recd of Dea. Green the Contribution of this Spring and Carryed it to Mr Adms. aftern at Wm Beebees."[18]

However, interspersed between the monotonous entries commenting on carting dung and fetching hay are lengthy narratives recounting Hempstead's geodetic activities. Significantly, these reports of his surveying coincide with his designated writing days (his being "at home most of the day writing"). In these entries Hempstead relates in great detail how he ran the surveyor's line to measure his land by "chain" and "link," "rod" and "pole," how he used the instrument of the "plain table," marked "exact angles," "turned" on proper "points," and took the "plot" of the land. Aside from geodetic practices, Hempstead also expands on the survey's textual outcome. He described that, after laying out a "lot" and demarcating its "Bounds," he drew a "plat." And he explained that the plat was derived by way of putting down rods, by "casting up" the numerical entries of his field notes, and finally how he "drew" and "wrote" the dual text of the plat.[19]

Indeed, in these passages Hempstead's prose becomes exhaustive and complex:

Thursd 25 fair. I was with Capt Lattimer Capt Stephn Prenttis and Thomas. Wee mett at Jno Champlins . . . to Renew the Town Bounds between us. wee began att the ditch by Champlins and Ran a Ransom Line North Six degrees West in ordr to find a true line between the Sd ditch and a line Tree at the Road by Minors. Wee Ran 78 Rod to a pond and Suposed itt to be 52 Rod a Cross and then up the hill 30 Rod to a Stake thenn Same Course 80 Rod to a Stake near a brook where a Tree is blown up and thn 58 Rod to a Cheesnut Tree Standing by the path from Oliver Beckwiths on the East Side the brook. then wee left of and went and Renewed the old Bounds. first wee took notice of the gray oak by the Road and then . . . wee went to an old Stump in Moors field wch was Somthing uncertain. Next we went to a heap of Stones . . . on the Southend of itt . . . then to a heap of Stones on the hill above Capt Lattimers house and . . . then to the Cornner Tree by a Run on the East Side of the hill.

18. *Diary of Joshua Hempstead of New London*, 196.
19. Ibid., 2, 12, 84, 96, 142, 196, 248, 275.

Expansive entries like this one recalibrate the basic premise of the diary form, positing a spatial, instead of a temporal, everyday consciousness. As the description of landed property recedes behind the description of geodetic practices, Hempstead recollects the construction of a double map. By describing minutely the topographic elements of the surveyed plot of land, he also charts a communal map that distinguishes contractual agreements ("old Bounds") and neighbors ("Oliver Beckwiths"). His narrative is concerned with stabilizing both the salable and social landscape. By the same token, his narrative implies that there is nothing more destabilizing to Hempstead than the inability to track a geodetic location of the land in absolute, legible terms. Underlying Hempstead's compulsively detailed account of measuring and marking the landscape according to "Six Degrees West" and "78 Rod" or "Cross" and "Tree" is the fear that the land resists being mapped, that there is always "Somthing uncertain" about the surveying record.[20]

Just as the verbal description of the survey functions to stabilize the colonial land record, it also converted the technical discourse of property into a narrative of selfhood. The geodetic record begins to assume the faint outlines of the narrative formula of story and plot. Even the crudest geodetic description has a beginning and an ending—it "began att the ditch by Champlins" and ended at "the Cornner Tree by a Run on the East Side of the hill." As the surveyor literally inscribes the land using field marks such as "a heap of Stones" or notable landmarks like "where a Tree is blown up," the surveyor's narrative begins to configure elements that in fictional writing constitute the outlines of a plot. The plat translates Captain Lattimer into the geodetic character, taking possession of the land by surveying it. When probed for further narrative action, the geodetic figure emerges as a textual device for establishing social contact between the "path from Oliver Beckwiths," the town bounds, and "Capt Lattimers house." Written in compliance with the colonial plat, the survey becomes a narrative space that is as much about the enactment of a spatialized individuality as it is about a spatially choreographed sociability. The survey's textuality here sets into motion a territorial narrative of emplacement in which communities and individual landowners articulate (and after selling land rearticulate) the territorial boundaries as well as their social position vis-à-vis family mem-

20. Ibid., 196–197.

bers and neighbors, as well as geopolitical entities such as townships or counties.

Yet, at the same time as the geodetic entries in the diary seemingly place the community on the land, they illustrate the diarist's personal concern of locating himself inside a permanent and easily accessible frame of reference. Indeed, the narrative persona of Hempstead records the beginnings of a rudimentary literary self-consciousness that is predicated not solely on individual landownership but on the ability to write oneself as a geodetic identity inside the narrative space of colonial records. As the diary fuses the survey's landmarks with the narrator's geodetically defined point of view, it creates a writing style that depends on the script of the plat. Hempstead's description of geodetic field marks confirms the diarist's stationary presence within the plat, as the constant repetition of the first person folds the geodetic figure of the platmaker into the spatial body of colonial society.

The Surveyed Self of William Byrd

In the writings of William Byrd, we find a different appropriation of the geodetic in the service of self-definition. Rather than focus on how the map and the survey work to position the individual within a larger human community connected by territorial relations, Byrd employs the language and practice of surveying to meld himself with the land. While scholarly attention has been focused on Byrd's *History of the Dividing Line* (the title of which is itself a testament to the interconnection of surveying and narrative) and its companion piece the *Secret History,* I want to look instead at his text *A Journey to the Land of Eden* (1733). Where *The History* tells the tale of the dividing line between Virginia and North Carolina and the social consequences thereof, the *Journey* relates the saga of Byrd's own private landownership; *The History* thus recounts geodesy on a macro scale, the *Journey* on a micro scale.[21]

21. William Byrd, *A Journey to the Land of Eden,* in Louis B. Wright, ed., *The Prose Works of William Byrd of Westover: Narratives of a Colonial Virginian* (Cambridge, Mass., 1966), 379–415. On the literary history of the *Journey* as a family manuscript, see Royster, *Fabulous History,* 4–5. For a modern reading of Byrd's *History of the Dividing Line,* its critical reception, and the surveyor's line as an organizing principle and polyvalent conceit for negotiating self-interest and interpersonal relations, see Douglas Anderson, "Plotting William Byrd," *William and Mary Quarterly,* 3d Ser., LVI (1999), 701–722. The best discussion of the *Journey* is by Wayne Franklin, *Discoverers, Explorers, Settlers: The Diligent Writers of Early America* (Chicago, 1979), 127–130.

The *Journey* is written in journal form, and its basic plot follows the generic conquest narrative: the narrator travels to the western parts of Virginia and North Carolina in order to survey and take possession of twenty thousand acres of prospective farmland. Similar to the two histories, the *Journey*'s narrator records the mundane events that surround a pack of men traveling in the colonial woods, suggesting diurnal episodes of drinking, eating, riding, and sleeping, which presumably were interspersed with riotous moments of male bonding and witty exchange. However, from the moment that Byrd travels into the space he claims as his property, the diary's narrative changes its mode from the mock-heroic imperial epic to the colonial rhetoric of land surveying. Or, to put this otherwise, instead of presenting the western territories as a vast pleasure ground to be traversed by Virginia's cosmopolitan elite, Byrd begins to enclose the land as his private property by using the localist narrative stance of the geodetic author.

Byrd begins his survey in narrative terms. He writes, "The beginning of my fine tract of land in Carolina [is] called the Land of Eden." The land thus assumes the position of a story, with its own plot (having a "beginning") and a title ("called the Land of Eden"). The survey also begins with a moment of authorial inscription: "I caused the initial letters of my name to be cut on a large poplar and beech near my corner, for the more easy finding it another time." This act of inscription serves a fourfold purpose that intertwines the pragmatic concerns of performing a survey with the more abstract principles of geodetic authorship. First, Byrd's initials act as an authorial attribution, especially in an age when it was common practice to publish a text under the initials of the author's name. Second, it performs the requisite function of beginning the survey. As we have seen, the survey relied upon alphabetic orientation; here, instead of using the more established form of "AB," Byrd begins with "WB." Third, it serves the practical purpose of allowing Byrd to find the tree where he started. And fourth, this act symbolically merges the body of the surveyor with the land he is surveying, as tree and man share an identity ("WB").[22]

Although the journal opens with an imaginative description of the fu-

22. Byrd, *Journey*, in Wright, ed., *Prose Works*, 394. Byrd elaborated the material fusion between surveyor and the survey in 1728. Having revisited the campsites of his official boundary survey, he discovered trees that bore the names of the North Carolina commissioners. Byrd went on to embellish the signatures by carving (in all likelihood unflattering) portraits into the trees, so as "to add to their Names a Sketch of their Characters" (cited in Royster, *Fabulous History*, 16).

ture contours of the estate (including the site or "situation for the manor house"), the dominant descriptive strategy quickly conveys us from the realm of fantasy to a world structured by chain and compass: "We were stirring early from this enchanting place and ran eight miles of my back line, which tended south 84½ westerly." From this point on, the daily narrative record supplements the linear construction of the geodetic plat. Like a surveyor's field notes, his account tabulates the daily progress: "[September] 27 Measuring and marking spent so much of our time that we could advance no further than eight miles, and the chain carriers thought that a great way." Or, on "[September] 29. In measuring a mile and a half farther we reached the lower ford of the Irvin [River], which branches from the Dan [River] about two miles to the south-southeast of this place." He refers almost exclusively to the controlled geodetic terminology of corner, line, distance, and compass direction. For the duration of the survey Byrd thus subordinates his narrative plot to the surveyor's plat.[23]

Following the logic of the surveying handbook, moreover, the technical skill of the surveyor folds the depiction of the earth into an anthropomorphic double of the surveyor-author. This slippage occurs when Byrd writes, "When we came to run our northern course of three miles to the place where the country line intersects the same Irvin higher up, we passed over nothing but stony hills and barren ground, clothed with little timber and refreshed with less water." The geodetic formula gives way to an essentialized account of the land as an impoverished human body that fails to perform according to biological ("barren") and social ("clothed") expectations. In the absence of external riches, the narrator looks to the land's deep, subterranean features:

All my hopes were in the riches that might lie underground, there being many goodly tokens of mines. The stones which paved the river both by their weight and color promised abundance of metal; but whether it be

---

23. Byrd, *Journey,* in Wright, ed., *Prose Works,* 394–396. As the analysis of eighteenth-century landscape description has emphasized, Byrd's descriptive phrases such as "enchanting place" were code signifying the economic agenda of the land speculator and surveyor in both England and America. Discussing landscape in relation to Byrd's *Journey* is Franklin, *Discoverers,* 127–130. On the relation of the aesthetic of landscape and enclosure laws, see Raymond Williams, *The Country and the City* (New York, 1973); John Barrell, *The Dark Side of the Landscape: The Rural Poor in English Painting, 1730–1840* (Cambridge, 1980); W. J. T. Mitchell, ed., *Landscape and Power* (Chicago, 1994).

silver, lead, or copper is beyond our skill to discern. We also discovered many shows of marble, of a white ground, with streaks of red and purple. So that 'tis possible the treasure in the bowels of the earth may make ample amends for the poverty of its surface.

In a desperate attempt to imbue the land with signs bearing the promise of intrinsic value, Byrd prepares the landscape in human, bodily terms: the white, marblelike skin of the plot of land displays on its surface the veinlike substructure that encloses the human body's "bowels."[24]

Eighteenth- and nineteenth-century American literature frequently represents the land as a female body, one that is prone to the rapacious desires of white male settlers. The reference to mining silver and gold in Byrd's account might immediately lead us to perceive this passage in that literary tradition; anatomical passages like this one situate Byrd's writings within a larger discourse of discovery and conquest, in which the literary strategies of territorial appropriation are predicated upon a feminized image of the land. Indeed, in *The History of the Dividing Line*, a text devoted to the surveying of political territories, Byrd's aggressive use of surveying lines does constitute an invasive maneuver, in which a feminized space is geodetically penetrated and mastered, as imperial modes of mapmaking imposed the power structure of patriarchy and masculinity upon the land.[25]

But in the *Journey*, a text devoted to the surveying of Byrd's private land, the chthonic anthropomorphizing serves a completely different function. Here, the land and the surveyor merge. It is significant that the land is described as white, and the area is circumscribed by the masculine rivers of the Dan and the Irvin. The *Journey* does not tell a story of male desires to dominate a passive, female, native landscape; rather, it provides an account of the surveyor's desire to become integrated with the land, inside a homosocial landscape governed by the codes of male proprietorship. Moreover, seeing the land with geodetic eyes, Byrd as the surveyor aims to inscribe himself into the space and to discover a reciprocity between his body and the earth. Just as the human letter-figures were subjected to the

24. Byrd, *Journey*, in Wright, ed., *Prose Works*, 396.

25. For the origins of this reading in early American literary studies, see Annette Kolodny, *The Lay of the Land: Metaphor as Experience and History in American Life and Letters* (Chapel Hill, N.C., 1975); Kolodny, *The Land before Her: Fantasy and Experience of the American Frontiers, 1630–1860* (Chapel Hill, N.C., 1984). Also, the line's "geographic dismemberings of a primordial 'Virginia' " has been reconsidered as an expression of Byrd's imperial impulse by Anderson, "Plotting William Byrd," *WMQ*, 3d Ser., LVI (1999), 714.

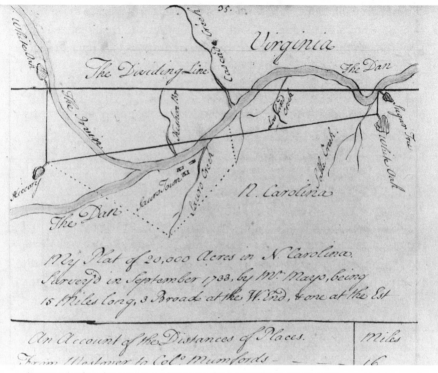

Figure 8. My Plat of 20,000 Acres in N. Carolina. *By William Byrd. 1733.*
Courtesy, The Virginia Historical Society

lines of the geodetic grid, Byrd emplaces his own body onto the form of
the plat. The deeply personal nature of this surveyor-land relationship is
manifested not only by his initials carved in trees but by the title that Byrd
gives his sketch, *My Plat of 20,000 Acres in N. Carolina* (Figure 8). The
oversized script of the first person possessive pronoun reveals a heightened sense of personal possession. Through inscribing the plat by his
own hand, Byrd invokes the ego and authorial persona of the modern
possessive individual ("my") in order to take possession of both the outcome of the survey and the land.

George Washington and Possessive Identity

While for the self-trained Byrd the exercise of writing and describing
the land becomes self-reflexive, the affective impulse of geodetic writing
also left its imprint in the work of the professionally trained surveyor
George Washington. Ideally, and in accordance with the writing instructions of surveying manuals, the surveyor displayed his professionalism

by writing up plats that were the product of applied literacy and mechanical skill—and not informed by personal interest. A look at Washington's school papers reveals that at age thirteen Washington was trained according to the professional surveyor's standards. Between 1745 and 1748, his copybooks show a constant overlap between surveying lessons and exercises geared toward the acquisition of basic literary competence ("cyphering") and social skills ("Rules . . . of Civility and Decent Behaviour in Company and Conversation"). Between reading the classics and solving mathematical problems, Washington copied out sets of surveying problems and practiced the drawing of plats. At least thirty-nine pages of his copybook were devoted to transcribing passages on the "Art of Surveying and Measuring of Land." Furthermore, his writing exercises were regularly supplemented by "practice surveys."[26]

This education prepared Washington for a short and intensive career as a local land surveyor. Working in the lucrative business of frontier surveying between the ages of seventeen and twenty, he conducted more than two hundred surveys, sometimes preparing three in a day. Unlike Hempstead and Byrd, Washington rarely took note of his surveying activities. Those diary entries that mention his geodetic work only do so in passing: for example, in March 1748, he wrote "Tuesday 29th. This Morning went out and Survey'd five Hundred Acres of Land and went down to one Michael Stumps on the So. Fork of the Branch. On the way Shot two Wild Turkies." But his surveying activities have survived in the standard documentary format, his surveying field books and meticulously drafted plats. Writing in compliance with Virginia's "surveyor's oath," Washington kept field books in which he entered the "essential information needed to produce the finished surveys that were later submitted to the proprietor's office." After finishing each survey, Washington transcribed his field notes by preparing a signed plat and description, which he "returned . . . to the proprietor's office, where [the plat] sometimes lay for several years before a grant was issued."[27]

26. See W. W. Abbot et al., eds., *The Papers of George Washington,* Colonial Series (Charlottesville, Va., 1983–), I, 1–3. An illustration of a practice survey written by Washington can be seen in Donald Jackson and Dorothy Twohig, eds., *The Diaries of George Washington* (Charlottesville, Va., 1976–1979), I, 14. Also see J. B. Harley, "George Washington, Map-Maker," *Geographical Magazine,* XLVIII (1976), 588–594; Lawrence Martin, *The George Washington Atlas* (Washington, D.C., 1932).

27. Abbot et al., eds., *Papers of George Washington,* Col. Ser., I, 8–33, esp. 12, 14; Jackson and Twohig, eds., *Diaries of George Washington,* I, 15.

The plats that Washington produced as a professional surveyor are textbook examples of good geodetic writing. In his finished surveys, the graphic components consist mainly of the property's outline into which were written innocuously descriptive words, such as "Area." There are no hints at information about the land's physical features, intended or imagined use, not to mention its social significance. The verbal part is executed in a legible round-hand style, demonstrating that Washington's mechanical competence extended from the art of surveying to the art of penmanship as well. His plats were ideal from the standpoint of the surveying manual because they were quite literally written like a textbook exercise; they avoided all references to the ungeodetic interference of human contexts that, for example, would suggest a tract's convoluted history of frontier landownership or personal investments.[28]

And yet, within only a few years after his surveying career had ended, Washington prepared a plat in which writing and describing the land became self-reflexive after all. In a 1766 plat of his estate on the Potomac River, Washington added a small decorative cartouche bearing this title: "A PLAN of my FARM on little Hunting Creek and Potomack River." Given that Washington is platting the survey of his private property, the appearance of the personal possessive pronoun "my" is not a surprise. Although the title doesn't bear the same suggestive clout as it did in the context of William Byrd's survey, especially if we consider that in Washington's handwriting it is not the pronoun "my" but the words "PLAN" and "FARM" that are capitalized, it nonetheless personalizes the property.[29]

For Washington to make the inscription of the plat visibly personal is a normative gesture in the larger context of the prevailing eighteenth-century country ideology. In this ideology, the British gentleman farmer on both sides of the Atlantic advertises his personal relationship to landed property by preparing—and stamping—the plot for his own possession. Through the plot the landowner was surveying not only to represent the land as proprietary property. Rather, as Washington's brief personal display of geodetic affect illustrates, surveying and plotting become

28. For examples, see Abbot et al., eds., *Papers of George Washington,* Col. Ser., I, 15, 21, 24.

29. For a reproduction of this plat, see Buisseret, "The Estate Map in the New World," in Buisseret, ed., *Rural Images,* 97. It can also be viewed on-line at the Library of Congress: http:/memory.loc.gov.

a symbolic shorthand for self-identification, a shorthand according to which the plat actualizes the *I*.[30]

PLATTING LAND AND IDENTITY

The profusion of colonial plats created a textual genre that fostered a strong sense of personal geodetic emplacement; although these plats were dutifully created in compliance with British imperial commands, they functioned as a colonial discourse of self-recognition and self-affirmation. In the final writing exercise of *Geodaesia*, Love advises the student, "Let the Arms of the Lord of the Mannor be fairly drawn," and, "Write down also in every Field the true Content thereof; and if it be required, the Names of the present Possessors, and their Tenures." While family crests were rarely to be found among colonial landowners, the landowner's written name became the dominant feature of the plat's geodetically constructed space. Family plats as well as local cadastral surveys marked landed property as discrete plots inscribed with proper names. This is the case for the single plat of "Capt. Henry Bull" (Figure 9) or for the multiple plat of Ipswich, Massachusetts, showing a list of names: "Wm Clark," "Enoch Wiffol," "Richd Baker," and so forth (Figure 10). These colonial plats here ostensibly resume the residual function of the imperial mapping project, representing British claims through the act of naming the land. But, as the colonial surveys inscribed the plot of land with personal names, they also linked the survey and the act of taking possession of the land to writing, literacy, and a process of individual literary identification: land here becomes private property because it is simultaneously made legible and legibly personalized.[31]

Indeed, writing proper names into the plat's empty space turns the survey into more than an act of personal identification. The colonial survey's

30. On country ideology, see Gordon S. Wood, *The Radicalism of the American Revolution* (New York, 1991), 269. Wood's reading corresponds with Alan Macfarlane's argument for the English custom of self-identification through landed property; see *The Origin of English Individualism: The Family, Property, and Social Transition* (Cambridge, 1978), 100–106. For an extended discussion on landed property, see C. B. MacPherson, *The Political Theory of Possessive Individualism: Hobbes to Locke* (Oxford, 1962); Richard Schlatter, *Private Property: The History of an Idea* (New Brunswick, N.J., 1951).

31. Love, *Geodaesia*, 144. The *Maryland Calendar of Wills* teems with references to land tracts that bear personal names; see I–XIV.

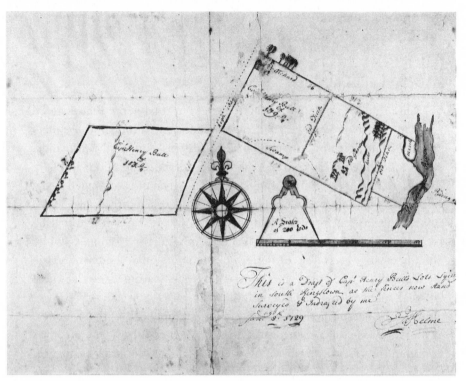

Figure 9. This Is Draft of Capt. Henry Bull's Lots Lying on South Kingstown as the Fences Now Stand. *By James Helme. 1729.* Ink and color wash on paper. RHi X3 7605. Courtesy, The Rhode Island Historical Society

overt emphasis on writing a person's name or signature into the map affiliates the plat with the "principle of individuation" as posited by John Locke, whose idea of modern autonomous existence argued for the necessity of owning a particular locus in space and time. Locke "established a principle in which individuality is linked to definitive placing—a place marked by the proper or 'appropriated' name which designates an individual identity and prevents it from being confused with another." In the colonial context, the act of "placing" the colonists' identity is performed by the act of geodetic writing. The colonial plat performs the rhetorical function of valorizing the individual: by representing the colonial subject through the simultaneous presentation of particular names and geodetic figures, it places the individual inside a land- and map-based economy. As a written text, the plat at once becomes the individual's index of

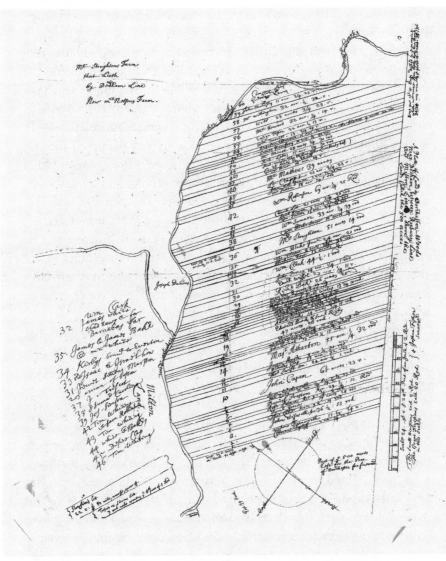

Figure 10. A Platt of Land in Dorchester Woods near Deadham, between Roxbury Line and Milton Line, above the Land Called the Five Hundred Acres. *By Joshua Fisher. Circa 1670.* Boston Public Library / Rare Books Department. Courtesy of the Trustees

socioeconomic distinction, a form of textual evidence describing a person's self-worth.[32]

Representing landed property in terms of identity suggests that geodetic writing performed at once an imperial and a nationalist function. It forced the colonist into a literary stance of self-articulation in which the geodetic terms of alphabetized points, graphic lines, and the materiality of the plat became the general foundation of geographic self-definition in British America. The individualized geodetic record disrupted the cartographic sway of the central Plantations Office over the documentation of its outlying properties. The surveyor's scripted point and compass rendered, rather than surrendered, local identity. The plat personalized, rather than depersonalized, the rhetorical process of territorialism. Descriptive geodetic writing even became a genre of self-distinction and an expression of self-love. As the events of the eighteenth century would show, the discourse of surveying provided some of the most effective grammars for an affective vocabulary: it pronounced the love of land to be a virtue and the love of self as an act of patriotism.

In some modern cultural and literary criticism, it has been argued that the act of mapping—an act involving numbers, mechanics, and a presumed technical and interpretive rigidity that is perceived as antithetical to the process of imaginative literary creation—is inherently oppressive. Important work on Native Americans, for example, tends to cast the map as a villain, asserting that the plat's representation of boundary lines hardened the division between the British American and the native people's cognition and figuration of land, place, and local identity. Similarly, it has been argued that the process of cultural differentiation turned on land titles, deeds, and thus implicitly the image of the plat: the language of surveying converted not only land but the native population into alienable property, as the plat transformed both land and people into staple goods and quantifiable objects intended for the European commodity market.[33]

---

32. Patricia A. Parker, "The (Self-)Identity of the Literary Text," in Parker, *Literary Fat Ladies: Rhetoric, Gender, Property* (New York, 1987), 155. She cites from the *Essay concerning Human Understanding,* in which John Locke writes that "therefore in their own species, which they have most to do with, and wherein they have often [occasion] to mention particular persons, they make use of proper names, and there distinct individuals have distinct denominations." Locke's passage is taken from III.3.4.

33. Eric Cheyfitz, *The Poetics of Imperialism: Translation and Colonization from the Tempest to Tarzan,* exp. ed. (Philadelphia, 1997), 46; Cronon, *Changes in the Land,* 70–81.

Central to these discussions of the rhetoric of land surveying is the understanding that through its geometrical representation the plat becomes the textual agent of alienation and ultimately of self-negation. They argue that through the survey land ceased to be defined by its use value. Instead, they emphasize how the specialized language of geodesy defined land in the terms of its exchange value, as a fungible object subject to the laws of commerce, the price of acreage, agricultural productivity, and the like. Once land had been marked as property, the discourse of surveying—the inscription of land and text with numerical ciphers and geometric patterns—essentially redefines human involvement with the land and its occupants because the scientific nature of geodetic representation disrupts the affective bond existing between land, labor, and the individual.[34]

While this argument in the main holds true in the context of the complex interactions between British Americans and the original inhabitants of the land, it seems less applicable to the colonists' practice surrounding the construction of the plats themselves. By adhering to the idea that the map and the act of mapping provide a disinterested counterpart to human subjectivity, or that the lines of the map can impose a rational and scientific framework upon the land, we inadvertently accept and perpetuate an eighteenth-century geographic ideal. But the plat, as it was put into practice, offers the antithesis of rational, bureaucratic disinterestedness. Its construction overtly revolves around the center of the surveyor, who, rather than transforming himself from a visible subject to an invisible object, boldly advertises and even celebrates his presence.[35]

Certainly officials in the Board of Trade and colonial land speculators did intend for a vast archive of plats to render the colonies utterly transparent to the investor's and politician's eye—correspondingly translating the land into commodity and political territory. But this fantasy of impe-

34. As if to further disrupt the Native American bond with the land, British colonists went out of their way to translate land deeds into the native language. See Jill Lepore, "Dead Men Tell No Tales: John Sassamon and the Fatal Consquences of Literacy," *American Quarterly,* XLVI (1994), 493–494.

35. In this context it is noteworthy that King Philip apparently had recognized the survey's role in creating emotive interest in the land. His Wampanoag negotiators also resorted to the plat and geodetic writing in the effort of engaging with (and possibly appropriating) the colonial codes of proprietary representation. See Margaret Wickens Pearce's fascinating study, "Native Mapping in Southern New England Indian Deeds," in G. Malcolm Lewis, ed., *Cartographic Encounters: Perspectives on Native American Mapmaking and Map Use* (Chicago, 1998), 157–186.

rial vision and domination was thwarted by the composition of the plats themselves, a process which propelled willing colonists to educate themselves and to take visual and textual possession of the land. If we look at the network of plats from the top down, we may see a dehumanizing, authoritarian system. If we look at the plats from the ground up, we see a genre that, perhaps unexpectedly even to those involved in their creation, provided through its mass application a creative form that affirmed the self. For British Americans, the plat was often a genre of self-assertion, not self-negation.

The social phenomenon of widespread plat writing affected British Americans' conceptions of text. On a very basic level, the directive to plat forced many to read about surveying practices (many of which were alphabetically oriented) and then to write a document that situated them as the discursive center. For many colonists, this enforced activity might have presented a rare occasion for authoring a public document. While the circulation of plats is not entirely analogous to, say, the aristocratic circulation of sonnets, it did offer an opportunity for writing. As the diary of Joshua Hempstead demonstrates, some colonists seem to have relished the opportunity for creative engagement through the composition of plats. As William Byrd's writings indicate, the plat could form the imaginative backbone for more self-consciously literary prose writing, and, as the poems of Steere and Chandler illustrate, the act of surveying inspired a particular form of poetic vision and expression. This vision turned the everyday act of geodetic writing into a touchstone that turned the pragmatic ciphers of the plat into an aesthetic production with which a vast number of colonists would have a direct personal involvement and through which they could imagine a concrete and localized individual identity. The extreme opposite and counterpart of the plat, the continental map, will illustrate how the art and science of cartography affected identity formation in British America, and how in public discourse the cartographic figures of the land provided a powerful persona for "American" self-fashioning.

chapter two

THE CONTINENT SPEAKS

GEOGRAPHY, ORATORY, AND

THE FIGURATION OF IDENTITY

IN REVOLUTIONARY AMERICA

The declaration "I am an American," while today a naturalized expression of national identity, was in its colonial context anything but an organic statement of personal and collective self-definition. Prior to 1764, the word "American" was rarely used for designating either the human occupants or the geographic space of the British provinces. Colonists writing to those living in England generally referred to themselves as "Englishmen" or "His Majesty's subjects" living in the "British dominions," "plantations," or "colonies." When expressing a local sense of identity, they turned to regional markers such as "New Englanders," "Pennsylvanians," or "Virginians." Then, almost immediately following the Stamp Act Crisis of 1764, colonial discourse became saturated with the appellation "American." In 1765, for example, Christopher Gadsden of South Carolina declared, "There ought to be no New England man; no New Yorker, known on the Continent; but all of us Americans." A decade later, the self-identification of "American" had become a regular firebrand in the arsenal of Revolutionary rhetoric; in 1774, Patrick Henry, already famous for incendiary statements and crowd-pleasing performances, thundered before the Continental Congress: "The distinctions between Virginians, New Yorkers, and New Englanders are no more, I am not a Virginian, but an American."[1]

1. Christopher Gadsden to Charles Garth, Dec. 2, 1765, cited in Edmund S. Morgan and Helen M. Morgan, *The Stamp Act Crisis: Prologue to Revolution* (1953; Chapel Hill, N.C., 1995), 113; Patrick Henry cited by D. W. Meinig, *The Shaping of America: A Geographical Perspective on Five Hundred Years of History*, I, *Atlantic America, 1492–1800* (New Haven, Conn., 1986), 306.

While individual Anglo-Americans had been using the term "American" occasionally, its first widespread application came during the Cartagena expedition of 1740 when the British press used the term mockingly to distinguish colonial from British troops. Twenty

Because of the term's sudden popularity in the wake of a pivotal political moment, the use of "American" was at first highly self-conscious, a move that carried the daring and frisson of a pre-Revolutionary people. For British Americans navigating the arena of public speech during the decade preceding the Declaration of Independence it represented a bold rhetorical move that, prima facie, hailed a geographic place-name as the foundation of a collective colonial identity and thus emphasized the discourse of geography as the constitutive rhetorical mode of colonial self-representation. The geographic self-designation was a striking move because of the term's historical and contextual symbolic freight, which made it an inherently problematic label for speakers intent on reaching colonial as well as overseas audiences.[2]

Colonial polemicists required a figurative persona through which they could enter into transatlantic political debates. For eighteenth-century speakers trained in classical rhetoric and elocutionary performance, the invocation of such personas was a standard feature for making a persuasive political argument. According to contemporary handbooks, rhetoric revolved around logic and affect, and colonial authors and orators exploited these two performative extremes. On the one hand, British-trained rhetoricians construed public speech along Ciceronian lines, emphasizing public speech as a ceremonial discourse that employed a pre-

---

years later, it was still used sparingly and as a derisive term to label colonial politics, social practices, and peoples. See Richard Middleton, *Colonial America: A History, 1585–1776* (Oxford, 1996), 414, 439; Meinig, *Shaping of America,* I, 305–307. This appellation coincided with other assertions of Americanness sweeping colonial discourse. Between 1762 and 1766 the use of American symbols (such as turkey, rattlesnake, and so forth) increased by 300 percent. See Richard L. Merritt, *Symbols of American Community, 1735–1775* (New Haven, Conn., 1966), 75; also see Lester C. Olson, *Emblems of American Community in the Revolutionary Era: A Study in Rhetorical Iconology* (Washington, D.C., 1991).

For late colonial administrative labeling practices, see James Otis, *A Vindication of the British Colonies . . .* (Boston, 1765), in Bernard Bailyn, ed., *Pamphlets of the American Revolution, 1750–1776,* I (Cambridge, Mass., 1965), 563; or [Silas Downer], *A Discourse, Delivered in Providence . . . at the Dedication of the Tree of Liberty . . .* (Providence, R.I., 1768), 8. For an example of regional self-address, see [John Dickinson], *Letters from a Farmer in Pennsylvania to the Inhabitants of the British Colonies* (Philadelphia, 1768).

2. The boundary between speaker and writer is blurred by the fact that many speech performances were not only heard but read; many others were written in imitation of oratorical precepts but remained unperformed. Thus, by referring to the speaker I invariably also imply the writer.

scriptive set of arguments and rhetorical commonplaces, delivered in a style of debate that was commensurate with the rules of civility. On the other hand, a new generation of rhetoricians understood public speech as the active art of moving the audience, of speaking directly to the listeners' feelings so as to engage their interests and excite their passions. Both of these schools frequently invoked figurative, classically inspired "characters" to persuade or move their audiences.[3]

Colonial audiences were accustomed to following political debates by reading or listening to a series of overdetermined and stereotyped characters. Pamphlets and newspapers rang with the voices of "Cato" and "Lycurgus," figures modeled on classical Roman orators. Colonial publications further echoed classical forms of rhetoric with Latinate characters such as "Publius" and his updated Anglophone counterparts, the "Farmer" and "Friend." Classical characters were modernized to suit eighteenth-century notions of taste and affect through the lachrymose persona of the "Child." And finally, the cast of oratorical characters had become adapted to the New World environment with the introduction of the "Indian." None of these voices, however, seemed truly representative of the collective identity of the colonists or capable of fully articulating their concerns. For a population struggling to define itself as a whole in the face of the geographic diversity of its parts, many of these characters were too local or too rarefied to be representative.[4]

3. In this context, the various public personas of American speakers fulfilled the dictates of the elocutionary revolution, a rhetorical movement in which, as Jay Fliegelman has demonstrated, mid-eighteenth-century Englishmen merged the rules of classical rhetoric with the demands of modern theatricality. See *Declaring Independence: Jefferson, Natural Language, and the Culture of Performance* (Stanford, Calif., 1993), 1–2, 28. See also Sandra M. Gustafson, *Eloquence Is Power: Oratory and Performance in Early America* (Chapel Hill, N.C., 2000), 118, 146; Christopher Looby, *Voicing America: Language, Literary Form, and the Origins of the United States* (Chicago, 1996); Adam Potkay, *The Fate of Eloquence in the Age of Hume* (Ithaca, N.Y., 1994). See also the older but immensely rich study by Wilbur Samuel Howell, *Eighteenth-Century British Logic and Rhetoric* (Princeton, N.J., 1971); and the essays on colonial rhetoric collected by Karl R. Wallace, *History of Speech Education in America: Background Studies* (New York, 1954).

4. My discussion of American speeches was guided by the texts anthologized or referenced in Bernard Bailyn, ed., *Pamphlets,* and Bailyn, *The Ideological Origins of the American Revolution* (1967; Cambridge, Mass., 1992); Thomas R. Adams, *The American Controversy: A Bibliographical Study of the British Pamphlets about the American Disputes, 1764–1783,* 2 vols. (Providence, R.I., 1980); Adams, "The British Pamphlet Press and the American Con-

Eventually, colonial rhetoricians would discover the figure they needed in the persona of the American continent itself. Speaking on behalf of the colonists, the voice of the North American continent made its rhetorical debut in the political pamphlet *The Rights of the British Colonies Asserted and Proved* (1764), in which James Otis wagered the geographic outline of "the continent of North America" against the dimensions of Great Britain. A decade later, at the height of the separatist debate, the figure of the continent had evolved into a full-fledged dramatic persona: having identified America as a *"formidable figure,"* Richard Wells imagined the transatlantic conflict as a ceremonial debate between British politicians and the American continent: "Let English statesmen clamor for power, let a British parliament boast of unlimitted supremacy, yet the *continent of America* will contend with equal fervency."[5]

The persona of a hulking landmass might seem antithetical to notions of performed reason and emotion. In colonial discourse, however, the continent became a repository and a mouthpiece for ideas about American identity. Wells presents a continent that not only speaks but is fervent. Taking its cues from Revolutionary speakers like Otis and Wells, this chapter suggests that geographic discourse and forms of rhetoric were, in fact, mutually informative, each inflecting the other with oratorical vivacity. In particular, maps displaying the North American continent to colonial audiences were deeply invested in the oratorical movement.

---

troversy, 1764–1783," American Antiquarian Society, *Proceedings,* LXXXIX (1979), 33–88; Gordon S. Wood, *The Creation of the American Republic, 1776–1787* (Chapel Hill, N.C., 1969); Philip Davidson, *Propaganda and the American Revolution, 1763–1783* (Chapel Hill, N.C., 1941).

Following the concept that colonies were bound to both crown and empire by the *"threefold cord* of duty, interest, and filial affection," colonists could hear "poor" America sigh and plead with "her Father," cry and argue with the English "Mother-country," or whisper and shout the offenses of the *"Parent State."* See Jonathan Mayhew, *The Snare Broken: A Thanksgiving-Discourse . . .* (Boston, 1766), vi–vii, 27; Richard Bland, *An Inquiry into the Rights of the British Colonies* (Williamsburg, Va., 1766), 13; Samuel Williams, *A Discourse on the Love of Our Country* (Salem, Mass., 1775), 18. For more pictorial examples, see Joan D. Dolmetsch, *Rebellion and Reconciliation: Satirical Prints on the Revolution at Williamsburg* (Williamsburg, Va., 1976), 18, 21, 123, 125, 127, 179.

On Indian eloquence in Revolutionary America, see Gustafson, *Eloquence Is Power,* chap. 3.

5. James Otis, *The Rights of the British Colonies Asserted and Proved* (Boston, 1764), in Bailyn, ed., *Pamphlets,* I, 436; [Richard Wells], *The Middle Line; or, An Attempt to Furnish Some Hints for Ending the Differences Subsisting between Great-Britain and the Colonies* (Philadelphia, 1775), 41 (my emphasis).

Wearing the imaginary costume of a map, the persona of the continent followed two oratorical strategies, aligning classical rhetoric with the new elocutionary movement. By locating their voice inside the setting of a map, American speakers animated the spatial concept of the Ciceronian rhetorical *topos* (the "commonplace"). In the strictly Ciceronian argument, the setting provided a dramatic place in which the skilled orator displayed the logic of his argument. A small but highly influential number of Anglo-American speechwriters turned this Ciceronian formula upside down. By announcing their American identity, they transfigured the setting into the orator's bodily character; using the trope of personification (prosopopoeia) in which the inanimate object becomes imbued with human qualities, these speakers developed a cartographic persona that bolstered intercolonial unity.

The road to establishing this figure as the representative American persona was neither easy nor self-evident. Before Anglo-Americans could claim the land itself as their spokesman, they first had to overcome the other figures with which Europeans identified the New World, in particular the figure of the Indian. Whether portrayed as a seminaked female or as a silenced male, the Indian often inhabited European maps of America, residing in the visual emblem of the cartouche. These decorative spaces on the map depicted rhetorically charged scenes and provided personas that, in the European imagination, epitomized the American speaker. To be taken seriously as international polemical sparring partners, the colonists needed to overcome the European association of the American voice with the figure of the native. Colonial rhetoricians, seeking to make themselves heard, needed to draw attention away from the figure in the map's cartouche and onto the land itself, which would be perceived as a persona in its own right, endowed with its own forceful voice.[6]

6. For the roots of colonial American anxieties regarding their identity, see Michael Zuckerman, "The Fabrication of Identity in Early America," *William and Mary Quarterly,* 3d Ser., XXXIV (1977), 183–214; Jack P. Greene, "Search for Identity: An Interpretation of the Meaning of Selected Patterns of Social Response in Eighteenth-Century America," *Journal of Social History,* III (1969–1970), 189–224. On the role of British nationalism in the context of empire and how it affected colonial American ideas of identity, see T. H. Breen, "Ideology and Nationalism on the Eve of the American Revolution: Revisions Once More in Need of Revising," *Journal of American History,* LXXXIV (1996–1997), 13–39; Eliga H. Gould, *The Persistence of Empire: British Political Culture in the Age of the American Revolution* (Chapel Hill, N.C., 2000). For a survey of additional character types and a synopsis of the national-imperial identity debate, see Stephen Conway, "From Fellow-Nationals to Foreigners: British Perceptions of the Americans, circa 1739–1783," *WMQ,* 3d Ser., LIX (2002), 65–100.

Just as early modern cartography played a significant practical and imaginative role in the representation of continents, it was the language of maps that made possible the European colonization of the Americas. Maps are now generally viewed as the product of an applied written language, consisting of distinct "signs, symbols, and rhetoric." With the aid of semiotic theory and discourse analysis, we now see maps as value-laden images, as subjective representations of historical practice rather than neutral mirrors of nature. Maps in general are considered distinctly political texts. Buttressing the power of European nation-states, cartographic writing itself facilitated the geographical expansion of social systems, using elaborate writing systems such as heraldic symbols, graded letter fonts, and graphic lines. British imperial maps—which by definition were interested in expanding a nation's territory—exported these codes, seeking to persuade the maps' readers on either side of the Atlantic of British ownership rights regarding the North American continent.[7]

British Americans frequently imported imperial maps during the eighteenth century. Decorative wall maps showing the British possessions in North America were favorite articles, purchased primarily by the colonial elite. Strategically displayed in the formal settings of the home or provincial office, these maps painted bombastic scenes of territorial conquest and signified the range of the British Empire.[8] For example, maps like

7. J. B. Harley, "Text and Contexts in the Interpretation of Early Maps," in David Buisseret, ed., *From Sea Charts to Satellite Images: Interpreting North American History through Maps* (Chicago, 1990), 4. On maps as language, see also Harley, "Maps, Knowledge, and Power," in Denis Cosgrove and Stephen Daniels, eds., *The Iconography of Landscape: Essays in the Symbolic Representation, Design, and Use of Past Environments* (Cambridge, 1988), 277–312, and "Deconstructing the Map," *Cartographica,* XXVI, no. 2 (Summer 1989), 1–20. For broader discussions of theoretical aspects of the history of cartography, including language, see the special issue of *Imago Mundi,* XLVIII (1996); Denis Wood and John Fels, "Designs on Signs: Myth and Meaning in Maps," *Cartographica,* XXIII, no. 3 (Autumn 1986), 54–103.

On the territorial rhetoric and politics implicit in maps, see Harley, "Maps, Knowledge, and Power," 282–287; James R. Akerman, "The Structuring of Political Territory in Early Printed Atlases," *Imago Mundi,* XLVII (1995), 138–154; Matthew H. Edney, "Reconsidering Enlightenment Geography and Map Making: Reconnaissance, Mapping, Archive," in David N. Livingstone and Charles W. J. Withers, eds., *Geography and Enlightenment* (Chicago, 1999), 165–198.

8. A growing and important body of work discusses the sociology underlying eighteenth-century map ownership. See J. B. Harley, "Power and Legitimation in the English

Henry Popple's *Map of the British Empire in America* (1733) reached American audiences upon special orders by the Board of Trade and Plantations (Figure 11), and colonial politicians like Benjamin Franklin eagerly requested Popple's map for public display.[9] Throughout the eighteenth century, the cartographic figure of British North America was made widely accessible to colonial audiences through the proliferation of inexpensive and rudimentary maps. These maps could be bought throughout the colonies in the form of broadsides, almanacs, magazines, book inserts, and

------

Geographical Atlases of the Eighteenth Century," in John A. Wolter and Ronald E. Grim, eds., *Images of the World: The Atlas through History* (Washington, D.C., 1997), 168–173; Harley, "The Map User in the Revolution," in Harley, Barbara Bartz Petchenik, and Lawrence W. Towner, eds., *Mapping the American Revolutionary War* (Chicago, 1978), 83–87.

On maps in British colonial material culture, see Margaret Beck Pritchard, *Degrees of Latitude: Mapping Colonial America* (New York, 2002), 43–53. Maps of all sizes and qualities were valuable household items among the mid-Atlantic well-to-do; they were advertised in wills, estate inventories, and colonial newspapers such as the *Pennsylvania Gazette* and the *Virginia Gazette*. See, for example, Richard Beale Davis, ed., *William Fitzhugh and His Chesapeake World, 1676–1701: The Fitzhugh Letters and Other Documents* (Chapel Hill, N.C., 1963); Clayton Torrence, *Virginia Wills and Administrations, 1632–1800* . . . (Baltimore, 1985). While the Fitzhugh records offer lines like "I give my son William . . . the Large Mapp in my Study" (379), the Virginia inventory of wills has references such as "in the large Room in lower House 1 Spy Glass, 1 bible, and 4 Maps" (will of Ishmael Moody, York County, Jan. 16, 1748 [vol. XX]). I am grateful to Margaret Beck Pritchard for sharing her research.

9. In 1746, Franklin asked for the delivery of a "large Map of the whole World, or of Asia, or Africa, or Europe, of equal Size with Popple's . . . to be hung, one on each side the Door in the Assembly Room" (Leonard W. Labaree et al., eds., *The Papers of Benjamin Franklin* [New Haven, Conn., 1959–], III, 77, also XIII, 214). Other influential wall maps circulating in British America were Herman Moll, *Map of the Dominions of Great Britain in North America* (London, 1720); John Mitchell, *Map of the British and French Dominions in North America* . . . (London, 1755); Lewis Evans, *A General Map of the Middle British Colonies in America* . . . (Philadelphia, 1755); Joshua Fry and Peter Jefferson, *A Map of the Most Inhabited Part of Virginia, Containing the Whole Province of Maryland, with Part of Pensilvania, New Jersey, and North Carolina* (London, 1751).

On the history of eighteenth-century maps in British America, moving from the general to the regional, see David Buisseret, ed., *From Sea Charts to Satellite Images: Interpreting North American History through Maps* (Chicago, 1990); Seymour I. Schwartz and Ralph E. Ehrenberg, *The Mapping of America* (New York, 1980); Barbara Backus McCorkle, *New England in Early Printed Maps, 1513 to 1800: An Illustrated Carto-Bibliography* (Providence, R.I., 2001); William P. Cumming, *The Southeast in Early Maps,* rev. and enl. by Louis DeVorsey (Chapel Hill, N.C., 1998); Cumming, *British Maps of Colonial America* (Chicago, 1974); Lester Jesse Cappon, "Geographers and Map-makers, British and American, from about 1750 to 1789," AAS, *Proceedings,* LXXXI (1971), 243–271.

Figure 11. A Map of the British Empire in America, with the French and Spanish Settlements Adjacent Thereto. *By Henry Popple. 1733.* Permission, Colonial Williamsburg Foundation

even card games. Often removed from their original bindings, magazine maps like Emanuel Bowen's *Accurate Map of North America* (1747) (Figure 12) not only popularized the image of the American continent but made the continent a conversation piece over which colonial pubgoers and coffeehouse patrons practiced the art of speaking while imagining their American identity. That the map of the American continent served colonists as a conversation piece becomes evident in the political cartoon *Liberty Triumphant; or, The Downfall of Oppression* (1774) (Figure 13). In satirical cartoons like this, the continental outline became the metaphorical

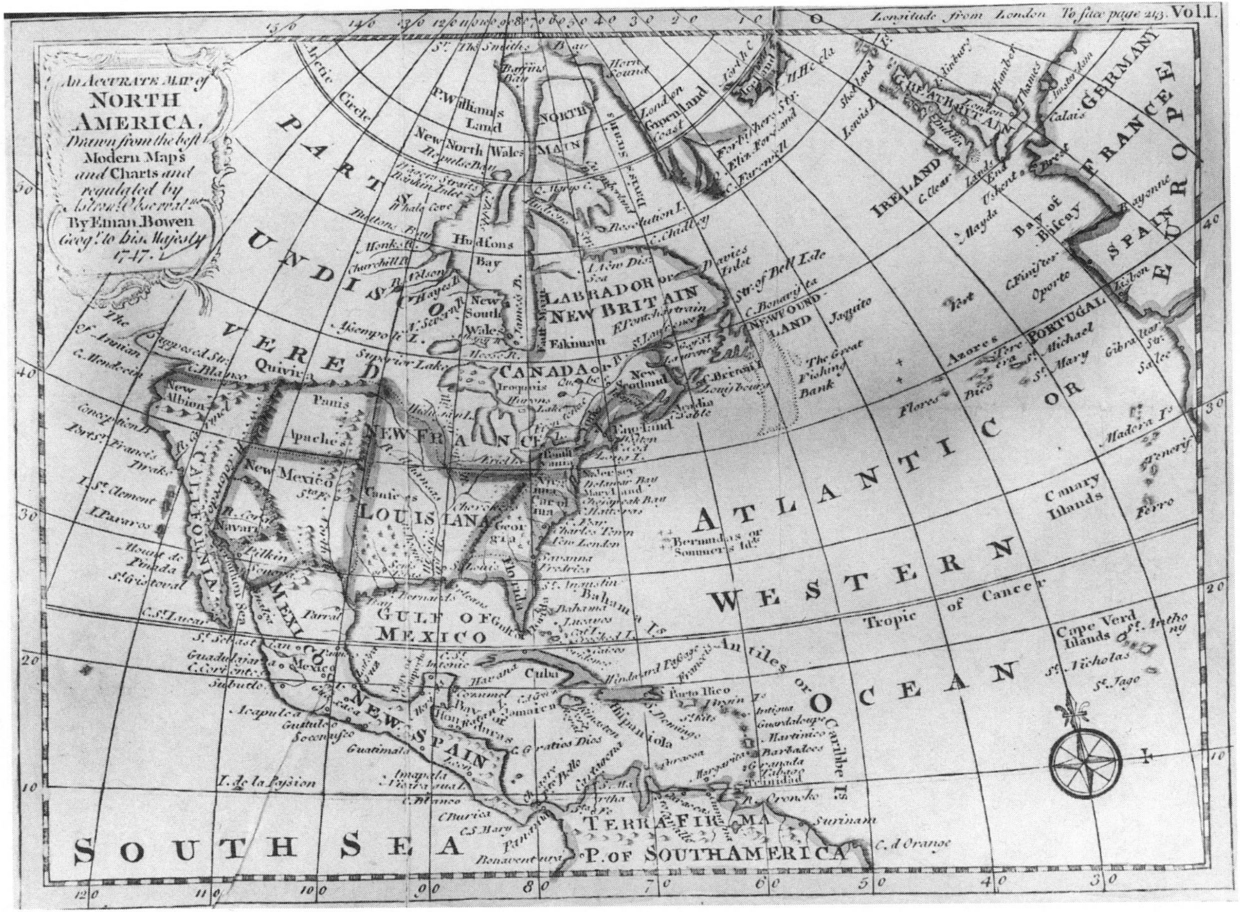

Figure 12.
An Accurate Map of North America.
By Eman[uel] Bowen. 1747.
Courtesy, American Antiquarian Society

*Figure 13.
Liberty
Triumphant;
or, The Downfall
of Oppression.
1774.
Permission,
Colonial
Williamsburg
Foundation*

soapbox from which the stereotyped figures representing the various European nations or members of the English political establishment could speak across the Atlantic to the quintessential American, the Indian. Scenes of such map talk—indicated by speech bubbles containing choice comments on current political affairs—took place inside gardenscapes, coffeehouses, and pubs and thus in settings reserved for conviviality and oral performances.[10]

That the cartoon *Liberty Triumphant* allowed English men and women to hear their concerns articulated by the eloquent Indian chief (the Indian figure calls out, "Aid me my Sons, and prevent my being Fetter'd") was the exception, not the rule. Since the Renaissance, artists and geographers had personified America by drawing the body of a voluptuous and usually naked indigenous woman, who was depicted as silent. By the mid-eighteenth century, the image of the quiet female native had become the dominant visual shorthand among Europeans representing North and South American people and goods. Thus, her figure loomed from Giovanni Battista Tiepolo's mural *America* (1753) as a sensual princess seated among the symbols of imperial commerce. While the latter figuration was never seen by most British colonists, they were able to catch a glimpse of her in printed genres ranging from geography and history books to city atlases like John Andrews's *Collection of Plans of the Capital Cities* (1771), where on the frontispiece the figure of America posed in the form of a limber-footed Diana (Figure 14). Indeed, permeating the venues of both eighteenth-century high and low art, the befeathered figure of America could be seen by British audiences performing on the stage, taking up ballet, and with naked splendor gracing English teapots and Meissen porcelain.[11]

10. For accounts of magazine maps as a new phenomenon, see Louis DeVorsey, "Eighteenth-Century Large-Scale Maps," in Buisseret, ed., *From Sea Charts to Satellite Images,* 67–71; David C. Jolly, comp., *Maps of America in Periodicals before 1800* (Brookline, Mass., 1989); Christopher M. Klein, ed., *Maps in Eighteenth-Century British Magazines: A Checklist* (Chicago, 1989); E. A. Reitan, "Expanding Horizons: Maps in the *Gentleman's Magazine,* 1731–1754," *Imago Mundi,* XXXVII (1985), 54–62. For maps in card games, see Geoffrey L. King, *Miniature Antique Maps* ([London], 1996). For political cartoons showing "map talk," see Dolmetsch, *Rebellion and Reconciliation,* 20, 29, 46, 75, 188.

11. See Julie Ellison, *Cato's Tears and the Making of Anglo-American Emotion* (Chicago, 1999), 91–96. All other references are illustrated by Hugh Honour, *The New Golden Land: European Images of America from the Discoveries to the Present Time* (New York, 1975), 87, 103, 109, 110; also see his exhibition catalog, *The European Vision of America* (Cleveland, Ohio, 1975); E. McClung Fleming, "The American Image as Indian Princess, 1765–1783," *Winterthur Portfolio,* II (1965), 65–81.

London, published according to Act of Parliament 15 Ma
M.ʳ de L'Etanville in Marylebone Street, Golden Sq.

Figure 14. Frontispiece to A Collection of Plans of the Capital Cities of Europe . . . ,
by John Andrews. 1771. Courtesy, The Library of Congress

Eighteenth-century maps showing the American continent consistently published images of the female or feminized native as silenced speakers. This representation of native speech appeared in the map margins, in the ornamental picture of a cartouche. Designed to introduce the map and mapmaker, the basic cartouche contains the map title, the author, and the scale. It thus functions as the literary key to the map. At the same time, however, a cartouche is more than a decorative or informative inset, serving also as a display of multiple, interrelated discourses "which bind the map within a series of ideological assumptions as to the way the land is viewed." A mixed medium linking the scientific and the descriptive as well as the verbal and the pictorial, the cartouche became the index to popular conceptions about the land. In the case of the cartouches introducing the colonies, the primary figure through which European mapmakers imagined America was the pictorial representation of Native Americans striking oratorical poses. These poses resemble in many ways the postures shown by eighteenth-century performance, gesture, and rhetoric handbooks. In a range of eighteenth-century cartouches, the essentialized representation of the Indian is predicated on a pattern of oral containment: natives engaged in the art of speaking are continually silenced. Or, to put it more strongly, in the language of eighteenth-century maps introducing the North American continent, the traditional voice of America becomes a dead voice.[12]

MAP CARTOUCHES AND THE
CONTAINMENT OF AMERICAN SPEECH

Perhaps the most influential example of how British cartographers associated oratory with the representation of the American continent is John Mitchell's *Map of the British and French Dominions in North America* (Figure 15). Mitchell's map was published in 1755 in response to French territorial encroachments, went through twenty-one English, French, Dutch, and Italian editions, and "was the cartographic document upon

12. G. N. G. Clarke, "Taking Possession: The Cartouche as Cultural Text in Eighteenth-Century American Maps," *Word and Image*, IV (1988), 455. In geographical writings, the female native figuration of America originally dates back to the mid-sixteenth century, when she was conceived to represent the southern parts of continents. By the eighteenth century, this figure was universally applied to both parts. See Stephanie Pratt, "From the Margins: The Native American Personage in the Cartouche and Decorative Borders of Maps," *Word and Image*, XII (1996), 349–365. On the cartouche, see Norman J. W. Thrower, *Maps and Civilization: Cartography in Culture and Society* (Chicago, 1996), 81. For examples of body postures, see Kellom Tomlinson, *The Art of Dancing, Explained by Reading and Figures . . .* (London, 1735); or William Scott, *Lessons in Elocution . . . [and] Elements of Gesture* (New York, 1799).

There has yet to be compiled a comprehensive guide to cartographic cartouches introducing "America." A representative sample of maps that were possibly circulating in the colonies can be found in the wonderful survey by Donald H. Cresswell, *The American Revolution in Drawings and Prints: A Checklist of 1765–1790 Graphics in the Library of Congress* (Washington, D.C., 1975).

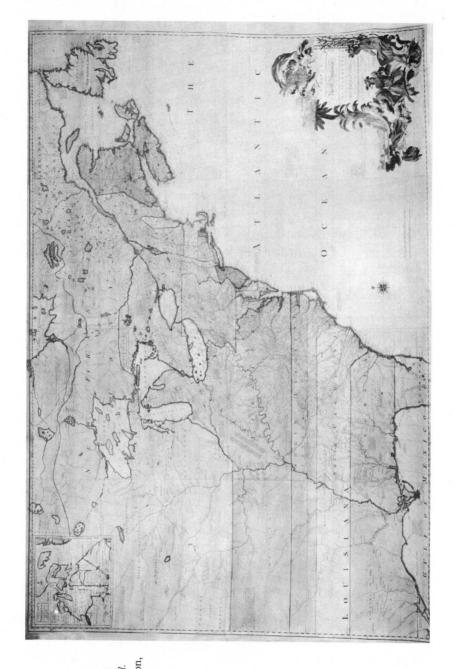

Figure 15.
A Map of the
British and
French
Dominions in
North America.
By John Mitchell.
1755. Permission,
Colonial
Williamsburg
Foundation

which Great Britain and the United States based their claims in the negotiations leading up to the treaty that terminated the Revolutionary War." The size of a wall map (about four by five feet), the *Map of the British and French Dominions* consisted of eight separate sheets, seven of which were devoted to the geography and geopolitics of the eastern continent; the eighth panel to the lower right contained the decorative cartouche.[13]

Looking at the cartouche's textual components—the map's title and the cartographer's signature—its iconographic narrative not only associates the continent with the stereotypical Indian body but offers a symbolic commentary on the condition of rhetoric and speech in America (Figure 16). The cartouche portrays the American peoples in contrast to the European through the categories of the natural and the feminine. Two native figures (one female and one male) are shown at the base of the map's inscription. Placed among the conventional symbols identifying the American continent (palm tree, beaver, fishing net, and cornstalks), both figures look upward. They are at once looking up to the map title and to the British flag billowing like a sail above the pictorial tableau and printed text. The Americans' body language (the male kneels down with his hands clasped as if praying while the female figure is touching her chest with her right hand) enacts the ritual surrender of America to British rule.

Significantly, this pictorial narrative revolves around orality and the representation of performed speech. The artist shows both the female and male figure engaged in the act of speaking; both are shown in partial or total relief so that the map viewer can see their parted lips and open mouths. Contrary to the allegorical typing of America as silent, the Americans are here understood to be active vocal performers. Their physical gestures indicate they are participants in an oral culture in which voice, rhetoric, and theatrical conventions of speech define the act of self-presentation. At the same time, however, the cultural representation of animated speech, that is, the implied ability to speak and be understood, is shown to be limited.

The stylized American speakers are reduced to the role of the praying

13. DeVorsey, "Eighteenth-Century Large-Scale Maps," in Buisseret, ed., *From Sea Charts to Satellite Images,* 67. For a general history of the Mitchell map, see Schwartz and Ehrenberg, *Mapping of America,* 159–160; Cumming, *The Southeast in Early Maps,* 25–26, 274–275; Walter W. Ristow, comp., "John Mitchell's Map of the British and French Dominions in North America," in Ristow, comp. and ed., *A La Carte: Selected Papers on Maps and Atlases* (Washington, D.C., 1972), 102–113.

Figure 16. Detail from A Map of the British and French Dominions in North America. *By John Mitchell. 1755.* Permission, Colonial Williamsburg Foundation

or pleading petitioner. Their hand gestures are modeled on a sign code that since the Renaissance was thought to provide a universal language through which Europeans and Native Americans could communicate without the aid of the spoken word and textual transmission. Gestural handbooks linked specific hand signs to various rhetorical tropes. The

Figure 17. Detail from A Map of the British Empire in America, with the French and Spanish Settlements Adjacent Thereto. *By Henry Popple. 1733.* Permission, Colonial Williamsburg Foundation

sign chart of John Bulwer's *Chirologia; or, The Naturall Language of the Hand* (1644), for example, identified the image of folded hands with the headline "ploro," "I plead."[14]

Mitchell's pictorial narrative was not the only prominent map developing a European tradition in which cartographers and geographers introduced Americans through the depiction of native peoples engaging in a partly gestural, partly dialogic performance. The cartouche presenting Popple's *Map of the British Empire in America,* for instance, has three native figures frame the map title (Figure 17). The title itself is shown to be chiseled out of rock (the continent) and covered with American symbols, including palm and fir trees, an alligator, birds, and monkeys. Thus situated, the American characters assume various dramatic postures of public speech. The female, maternal figure reports the arrival of the European merchant marine to a lounging American princess by pointing in a dramatic and questioning gesture (her outstretched palm faces upward) to a

14. See James Knowlson, *Universal Language Schemes in England and France, 1600–1800* (Toronto, 1975), 212–214.

group of sailors who are unloading European merchandise from a ship on the American beach. Her figure is balanced by a male figure who points his open hand in declamatory fashion to the letter *A* of the word "America," indirectly inviting the map reader to enter the space of the continent through the printed text of the map. Both characters here stage the persona of America along the lines of classical representations of oratory, as body postures and hand gestures lend dignity to the speakers and pathos to the message.[15]

Yet, by the same token that the cartouche emphasizes the physical trappings of oratorical performance, its composition in fact negates the success of proper dialogue and actual speech. In eighteenth-century rhetoric manuals, the speaker ideally addressed the viewer by pointing, looking, and talking directly to the audience. But here the cartographic staging of American speech is designed to disrupt the elocutionary moment by keeping the dialogue locked up inside the cartouche. The cartouches reduce the natives' expression to an essentially wordless state. In the case of Mitchell's map, the cartouche shows how their supplications are directed at a faceless receiver, the institutional authority of the British state (signified by the flag) and are therefore implicitly subject to offstage negotiation, misrepresentation, and censorship. In the case of Popple's cartouche, the male American is looking sideways to the west and thus avoids eye contact with the map reader; while seemingly talking with an invisible audience outside the map, his voice is yet again staged to be inaudible. Without a visible human addressee or face-to-face exchange, the voice of America is caught in the prison of ecphrastic stasis: like the representation of a speaking statue inside a poem, American voices can never be heard outside the map but only guessed at by the map reader.[16]

15. In addition to hand gestures, speakers received exact instructions about the placement of their hands in relation to their bodies; see Scott's *Lesson in Elocution,* and Fliegelman's discussion of Scott in *Declaring Independence,* 106.

16. Seeing the face of the speaker is a crucial component in the elocutionary revolution; the face and the "language of the eye" become the register of the speaker's expression of private feeling, and it thus was considered a guide to his truthfulness. See Fliegelman, *Declaring Independence,* 2–3, 37, 48–49.

That the male figure is looking out of the map frame is the result of this cartouche's publication history (and indicative of the longevity of cartographic signs); originally placed to the right of the continent, the cartouche's male figure would have looked at the land but still pointed to the map title. This does not diminish my suggestion that, informed by oratorical body postures, the male figure undercuts the implied theatricality of native speech.

The cartouche's disruption of text-reader relations turns upon the implied understanding that any form of American speech is not only inaudible but inherently unintelligible. This becomes apparent when examining Popple's cartouche more closely. The dominant, overarching figure of America, though lording over her two subjects, is flanked by a parrot to the left and two monkeys on the right. Popple here taps into a symbolic tradition in which draftsmen and engravers since the sixteenth century had located the species of the American inside the animal kingdom. A lesser known cartouche introducing the map *America Septentrionalis* (1772) by Tobias Lotter illustrates the pervasiveness with which European mapmakers invoked the link between the American and the animal (Figure 18). Separated by a blazon bearing the map's title, a Native American timidly offers food to a sleeping lion (England) in the presence of a European merchant. Compared to the well-drawn features of the trader's physiognomy, the face of the Indian figure is ambiguously marked, showing disproportionate ears and apelike facial features. Moreover, whereas the fully dressed trader is standing upright, the half-naked American figure crouches on all fours while performing his menial tasks. The merchant's intellectual superiority is marked by his ability to read a paper from his account book. By contrast, the subhuman figure of America associates American speech with the unintelligible chatter of animals; or, rather, considering Popple's stylized scene that frames the dominant female figure of America with parrots and monkeys, American speech is marked as a form of apish imitation, not a studied exercise in classical rhetoric and modern eloquence.[17]

Both Popple's and Lotter's cartouches here complicate the early modern European celebration of Native American oratory, playing down native eloquence as a barely human, underdeveloped form of rhetoric. Eighteenth-century rhetoric handbooks describing the history and origins of language tended to cite Amerindian languages as examples of nascent

17. At least since the sixteenth century the European culture industry has associated Native Americans with monkeys and parrots. See the Italian ballet costume designs for *Peregrine Margherita* (1660) and *Fenice Rinnovata* (1644) shown in Honour, *New Golden Land,* 103. For a more contemporary cartouche, see also the cartouche decorating Emanuel Bowen's magazine map "A Map of the British American Plantations," prepared for *Gentleman's Magazine; and Historical Chronicle,* XXXIV (July 1764). Mary Louise Pratt demonstrates more generally the way in which Europeans have represented colonial populations as animals, especially monkeys. See *Imperial Eyes: Travel Writing and Transculturation* (London, 1992).

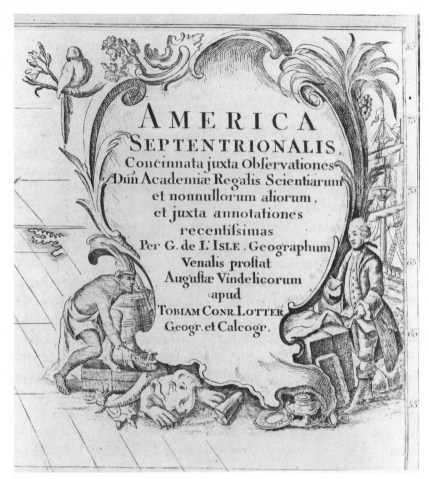

Figure 18. America Septentrionalis. *By Tobias Conr. Lotter. 1772.*
Courtesy, The Library of Congress

rhetorical cultures. Tracing the "gradual progress towards refinement," for example, Hugh Blair writes in his influential *Lectures on Rhetoric and Belles Lettres* (1759) "that all Languages are most Figurative in their early state." Examining the history of language from a Eurocentric perspective, this meant that, during the formative period of modern culture, "language is then most barren; the stock of proper names, which have been invented for things, is small; and, at the same time, imagination exerts great influence over the conceptions of men, and their method of uttering them; so that, both from necessity and from choice, their Speech will, at that period, abound in tropes." It is telling that, when giving a specific example, Blair writes, "We find, that this is the character of the American and Indian languages: bold, picturesque, and metaphorical; full of strong allusions to sensible qualities, and to such objects as struck them most on their wild and solitary life." Blair's exposition here sums up the popular eighteenth-century conception that language and rhetorical performance evolve parallel to a progressive model in which society moves from an isolated natural or savage state to a sociable cultivated or civilized one. In a surprising slippage, and one that echoes the deterministic theories of natural historians, Blair distinguishes and simultaneously confuses the difference between "American and Indian languages." For British students of rhetoric, Blair creates the impression that in America—regardless of cultural origins—speech acts and speakers devolve into the unrefined state of language and become immured inside a banal figurative code that prevents the dramatization of more emotionally or, for that matter, forensically argued subject matters.[18]

Blair's description of American language as "bold, picturesque, and metaphorical" becomes literalized within the cartographic context. Maps, it has been argued, are an extreme form of metaphor, an entire communicative system based on substitutive representation. This principle of substitution, of figurative language, is exemplified in the frontispiece of Tobias Lotter's *Atlas Novus sive Tabulae Geographicae* (1772?) (Figure 19). The illustration expands the familiar iconographic narrative used by European artists to imagine the voluntary surrender of America by Native Americans through the ceremonial submission of maps to the colonizer—a trope that was still popular on the eve of the Revolutionary conflict (see, for example, the frontispiece in Bernard Romans, *A Concise Natural History of East and West Florida* [1775] [Figure 20]). Lotter's version of this scene, however, marginalizes the European, relegating the bearded merchant to the background. The frontispiece instead foregrounds an emblematic scenario in which the native speaker's oratorical posture competes with the pictorial language of the map. While the Native American strikes the pose of the classical orator, complete with outstretched hand, the rhetorical posture is rendered absurd by the attentive audience of the parrot (at his feet) and the monkeylike creature (on his far left). The figure's capacity for speech is further compromised by his gestural act of

18. Hugh Blair, "Origin and Nature of Figurative Language," lecture 14 of Blair, *Lectures on Rhetoric and Belles Lettres,* reprinted in James L. Golden and Edward P. J. Corbett, *The Rhetoric of Blair, Campbell, and Whately* (New York, 1968), 78. See also Adam Smith, "Lecture 3d," in Smith, *Lectures on Rhetoric and Belles Lettres,* ed. J. C. Bryce (Oxford, 1983), 9–13.

Figure 19. Frontispiece to Atlas Novus sive Tabulae Geographicae Totius Orbis . . . .
By Tobias Lotter. 1772. Courtesy, The Library of Congress

Figure 20.
Frontispiece to A Concise
Natural History of East and
West Florida, *I, by Bernard
Romans. 1775.* Courtesy, The
Library of Congress

pointing at the map of the American continents. While this calls upon the cartographic design of America as a form of self-identification, it also turns to the map's silent mode of communication. Unlike more conventional scenes in which the native figure surrenders the map to the dominant European, the American surrenders his voice to the map. The map image refracts the speaker's bodily reflection into that of the geographic figure of the continent, suggesting that the allegorical figure of the eloquent Indian is as silent as the land or, rather, as silent as the map's representation of the American continent.[19]

19. Rudolf Arnheim, "The Perception of Maps," in Arnheim, ed., *Essays on the Psychology of Art* (Berkeley, Calif., 1986), 194. Arnheim argues that, while the textual components classify the map as a conventional material sign, maps can be read as a thickly layered

In the absence of the familiar symbols linking the native figure to human speech, the sketchy outline map of Lotter's cartouche renders the continent not only mute but unspeakable, since it is impossible to pronounce purely pictorial, nonglottic signs. In this context, mediation transforms the map's graphic form into a silent allograph, here a substitute sign for speech. At the same time, the map image introduces the written name, or rather the signature of the continent, through the phonetic alphabet. By combining linear graphics and the printed word "America," Lotter's scene seems to replace the agency of the speaking human figure with either the written word or the abstract figures of cartography. The continent here signifies the end of American speech; its mode of identification is no longer performed by dramatic dialogues, but is now represented by a map and name fragment ("AME" and "RICA"). Here the cartographer's representation of American speech is not defined by the logocentric, face-to-face arrangement of speaking subjects, but rather by the emerging rules of a print-based culture and its detached engagement with geography. The American character, and with it the subject position of the American orator, is permanently suspended in the silence of the map.[20]

SILENCED BY DEFAULT:
AMERICAN FIGURES AND COLONIAL SPEECH

A corollary of this dynamic between ideas of oratorical practice and the figure of the Native American is how British American rhetoricians appropriated and integrated the negative representation of native speech. In many ways the educated colonial speaker found himself in a position similar to that of the Native American depicted in the cartographic cartouche. That figure, trapped and compartmentalized within the confines

---

discursive system similar to metaphors. These are observations that overlap with studies by art historian Ernst Gombrich and his definition of the "Schema" (E. H. Gombrich, *Art and Illusion: A Study in the Psychology of Pictorial Representation* [Princeton, N.J., 1969]).

20. Lotter's frontispiece here provides a pictorial analogy of the mid- to late-eighteenth-century cultural shift from orality to a print-based literacy. For scholarship discussing the abstractness of print in colonial America, see Michael Warner, *The Letters of the Republic: Publication and the Public Sphere in Eighteenth-Century America* (Cambridge, Mass., 1990); Larzer Ziff, *Writing in the New Nation: Prose, Print, and Politics in the Early United States* (New Haven, Conn., 1991); Grantland S. Rice, *The Transformation of Authorship in America* (Chicago, 1997); Gustafson, *Eloquence Is Power*, 150–170.

of the decorative image, could only gesture to the greater map that she could never reach. Colonists intent on dramatizing the differences between British America and England imagined themselves as relegated to a marginal and circumscribed position within British political discourse. As speakers expounded how their portrayal as Indians largely silenced or muted their attempts to participate in a reasoned, logical transatlantic dialogue, they increasingly took exception to the way in which their voices were diminished if not negated by the oratorical setting, the geographic representation of the American continent.

To begin, American colonists were appalled that, in the context of a transatlantic debate over political representation, the British failed to address them by their proper geographic name. In *An Inquiry into the Rights of the British Colonies* (1766), for example, Richard Bland calls attention to how British rhetoric continually deferred the nominal acknowledgment of America:

> You can discover two Species of virtual Representation; the one to respect the Subjects in *Britain,* and always existing in Time of Parliament; the other to respect the Colonies, a mere Non-Entity, if I may be allowed the Term, and never existing but when the Parliament thinks proper to produce it into Being by any particular Act in which the Colonies happen to be named.

Protesting the colonists' lack of political representation in the British Parliament, Bland emphasizes the collective, generalizing label "colonies" as the nominal strategy that rendered the American territories into "Non-Entities."[21]

What may appear as a minor quibble over proper naming practices was for Bland and his contemporaries a crucial, debilitating feature in discussions over the situation of British Americans. The bureaucratic label "colonies" understated the colonial speaker's specific geographic context and thus denied him a concrete place or geographic location in the political debate. That the British failed to address the colonists by their proper place-name was also the concern of Silas Downer, who detects a generally possessive terminology in British political discourse that was geared toward downplaying the colonists' specific continental identity:

> The language of every paultry scribler, even of those who pretend friendship for us in some things, is after this lordly stile, *our colonies—*

21. Bland, *An Inquiry,* 12–13.

*our western dominions—our plantations—our islands—our subjects in America—our authority—our government—*with many more of the like imperious expressions.

This survey reads like the publication catalog of eighteenth-century cartographers, whose maps reflected and inscribed this sense of imperiousness the colonists found so odious. Positioning the name "America" grammatically as a locative object prevented the nominal recognition of the colonist as a non-British identity living in a non-European environment.[22]

In the opinion of many colonial speakers, British naming practices were emblematic of British geographic ignorance or illiteracy. Otis pretends to be shocked in *The Rights of the British Colonies Asserted and Proved* when he discovers that British politicians have been making decisions based on a rather faulty sense of continental geography. He is puzzled by the British lawmakers' condescension toward the colonies—"some of [England's] great men and writers, by their discourses of, and conduct towards them, consider [the American colonies] all rather as a parcel of *little insignificant conquered islands* than as a very extensive settlement on the continent." Otis blames British attitudes on the way in which "their lawbooks and very dictionaries of law, in editions so late as 1750, speak of the *British* plantations abroad as consisting chiefly of islands; and they are reckoned up in some of them in this order—*Jamaica, Barbados, Virginia, Maryland, New-England, New-York, Carolina, Bermudas.*" Otis goes on to mock at length such geographical ignorance and how it undermines the authority of the British political establishment: "Letters were often received, directed to the Governor of the *island* of New-England. Which *island* of New-England is a part of the *continent* of North-America, comprehending two provinces and two colonies; and according to the *undoubted* bounds of their charters, containing more land than there is in the three

22. [Downer], *A Discourse,* 8. Maps showing the British colonies in America were entitled *Map of the Dominions of Great Britain in North America* (1715), *Map of the British Empire in America* (1733), and *The British Colonies in North America* (1777). These maps are in the atlases of Herman Moll, *The World Described . . .* (London, 1708–1720); John Popple's wall map cited above; and William Faden's *North American Atlas . . .* (London, 1777). Each map marked the American continent as a geopolitical possession belonging to a European power but not as a space inhabited by a local population. A closer look at these maps reveals that the American place-name itself is even written out of the actual continental image; as the same maps subdivided the continent into regional administrative units, they assigned each unit the name of the supervisory provincial agency instead of the geographic region.

kingdoms. But I must confine myself to matters of more importance than detecting the geographical blunders, or refuting the errors of dead, super-annuated or any otherwise stupefied secretaries of state."[23]

For Otis, British geographical ignorance leads to a gross misrepresenta-tion of the colonies' inhabitants. When seeking to correct the mistake, he feels compelled to comment that the colonies "are well settled, not as the common people of *England* foolishly imagine, with a compound mongrel mixture of *English, Indian* and *Negro,* but with freeborn *British white* sub-jects, whose loyalty has never yet been suspected." Daniel Dulany makes a similar observation in his treatise *Considerations on the Propriety of Impos-ing Taxes in the British Colonies* (1765) when he asks his audience,

> What a strange animal must a North American appear . . . to the gener-ality of English readers, who have never had an opportunity to admire that he may be neither black nor tawny, may speak the English lan-guage, and in other respects seem, for all the world, like one of them![24]

Both Otis and Dulany are concerned that geographic descriptions of the colonies define the colonists according to theories of an environmentally determined degeneracy. They confront the idea, popularized by natural historians and physiocrats, according to which the American continent's southern geographic position (relative to Europe) subjected its occupants to a generally labile environment in which the warmer climate, summers of excessive heat, coastal swamps, and so forth fostered biological and moral decay. According to this theory, it was feared that, once Europeans moved to America, the continent's physical geography (position, size, and biomaterial contents) would corrupt the colonists' bodies, minds, and overall characters, in the end transforming them into a people that resem-bled the local native rather than European culture. This geographic inter-pretation of America threatened the colonists' status as British citizens and with it their inalienable rights to property, protection, and political representation. Within the colonial context of rhetoric and debate, the widespread geographic misrepresentation of Americans as "mongrels" and "animals" seriously impeded colonial speakers' acceptance as rhe-torical partners in a political dialogue. Concerns about British under-

23. Otis, *Rights of the British Colonies,* in Bailyn, ed., *Pamphlets,* I, 435. Otis's critique of the English identification of colonists with islands is also an overstatement on his part; if we take England's perspective, the most profitable colonies were islands.

24. Ibid.; Daniel Dulany, *Considerations on the Propriety of Imposing Taxes in the British Colonies* [Annapolis, Md., 1765], in Bailyn, ed., *Pamphlets,* I, 633.

standings of geography were thus inherently concerns about colonial speech. British ignorance about the racial character of the American, stemming from the mislocation of the colonies, threatened to reduce the colonists to the familiar inarticulate position of the monkey within the cartographic cartouche.[25]

Discussing English geographic knowledge confirmed for many speakers the fear that their misrepresentation was the result of the physical distance separating the colonies and Great Britain. Speakers worried that they were becoming disfigured and silenced because the distance allowed the press to alter the transmission and reception of British American speeches. When referring to America, colonial speechwriters made a habit of citing the numeric figures of geographic distance ("3000 miles") and size ("eighteen hundred miles in length"). Indeed, whether performing live or on the printed page, American speakers compulsively invoked the trope of distance. Having cast the persona of America in the character role of the daughter who does "nothing but call [England], over and over again, her FATHER," Jonathan Mayhew observes in his sermon *The Snare Broken,* "What wonder is it, if after groaning with a low voice for a while, to no purpose, we at length groaned so loudly, as to be heard more than three thousand miles."[26]

Mayhew here explores a rhetorical model similar to that of modern linguistic communication—consisting of sender, receiver, and message— in order to demonstrate how physical geography, expressed by mathematical figures, at once muffled colonial speech and discredited the speaker. Considering that oratorical performances depended on close spatial quarters to ensure face-to-face contact between speaker and audience, the distance of "3000 miles" was the perfect metaphor illustrating not only

25. On the trope of biocultural or racial degeneracy in late colonial discourse, see H. Roy Merrens, "Historical Geography and Early American History," *WMQ,* 3d Ser., XXII (1965), 529–548; Greene, "Search for Identity," *Jour. Soc. Hist.,* III (1969–1970), 208–210; Zuckerman, "The Fabrication of Identity," *WMQ,* 3d Ser., XXXIV (1977), 194–196; Alden T. Vaughan, "From White Man to Redskin: Changing Anglo-American Perceptions of the American Indian," *American Historical Review,* LXXXVII (1982), 917–953.

26. Mayhew, *The Snare Broken,* 14; see also Otis, *Vindication,* in Bailyn, ed., *Pamphlets,* I, 564; and [John Joachim Zubly], *An Humble Enquiry into the Nature of the Dependency of the American Colonies* . . . ([Charleston, S.C.], 1769), 25. Here I want to acknowledge Christopher K. Brooks, whose observation that "Americans seemed to understand that distance negates rhetoric" informed my thinking and research for this chapter. See his different argument in "Controlling the Metaphor: Language and Self-Definition in Revolutionary America," *Clio,* XXV (1996), 248.

political differences but the conditions of American speech and speakers inside the transatlantic forum. Distance thwarted the most eloquent performance. Overseas transportation and time lags caused a tightly argued case to appear late in print, rendering, as some colonists feared, their arguments moot and inviting ridicule. This perceived condition of communication seemingly forced colonial speechwriters to raise their voices at least in stylistic terms, thus violating at once the gentleman's code of conduct and the rhetorician's rules of "political, forensic, and ceremonial discourse." As the continental situation forced the speaking subject's voice to amplify the volume in order to compensate for the communicative delays, American speeches inadvertently became inscribed by class markers. The figuratively brass and shockingly impolite rhetoric of James Otis or, later, Patrick Henry made the colonial orator indistinguishable from the noise created by the British mob.[27]

Finally, for several writers geographical and cartographical representations threatened to eliminate the colonists' very geographic position, that is, their identity as a speaking subject. In *A Vindication of the British Colonies* (1765), James Otis protested the empire's empirical recording practices, which seemingly discounted the voice of America by presenting colonists in the form of numbers:

> Should a mother state even think it reasonable to impose internal, as well as external taxes, on six millions of subjects in their remote dominions, without allowing them *one voice,* it would be matter of wonder and astonishment. . . . Those six millions must on such an event, unless blind, see themselves reduced to the *mortifying condition of meer ciphers and blanks* in society.

Invoking the numbers printed on maps and in geography books as a rhetorical commonplace, Otis shows how the bureaucratic writings of political arithmetic embarrassed colonial endeavors to gain proper representation. Being reduced from "six millions" to "one voice" diminished the volume of the representative American speaker. Moreover, by using numbers rather than words to describe the voice of Americans, Otis suggests that the British representation of America was substituting the traditional means of representing voice with abstract, reductive signs. Otis

27. Fliegelman, *Declaring Independence,* 29. Sandra Gustafson traces the symbolic meaning underlying the term "mob" in the writings of James Otis and John Adams to their opinion that it meant a "mixed crowd," "as lower class and foreign in origin, impure through its mixture of people" (*Eloquence Is Power,* 180).

here draws on the binary understanding by which contemporary rhetoricians distinguished speech from writing as the living voice from the dead letter. Conveying their presence through mathematical ciphers only, the colonists' "voice of America" becomes reduced to an empty signifier, a voice detached from either a living body or a language. Once reduced to "blanks," colonial Americans do not have to be "blind" to realize that they have become completely invisible to English readers. Colonial speakers here find themselves in a rhetorical position worse than that of Shakespeare's Caliban: hailed as "thou Earth, thou," this representative American figure at least had a voice and language through which to curse Prospero and to challenge (though unsuccessfully) his rule. By contrast, the colonist who perceives himself to speak as a cipher or blank does not even have a place or space from which to address the imperial establishment.[28]

THE AMBIGUITY OF AMERICA; OR, WHAT IS A CONTINENT?

The exposure and denunciation of British geographical ignorance in colonial speeches fulfilled the colonial rhetorician's need to position himself against the dominant, imperial frame of cartographic discourse. More important, it called attention to the speaker's general lack of a common geographical self-definition. Throughout the speeches discussed above, the colonists repeatedly associate themselves with the North American continent, invoking geographic distance and dimensions—or to quote Thomas Paine, "at least one eighth part of the habitable globe." Yet, to use the continent as the discursive basis of identification was vexed in part because of the lack of a coherent conceptual geographic definition of the meaning of "continent." The idea of an American continent was only beginning to emerge as a concrete imaginative construct. Before the mid-eighteenth century, North America was represented as a fragmented, elusive territory. The typical map circulating in the colonies showed the continent to consist of anything from multiple islands to a series of peninsulas to one or two continental landmasses. On the eve of the American Revolu-

28. Otis, *Vindication,* in Bailyn, ed., *Pamphlets,* I, 563–564 (emphasis added). The distinction between speech and writing developed out of the early modern tension between orality and print but persisted as late as 1765, when John Rice, for example, writes, "Now the Art of Reading, being in fact the Art of converting Writing into Speech, the Relation which the living Voice bears to the dead Letter, becomes a very peculiar Object of the Reader's Attention." See Rice, *An Introduction to the Art of Reading* (1765; rpt. Menston, Eng., 1969), 194.

tion, most of the political maps representing the British colonies in magazines and bookplates depicted North America as a semicontinent in which the eastern landmass fills out the map image and the Appalachian Mountains or the Mississippi River posed as the boundary dividing the American continent into a terra cognita and the great unknown.[29]

While the cartographic representation of North America as a continental form was incomplete for very practical reasons (lack of surveys and geographical observations), it was systemically rendered ambiguous because the definition surrounding the term "continent" itself was in flux and a site of competing political ideologies. In the eighteenth century, the continent was only one of several conceptual building blocks of world geography. Unlike the Renaissance cosmographers who differentiated between celestial, terrestrial, and human geographies, Enlightenment cartographers and geographers concentrated on metageographical concepts that included continents, nation-states, and supracontinental blocks, such as the Orient and Occident, or the Northern and the Southern Hemispheres. Through such a metageographical organization, conventional geographic thinking came "to treat the earth's surface as if it were amenable to taxonomic classification in neat hierarchies of territorial units." This graded classification of metageographical territories became the geographic rule during the late seventeenth and throughout the eighteenth century and was made salient in the various archival mapping projects that surrounded the national consolidation and imperial overseas expansion of states like England, France, and Spain.[30]

29. Martin W. Lewis and Kären E. Wigen, *The Myth of Continents: A Critique of Metageography* (Berkeley, Calif., 1997), 1–46.

For maps illustrating the state of eighteenth-century geographic knowledge, see Buisseret, ed., *From Sea Charts to Satellite Images;* Schwartz and Ehrenberg, *Mapping of America;* Cumming, *The Southeast in Early Maps* and *British Maps of Colonial America.*

30. Lewis and Wigen, *Myth of Continents,* 11. On the history of the mapping of continents, see Rodney W. Shirley, *The Mapping of the World: Early Printed World Maps, 1472–1700* (London, 1983); Philip D. Burden, *The Mapping of North America: A List of Printed Maps, 1511–1670* (Rickmansworth, Eng., 1996).

For an east-west bias in representations of North America, see the work of the English mapmaker Herman Moll and the Frenchman Guillaume Delisle described by Dennis Reinhartz, *The Cartographer and the Literati: Herman Moll and His Intellectual Circle* (Lewiston, N.Y., 1997). On the north-south bias in colonial maps, see my "Mapping the 'American South': Image, Archive, and the Textual Construction of Regional Identity in the Age of Washington," in Tamara Harvey and Greg O'Brien, eds., *George Washington's South* (Gainesville, Fla., 2004), 42–68.

Figure 21.
A New Map of
North
America. . . . By
Edward Wells.
1715.
Permission,
Colonial
Williamsburg
Foundation

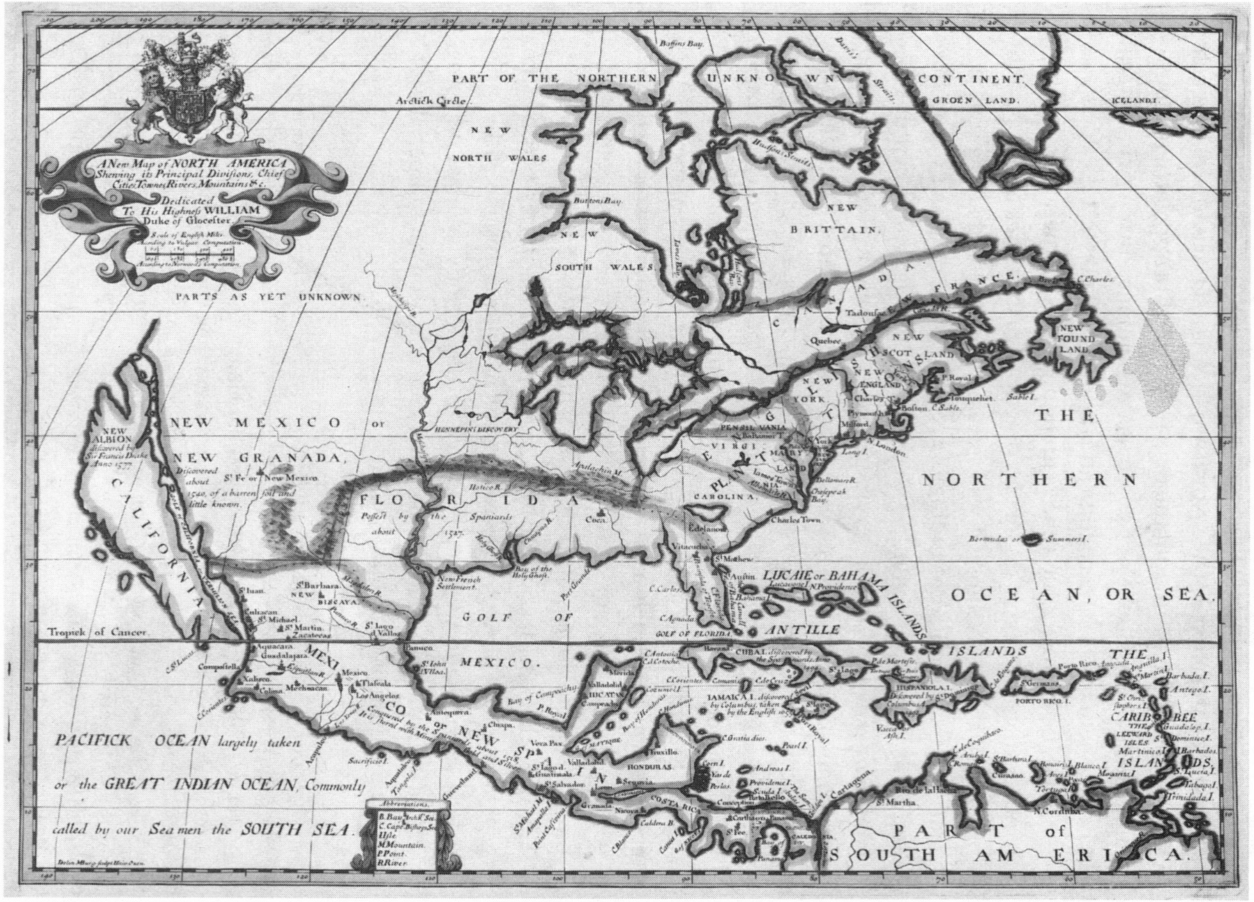

The hierarchical order of these metageographies becomes visible in British atlas maps that were published throughout the first half of the eighteenth century and, given the map reader's sentimental attachment to the material artifact, circulated for many years later. Maps presenting North America depicted an array of land segments that failed to resemble the modern definition of a coherent continental form. Edward Wells's *New Map of North America* (1715) offers the map reader a cartographic collage showing the mainland British colonies, the islands of the West Indies, and the island of California (Figure 21). This picture of North America is framed to the north by the "Continent Groen Land" and to the south by a "Part of South America"—Greenland, a territory in which the British had little investment, is promoted to continental status while the Americas are reduced and dissected. Wells renders the American continental frame incomplete, revealing to the west the blank spaces of "Parts as Yet Unknown" and the "Part of the Northern Unknown."

The omission of parts unknown, of course, resulted from a lack of information. Eighteenth-century expeditions that would survey the northwestern parts of America were in progress or yet to come. But, leaving this point aside, it is important to remember how in the history of map reading (as opposed to professional mapmaking) the map of North America projected an inchoate and fundamentally anticontinental image. This map image informed readers and students throughout the first half of the eighteenth century. Turning to a second example, Thomas Bakewell's map *America: A New and Most Exact Map Laid Down according to the Observations Communicated to the English Royal Society and French Royal Academy* (1740) demonstrates how the northern parts of America are shown to be visually incoherent when compared to the neat outline of South America (Figure 22). The cartographic figure of North America gives the impression of a pseudo-archipelago, as real islands blur optically with the territorial design of California and the political lines demarcating the colonial provinces. The map emphasizes the geographic integrity of England; by contrast, the unit called North America takes on quite the opposite appearance. Looking as insular as the mother country, the North American continent appears unsound, with the veneer of a work in progress rather than a complete metageographic entity.[31]

31. On California's cartographic history as an island, see Glen McLaughlin and Nancy H. Mayo, *The Mapping of California as an Island: An Illustrated Checklist* ([Saratoga, Calif.], 1995); R. V. Tooley, *California as an Island: A Geographical Miosconception . . .* (London, 1964).

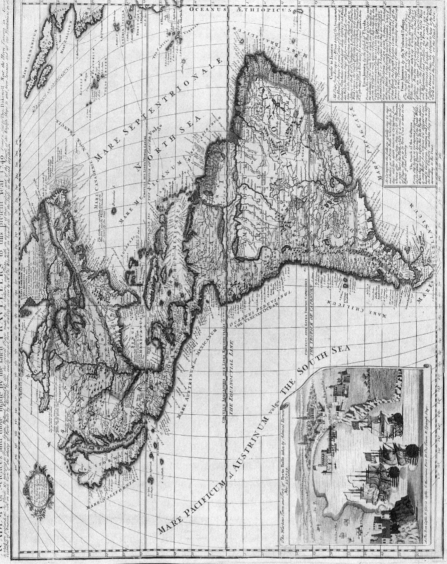

Figure 22.
America: A New and Most
Exact Map. . . . *By Thomas
Bakewell. 1740.* Permission,
Colonial Williamsburg
Foundation

Colonial students who were trained in classical rhetoric and modern elocution most likely encountered the ambiguity surrounding the continent in textbooks like Patrick Gordon's *Geography Anatomized; or, A Compleat Geographical Grammer* (1693; 1754). Unlike other geographers, this textbook author sought to ally the study of geography explicitly with language instruction and the spoken word. Gordon writes in the introduction, "I have given it the Title of Grammar, having reduc'd the whole body of Modern Geography to a true Grammatical Method; this Science as capable of being taught by Grammar as any Tongue whatsoever." According to seventeenth- and eighteenth-century pedagogy manuals, lessons in all subjects were ideally taught orally through rote memorization. As teachers completed textbook lessons by having students stand up before the class, geography lessons became recitals of Gordon's tables and maps.[32]

Gordon's *Geography* offered not only a lesson in memorization but a typical geography lesson, one that shaped many British colonists' basic assumptions about geographical space and its representation. Studying the textbook, the reader discovered that the concept of the American continent emerged in the encyclopedic form. The textbook presented a taxonomic world order that revolved around early modern nation-states. It condensed the geography of the world into parenthetical lists, showing the names of countries like England and geopolitical units like New England (Figure 23). This list arranged the display of continents according to early modern geographic convention: the roll call began with Europe and ended with North and South America.[33]

32. Pat[rick] Gordon, *Geography Anatomized; or, A Compleat Geographical Grammer* . . . (London, 1693), A2d. On the oral component in colonial education, see Lawrence A. Cremin, *American Education: The Colonial Experience, 1607–1783* (New York, 1975); E. Jennifer Monaghan, "Literacy Instruction and Gender in Colonial New England," in Cathy N. Davidson, ed., *Reading in America: Literature and Social History* (Baltimore, 1989), 53–80; David D. Hall, "The Uses of Literacy in New England, 1600–1850," in William L. Joyce et al., eds., *Printing and Society in Early America* (Worcester, Mass., 1983), 1–47. On eighteenth-century geographic knowledge as conveyed by popular textbooks, see the brief discussions by Margarita Bowen, *Empiricism and Geographical Thought: From Francis Bacon to Alexander von Humboldt* (Cambridge, 1981), 144–154; David N. Livingstone, *The Geographical Tradition: Episodes in the History of a Contested Enterprise* (Oxford, 1992), 111–113.

33. Originally published in 1693 and with its twentieth edition coming out in 1754, Gordon's *Geography* stands out because of its widespread diffusion and multigenerational ownership among the many works that were made available in British America. Much cheaper than previous tomes on geography, this textbook—explicitly designed for use in "publick schools"—reached an audience previously unable to purchase the lavishly illus-

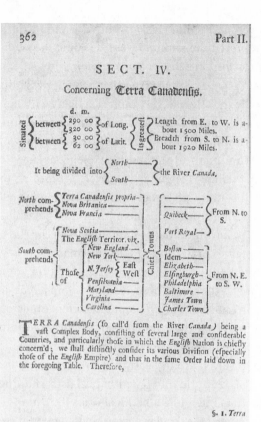

S E C T. IV.

Concerning Terra Canadensis.

Figure 23.
"Concerning Terra Canadensis." From Geography Anatomiz'd; or, The Geographical Grammar, *by Pat[rick] Gordon. 1711.* By Permission of the Houghton Library, Harvard University

While Gordon's textbook thus established a Eurocentric world order that was predicated upon the nation, built into its representation of America was a fundamental ambivalence toward giving it continental status. As the student rehearsed place-names and local facts, he was supposed to pronounce and enunciate the world's political units and divisions from north to south. For Europe this meant the oral reading lesson would start with the names of England and the Scandinavian countries. Reciting the

trated, leatherbound folio editions. Reading-diaries and notebooks, too many to cite here, demonstrate how Gordon's textbook pervaded the pedagogic settings of city schools and frontier homes. Furthermore, when examining the bookbindings, personal inscriptions and signatures reveal that this geography book had a lasting influence; its pedagogic authority gained in stature as it was passed on from one generation of geographic scholars to the next.

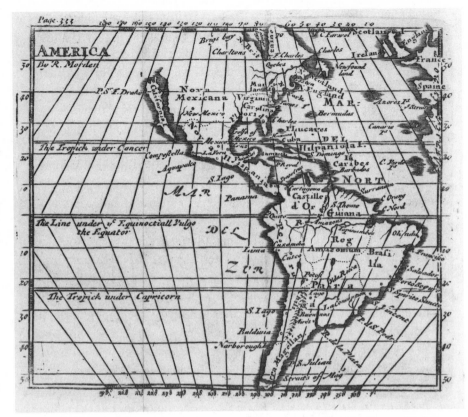

Figure 24. "America." By R. Morden. From Geography Anatomiz'd; or, The Geographical Grammar, *by Pat[rick] Gordon. 1711.* By Permission of the Houghton Library, Harvard University

place-names and dimensions of America, however, Gordon makes an exception: there the student is supposed to call out the names, not in a political microterritorial order, but rather by following the larger geographic continental framework, beginning "at the Pole."

Conversely, Gordon's *Geography* seeks to control the continental status of English overseas possessions. Attached to the table was a foldout map showing the continent of "America" (Figure 24). As the map reveals, the continental landmass is partitioned into European-controlled geopolitical units. It includes capital cities and trading posts. It shows North America to be open-ended and incomplete. And finally, characteristic of the period, the mapmaker's representation of the Atlantic is designed to foreshorten the distance separating England, France, and Spain from their respective overseas possessions. If we assume the viewpoint of the British-based reader, the map is designed to assert an imperial spatial hierarchy: a much-exaggerated England peeks out from the map's top right margin, supervising its colonial turf from unrealistically close quarters.

Within this eighteenth-century context, then, the idea of the continent became politicized; "continent" was not simply a neutral signifier for a large tectonic landmass but a malleable geopolitical term that was deployed to uphold particular ideologies. Used as much to indicate a political order as a geographic space, however, the continent assumed its own competing and often contradictory definitions. The status of the continent was of particular importance to British authors confronting the colonies in North America. Defining themselves as an island nation discrete from the European continent, the British needed to negotiate the power relations between their own small geographic space and the vastness of the American continent housing the inferior political order of the British colonies. One approach was to create a sense of a geopolitical aesthetic, in which the form of the island—with its clear borders and self-containment—was subtly portrayed as the idealized geographic form of the nation-state. To this end, British geographers, especially those who were writing textbooks, tended to promote the form of the island and to downplay the metageographical status of the continent. Sir Isaac Watts, for example, defined land forms in his textbook *The Knowledge of the Heavens and the Earth Made Easy* (1736) as "called either an Island, a Continent, a Peninsula, an Isthmus, a Promontory, or a Coast." The list presents a set of geographical forms that reflect British national thinking; by privileging islands over mainlands, Watts subordinates the world's geography to the form of the British nation-state.[34]

Watts continues to present Britain (or, more specifically, southern England) as the idealized geographic space in his illustration "A Map of a Country Exemplified" (Figure 25). Here a fictional land is created to graphically display the different types of topographic features, such as an isthmus, a peninsula, and a gulf. While the country presented is not an exact depiction of a known European state, the shape bears an obvious graphic similarity to southern England, with a river to the east in the place of the Thames, an island to the south in the place of the Isle of Wight, and

---

34. Isaac Watts, *The Knowledge of the Heavens and the Earth Made Easy; or, The First Principles of Astronomy and Geography Explain'd by the Use of Globes and Maps* (London, 1736), 55.

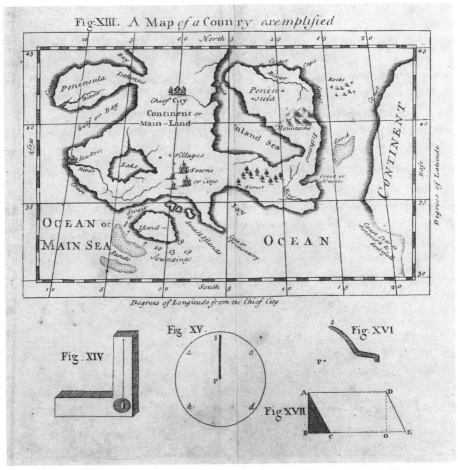

Figure 25. *"A Map of a Country Exemplified." From* The Knowledge of the Heavens and the Earth Made Easy . . . , *by Isaac Watts. 1736.* By Permission of the Houghton Library, Harvard University

a continent to the east in the place of mainland Europe. If Watts's listing of geographic forms created a hierarchy of islands over continents, his map performs a different function, conflating the notion of islands and continents. The shape of the English island is here labeled as a "Continent or Main-Land": not only are island and continent rendered coterminous, but with the title of "Main-Land" the small "Country" takes precedence even over the large "Continent" depicted to the east. Island, continent, and country (or nation-state) here become one, as Britain again becomes the ideal model of geographic and political organization.

As eighteenth-century atlases and schoolbooks showing the American possessions of England resisted, like Watts's fictional map, North America's continental status, colonial speakers choosing the label of "American" therefore seemed to be grounding their identity in an ungrounded, ephemeral space. For the skilled orator this rhetorical ploy seemed self-defeating, if not absurd. To speak from the position of the American continent was to speak without a concrete physical base, as the undefined geographical space prevented the location and identification of the colonial speaker inside the transatlantic theater of rhetoric. Paradoxically, it was through the vociferous denunciation of British geographical knowledge that the colonist exercised his voice and honed his rhetorical skills. More specifically, while denouncing the kind of geographical knowledge that was designed to silence the native figure of America, the newly identified British American appropriated the figure of the continent not only to find his voice but to create a persona who could dramatize a collective sense of identity.

Those colonial rhetoricians who set out to define the colonies in "American" terms did so by reeducating the audience, providing virtual geography lessons that stabilized the continental map. In order to do this, speakers and writers alike appropriated the textbook protocol of map reading. A recurrent theme of American political discourse became the continent's parameters, as speeches sketched out the basic map image of America. Jonathan Mayhew defined "this continent, from Canada to Florida, and the West-India islands," and Samuel Williams, in his aptly titled manifesto *A Discourse on the Love of Our Country* (1775), describes "that vast extent of country which reaches from *Labrador* to *Florida*." Speakers like Williams expanded this map lesson into one on physical geography ("We view this country in its extent and variety of climates, soils, and produce, etc.") or, as John Zubly did, into one on political geography ("BRITISH EMPIRE is a more extensive word, and should not be confounded with the kingdom of Great-Britain; [the kingdom] consists of *England, Scotland, Ireland,* the Islands of *Man, Jersey, . . .* and the Islands and Colonies in *North-America,* etc."). Celebrating America's continentality, Williams begins his lesson by imitating a geography textbook's table of contents: "In that vast *extent* of country, which reaches from *Labrador* to *Florida,* there is a *climate* adapted to health, vigour, industry, liberty, genius, and happiness. Our *soil* is adapted to the most useful kinds of *produce;* and our *situation* is not unfriendly to *commerce.*" To this he adds the inventory typical of most contemporary geography books. Having listed the natural aspects of British America, he enumerates its cultural achievements—the militia, public academies, discoveries in electricity and inoculation, various "natural productions," and, as a specimen of the continent's "genius," Benjamin Franklin.[35]

The cumulative effect of this rote repetition of geographic names and facts was the emergence of the continent as a comprehensive spatial and geopolitical entity. Colonial rhetoricians stressed the sheer magnitude of the continent itself. (Again, while today the knowledge that North America comprises an entire continent seems self-evident, colonial audiences needed to be systematically trained to absorb this concept.) They needed to overcome the legacy of sixteenth- and seventeenth-century cartographic and narrative traditions and their conceptual understanding of America as a series of islands. Florida, for example, was long perceived as a fabulous isle, and it was not until the 1730s that the "island" of California was cartographically attached to the continental landmass. The image of Edward Wells's North American archipelago persisted far into the century. As evidence of the persistence of this tradition we need only return to Otis's complaint about letters addressed to the "Governor of the *island* of New-England."

By establishing America as a continental landmass, colonial speakers and authors could then turn this knowledge to their forensic advantage by comparing the massive continent of America to the diminutive island of Great Britain. Audiences were asked to imagine the figure of the continent through maps that juxtaposed its graphic and empty outline against the shape of England, as in Patrick Gordon's *Geography Anatomized.* When read from a colonial vantage point, Gordon's map illustrates how the weighty image of the Western Hemisphere overshadows the much smaller figure of England. This strategy of comparative mapping became, in the words of colonial rhetoricians, one of the more effective tools for asserting American claims of sovereign authority.

The most prominent case for claiming sovereignty was made by Thomas Paine's widely read and recited pamphlet *Common Sense* (1776), where the figure of the continent provided the clinching metaphor for redefining both the transatlantic rationale of power relations and

35. Mayhew, *The Snare Broken*, 16; Williams, *A Discourse*, 4, 23; [Zubly], *Humble Enquiry*, 3–4.

the basis of political speech: "Small islands not capable of protecting themselves, are the proper objects for kingdoms to take under their care; but there is something very absurd, in supposing a continent to be perpetually governed by an island . . . as England and America, with respect to each other, reverses the common order of nature, it is evident they belong to different systems: England to Europe, America to itself." Moses Mather packages the comparison more directly in the didactic terms of geographical literacy. Assuming the tone of the schoolmaster, he lectures: "REALM signifies kingdom; and kingdom signifies the country . . . subject to one sovereign prince. . . . Should a schoolboy be asked, whether America, which is three thousand miles distant, was within the kingdom of Great-Britain, both being subject to one prince, he must answer that it was not." And he concludes: "They are two countries, three thousand miles distant from each other, inhabited by different people, under distinct constitutions of government, with different customs, laws and interests."[36]

In what appears a pedantic exercise, the references to the continent prove an unlikely source of elocutionary animation. The colonial appropriation of cartographic discourse here comes full circle. Having shed the image of the personified character of America by emphasizing the abstract graph of the map or the rote recitation of geographic facts, the continent itself now becomes a character within colonial oratory. According to Richard Wells, writing in 1775, the continent had evolved into a full-fledged persona, including body, voice, and opinions. Contending that the continent is a "formidable figure," he imagines it engaged in a lively debate with British politicians: "Let English Statesmen clamor for power, let a British parliament boast of unlimitted supremacy, yet the continent of America will contend with equal fervency." America the continent is

36. Thomas Paine, *Common Sense,* in Michael Foot and Isaac Kramnick, eds., *The Thomas Paine Reader* (New York, 1987), 86. Here I wish to amend Paine's often-noted planetary metaphor, which is usually used to locate his rhetoric inside the world of Newtonian physics. [Moses Mather], *America's Appeal to the Impartial World* . . . (Hartford, Conn., 1775), 30, 47.

On the popular reception and public reading of Paine's pamphlet, see Eric Foner, *Tom Paine and Revolutionary America* (New York, 1976); Evelyn J. Hinz, "Thomas Paine," in Everett Emerson, ed., *American Literature, 1764–1789: The Revolutionary Years* (Madison, Wis., 1977), 39–57. For a discussion of the rhetorical radicalism of *Common Sense,* see Jon P. Klancher, *The Making of English Reading Audiences, 1790–1832* (Madison, Wis., 1987).

thus placed on equal ground with the human agents of statesmen and Parliament. The "name of AMERICAN" becomes subtly anthropomorphized; it appears atop newspapers and pamphlets and thus was billed in much the same way that colonial printers promoted the stage performances of religious and political speakers. The name America takes on sartorial properties; it can "carry honour and majesty in the sound," just as men would "esteem it a blessing to wear" that "venerable and commanding stile." Thomas Paine completes the anthropomorphization of the continent when he comments in *Common Sense* on its wardrobe: "The Continental Belt is too loosely buckled." The continent even had an emotional identity, for "until an independance is declared, the Continent will feel itself like a man who continues putting off some unpleasant business from day to day." And, finally, the dramatic figure of the continent assumes a voice in political debate. It becomes the arbiter on the weighty matter of American sovereignty. Paine writes that "nothing but Continental authority can regulate Continental matters" and that "the appeal was the choice of the king, and the continent hath accepted the challenge."[37]

The American continent provides Paine with the ideal dramatic rhetorical figure scripted for making radical and subversive arguments. Having established the continental persona, Paine redefined the character of international dialogue. He purposefully stages the continent vis-à-vis the king, thus invoking the most prominent corporeal image defining English notions of sovereignty. This notion of sovereignty was often imagined in terms of an elocutionary performance, as is witnessed by the famous frontispiece of Thomas Hobbes's *Leviathan,* which was a critical influence on American deliberations about statehood and self-government (Figure 26). There the figure of the king looms large over his territorial domain; his outstretched arms hover above the land while a sword and staff signify his civic and ecclesiastical powers. A closer look reveals that the king's

37. [Wells], *The Middle Line,* 5, 6, 8, 31, 42; *Royal American Magazine,* I (1774), 10, cited in Jack P. Greene, *The Intellectual Construction of America: Exceptionalism and Identity from 1492 to 1800* (Chapel Hill, N.C., 1993), 164; Paine, *Common Sense,* in Foot and Kramnick, eds., *Thomas Paine Reader,* 79, 99, 103, 107. The following rhetoric handbook lesson applies here perfectly: "For polite and elegant speakers distinguish themselves by their discourse, as persons of figure do by their garb; one being the dress of mind, as the other is of the body. And hence it comes to pass, that both have their different fashions, which are often changed." John Ward, *A System of Oratory . . . ,* I (London, 1759), 309–310.

Figure 26. Detail from Frontispiece to Leviathan, *by Thomas Hobbes. 1651.*
Courtesy, University of Delaware Library

body is an empty shell filled by the bodies of the people. The sovereign's personal body is thus shown to be a constitutive form, posing as the embodiment of the collective. What is significant about this body politic is its dramatization of speech. The frontispiece shows, on the one hand, the sovereign's subjects as a crowd that collectively turns its back on the viewer, rendering the individual members faceless and implicitly voiceless. On the other hand, the image delineates the face of the king, showing his mouth and lips partly opened as if he were caught in the act of speaking. The frontispiece here anticipates the theatricality of the modern state apparatus, in particular the elocutionary practice of interpellation, which subordinates the subject to the state through the simple utterance of commands. By emphasizing the king's body language and facial expression, the artist illustrates how the king becomes not only the exclusive figure capable of speaking for the people but also the figuration of speech as a sovereign voice. Being the only voice heard throughout the imperial territory, the image declares the figure of the king to be the natural proprietor of the land and his geographically embedded voice as the measure by which political selfhood is performed.[38]

From the moment that the colonists had the continent speak, the speaker's use of geographic figures inverted the symbolic structure of Hobbes's frontispiece. The land, which in British theories of sovereignty served as the indispensable base for maintaining the material desires of the king, now had not only come alive but slipped into the rhetorical subject position of the king's body. The king's rhetorical eclipse by the American continent was prepared by printers or writers who purposefully abridged the king's name. For example, in *Common Sense* Paine refers to the king exclusively as the "K— of England." He thus erases the symbolic speaker of his hereditary title while opening up a typographic slot into which readers and listeners could now enter a new character representing the imperial body politic, such as the American continent.

As with the manuscript figure of the plat, the rhetorical figure of the continent was again grounded simultaneously in figures of land and literacy. Through the act of writing, the colonists' geodetic representation of land on the American continent had fostered individualistic attitudes within the larger British American imperial community. Similarly, the oratorical adaptation of the cartographic figure of the continent now blurred the map's Anglocentric communal connotation: by speaking from the space of the continent, colonial speakers made the map an expression of both individual and collective identity. Indeed, from the perspective of the individual speechwriter, geographical literacy proved to be the elocutionary lifeline. By reciting the map image of the continent, speakers developed a didactic mode of geographical oratory that confirmed the geographic character of the speaker; it situated the speaker's body while also providing him with a mouthpiece through which to assert his voice as that of a sovereign. In dramaturgical terms, nothing sounded more persuasive than having political demands announced by the figure of the continent whose base was as wide as North America, and who carried a bodily emphasis derived from the speaker's personal geographical identity.

Choosing the figure of the American continent, however, confirmed one's metageographical rather than local situation. Masked as the continent, the colonial speaker inevitably conjured up the idea of a continental

38. Wood, *Creation of the American Republic*, 348.

community. Or, to put it more directly, the rhetorical construction of the figure of the continent concluded a larger public debate over the virtue and logistics of expansion by the colonists, with or without the empire's blessing. It is not a coincidence that many of the speakers who were rehearsing the figure of the continent—including James Otis, Jonathan Mayhew, Benjamin Franklin, and Christopher Gadsden—have been identified as the leading members of the expansionist camp in the British colonial political arena.[39]

For members of this group, the oratorical figure of the continent provided the logical continuation of the existing cartographic rhetoric used by imperial institutions. As they made the voice of the colonial distinctly audible through translation—a process that turned the nonalphabetic ciphers of geography (the coordinates, map images, and textbook numbers) into an expressive tool of colonial self-representation—they established a persona compatible with the symbols representing the British Empire. Such a figure made it very easy to speak with one voice for "six millions," as James Otis would have it. Its expansive girth more or less served as rational evidence when making a case for western expansion, and its collective persona ultimately declared the existence of a new body politic of imperial proportions.

Calling on the American as a continental figure provided in the end not only a persuasive forensic figure in eighteenth-century political discourse but also an emotionally moving figure that evoked public interest and, more important, a sense of patriotic affection. Just as we must imagine that geographic boundaries marking land and water shifted from one map publication to the next, the imaginary body politic of the American continent expanded or contracted depending on a transatlantic debate in which modern bureaucratic imperialism competed against traditional definitions of English nationalism. The same rhetorical conceits—references to distance, area, and fantastic descriptions of a fertile American empire—that made the figure of the continent into an extroverted figure of territorial ambition also served as a narrative blueprint guiding the audience in the opposite direction. As colonial speakers

39. The expansionists were a group of "upper class individuals, who," as Marc Egnal writes, "were actively committed to promoting the ascendancy of America." "These well-to-do men and, in rare instances, wealthy women generally agreed on a variety of issues, including the need for strengthened local sovereignty, a healthy domestic economy, thriving maritime commerce, and new land." *A Mighty Empire: The Origins of the American Revolution* (Ithaca, N.Y., 1988), 7.

sought to move the audience and awaken their passions, by hailing them-selves as cartographically defined characters they realigned the British colonists' national affect (their "love of country") by shifting their emo-tional investment from the map of England to that of North America. Through the figure of the continent, a few prominent colonial speakers—having reconciled the structural rationale of rhetorical argument with the elocutionary ideals of sentimentality—ultimately turned to geographical literacy as the basis of an Anglo-American variant of patriotism.

chapter three

MAPS, SPELLERS, AND THE

SEMIOTICS OF NATIONALISM

IN THE EARLY REPUBLIC

After the Revolutionary war, it was a bitter irony for Anglo-Americans, eager to sever all representational ties with the former imperial power, that their discussions about Independence and self-government were by necessity conducted in the very language of the former oppressor. While some of the founders debated whether Hebrew or German should become the Republic's first language, diplomats at the Paris peace conference found it easy to imagine a future in which "the thirteen United States wou'd form the greatest Empire in the World" but also anticipated that such an American empire "from a similarity of Language, Manners and Religion . . . wou'd be *English*." The new American citizens also recognized English as the dominant language and lingua franca connecting the larger community of polyglot peoples living within the new national borders. However, the linguistic proximity to imperial England and its legacy of institutions, political practices, and concepts of national culture raised the question whether English, or for that matter any language, was truly capable of representing the new Republic and the meaning of independent citizenship.[1]

If we turn to the political arena during the first decade after Independence, Federalists and Antifederalists alike frequently expressed concern about how their reliance on the medium of language obstructed the definition of government. The Federalist James Madison questioned the efficacy of the spoken and written word for negotiating federal and state interests. Discussing the "arduous . . . task of marking the proper line of partition between the authority of the general and that of the State govern-

1. "Anecdotes of the Negotiations," in W. A. S. Hewins, ed., *The Whitefoord Papers: Being the Correspondence and Other Manuscripts of Colonel Charles Whitefoord from 1739 to 1810* (Oxford, 1898), 187, cited in Eliga H. Gould, "A Virtual Nation: Greater Britain and the Imperial Legacy of the American Revolution," *American Historical Review,* CIV (1999), 481.

ments," he despairs that the use of "words" and "language" fails to convey "complex objects" (such as the idea of a federal union) via "human faculties" to a self-interested people. He writes in Federalist No. 37:

> The medium through which the conceptions of men are conveyed to each other adds a fresh embarrassment. The use of words is to express ideas. Perspicuity, therefore, requires not only that the ideas should be distinctly formed, but that they should be expressed by words distinctly and exclusively appropriate to them. But no language is so copious as to supply words and phrases for every complex idea, or so correct as not to include many equivocally denoting different ideas.

Antifederalists seemingly shared Madison's sense of a linguistic crisis. "And where is the man," asked the voice of Denatus in the *Virginia Independent Chronicle,* "who can see through the constitution to its effects? The constitution of a wise and free people, ought to be as evident to simple reason, as the letters of our alphabet."[2]

Self-consciously inhabiting a logocentric world that revolved around the English language and its alphabetic writing code, both sides were flustered by the fact that the Constitution as a verbal construct lacked transparency and immediate recognition. For Madison, the new Republic's constitutional process was inherently threatened because its foundational document was "rendered dim and doubtful by the cloudy medium through which it is communicated." Similarly, those who opposed the idea of federal union feared that the Constitution's "dim" words ("Who can see through the constitution?") would become precisely the tool by which a central government would obfuscate the practices of power.[3]

For the union to work at all, both the Federalist and Antifederalist voices asserted that the Constitution would have to display its meaning as did the spelling book or picture primer, the most basic of literacy tools. For its meaning to be evident to simple reason, the Antifederalists pro-

2. James Madison, Federalist No. 37, in William R. Brock, ed., *The Federalist; or, The New Constitution* (London, 1992), 179, 180–181; "Address by Denatus," in Herbert J. Storing, ed., *The Complete Anti-Federalist* (Chicago, 1981), V, 262.

3. Madison, Federalist No. 37, in Brock, ed., *The Federalist,* 181. For materials discussing the fears and uses of logocentrism in the constitutional debates, see Robert A. Ferguson, " 'We Hold These Truths': Strategies of Control in the Literature of the Founders," in Sacvan Bercovitch, ed., *Reconstructing American Literary History* (Cambridge, Mass., 1986), 1–28; Michael Warner, *The Letters of the Republic: Publication and the Public Sphere in Eighteenth-Century America* (Cambridge, Mass., 1990), 97–117.

posed the symbolic order of the letter alphabet. If we consider the Federalists' invocation of visual perception in relation to the medium of the word, their implied solution to ambiguous language invoked the picture pedagogy of the eighteenth-century alphabet lesson. For Federalist and Antifederalist alike, then, in the ideal world of post-Revolutionary communication the Constitution would operate like a picture primer, displaying its subject matter like an alphabet lesson in which words become meaningful through the visual representation of objects. Such a pictorial language would disperse the fear of linguistic opacity and make the Constitution "evident to simple reason," that is, accessible at once to the literate and illiterate American. To expand on the idea of a constitutional primer even further, the two political factions hoped to discover in the Constitution a language teaching a lesson similar to that of the alphabet primer: instead of reading "A stands for apple," ideally the Constitution would convey the meaning of a "free and wise people" so that "A stands for American."

The perceived linguistic crisis was resolved at least temporarily by the framers' shared culture of geographical literacy. When the time came to ratify the nation's founding document, the signers of the Constitution ceremoniously bypassed both the alphabet and the vexing ambiguity underlying the English language. As Robert A. Ferguson has pointed out: "The signers of the Constitution appear neither in alphabetical order, nor by presumed importance or seniority, nor in haphazard fashion. They are grouped, instead, by state with the states themselves appearing in *geographical* order from north to south, starting with New Hampshire in the north and working in sequence through Georgia in the extreme south." "The United States thus appear," he continues, "on the page in familiar map form—the perfect icon in answer to Madison's fears about indistinct objects, imperfect perception, and faulty language." Neither the alphabetically constructed word nor the collaboratively composed text of the Constitution, but the implied form of the national map thus capped at once the political debate over the Republic's new Constitution and the pervasive sense of language crisis that emerged from this debate.[4]

The national map had become so integral to the early national linguistic consciousness that even the country's fundamental documents were innately structured by the diction and grammar of the national map.

4. Robert A. Ferguson, "The American Enlightenment, 1750–1820," in Sacvan Bercovitch, ed., *The Cambridge History of American Literature*, I, *1590–1820* (Cambridge, 1994), 484.

Thus, early on, the map entered into the national linguistic reform move-ment, and the textuality of the national map informed primers and ele-mentary lessons in print literacy in the early Republic. Many Americans self-consciously turned to the material form and rhetoric of the national map in order to negotiate and reconcile the competing interests laid bare by the Federalist crisis. Through geographical literacy, the new citizens adopted the national map as a proleptic text that enabled American politi-cians to ratify the Constitution and became a popular language by which ordinary citizens learned to imagine the contested idea of national unity.[5]

WEBSTER'S SPELLERS AND THE ACOUSTIC MAP

Prompted by the Revolutionary momentum, educational, linguistic, and political theorists did their best to redesign the English language. Sev-eral authors sought to revise the most basic element of language, the alphabet. Devising a national alphabet, James Ewing and Abner Kneeland expanded the number of letters from twenty-six to thirty-three; in an effort to provide a proper transcript of American speech habits they designed new symbols that represented these distinctive sounds. Thomas Embree went so far as to substitute syllabic letter combinations with numbers, such as "2 aw, 3 ah, . . . 8 ezhay, 9 eng." At their extreme, linguistic reform efforts went beyond the building of lexicons, pronunciation, and orthog-raphy; William Thornton suggested the gradual revision of the alphabetic code itself. Making his case for a whole new script, he exhorted the Ameri-can audience, "You have corrected the dangerous doctrines of European powers, correct now the languages you have imported," which he then transcribed into print type as "Iu hav korektid þɪ deendjra doktrinz ov Iuropiiɔn pouɪrz."[6]

5. The idea of a larger American nation-state and national culture was anything but well received. Historians have reminded us of the vehemence and pervasiveness with which local cultures resisted nation building in post-Revolutionary America. See David Waldstreicher, *In the Midst of Perpetual Fetes: The Making of American Nationalism, 1776–1820* (Chapel Hill, N.C., 1997), chaps. 2, 5; James Roger Sharp, *American Politics in the Early Republic: The New Nation in Crisis* (New Haven, Conn., 1993); Peter S. Onuf, "Federalism, Republicanism, and the Origins of American Sectionalism," in Edward L. Ayers et al., *All over the Map: Rethinking American Regions* (Baltimore, 1996), 11–37; Cathy D. Matson and Peter S. Onuf, *A Union of Interests: Political and Economic Thought in Revolutionary America* (Lawrence, Kans., 1990).

6. James Ewing, *The Columbian Alphabet: Being an Attempt to New Model the English Alphabet . . .* (Trenton, N.J., 1798); Abner Kneeland, *A Brief Sketch of a New System of*

More moderate linguists such as John Witherspoon, the teacher of James Madison, deplored the lack of federal English. He encouraged the incorporation of "Americanisms," advising his students to compile new dictionaries. The most prominent compiler and reformer of the English language was Noah Webster, who initially began his reform efforts by concentrating on the received standards of English pronunciation. Using the linguistic theory that written words follow the ear, he demanded that common schools adopt a new orthography in which alphabetic letters functioned like modern phonetic signs. To illustrate his argument, for example, he wrote, "There iz no alternativ."[7]

In Webster's 1783 primer, *A Grammatical Institute of the English Language,* his first successful publication in a series of spelling books, the alphabet lesson combined the pedagogic elements of reading and elocution manuals. Its directions maintained that "a child be taught, first the Roman letters, both small and great—then the Italics—then the sounds of the vowels." The various spelling exercises depended on a pronouncing-form method, which meant that students learned to cipher and spell the written word through the imitation of the stresses, breaks, and pauses that marked the word's spoken performance. Moreover, because these lessons in pronunciation required students to stand up as a group, the early national spelling exercises resembled a choral performance. Each of Webster's spelling lessons entailed a graduated theatrical element: students recited numerous tables that progressed from syllabic fragments

---

Orthography (Walpole, N.H., 1807); Thomas Embree, *Orthography Corrected: or, A Plan for Improving the English Language* . . . (Philadelphia, 1813), vii; William Thornton, *Cadmus; or, A Treatise of the Elements of Written Language* . . . (Philadelphia, 1793), [iii–vii].

For extensive discussions of the linguistic reform efforts, see Dennis E. Baron, *Grammar and Good Taste: Reforming the American Language* (New Haven, Conn., 1982); David Simpson, *The Politics of American English, 1776–1850* (New York, 1986), esp. 19–28; Michael P. Kramer, *Imagining Language in America: From the Revolution to the Civil War* (Princeton, N.J., 1992), 35–63; Jill Lepore, *A Is for American: Letters and Other Characters in the Newly United States* (New York, 2002), 15–60.

7. John Witherspoon coined the term "Americanism" in "The Druid" (1781), in M. M. Mathews, ed., *The Beginnings of American English: Essays and Comments* (Chicago, 1963), 17; Noah Webster, *A Collection of Essays and Fugitiv Writings* . . . (Boston, 1790), xi. Webster's phonetic orthography was anticipated and influenced by Benjamin Franklin, whose pamphlet *A Scheme for a New Alphabet and Reformed Mode of Spelling* (1768) already bent the rules of English to reflect an American variant of English speech. See also Thomas Gustafson, *Representative Words: Politics, Literature, and the American Language, 1776–1865* (Cambridge, 1992), 39–40; Lepore, *A Is for American,* 31–37.

(table 1: "ba, be, bi, bo . . ."), to monosyllabic words, to the polysyllabic (table 2: "bag, big, bog . . ."; table 6: "ab so lute, ab sti nence . . ."), until they finally rehearsed short didactic narratives (table 42: "The Story of Tommy and Harry").[8]

In order to give the American language its own "sound" (and make it at the same time the basis of a new language), Webster focused on the oral component of the elementary spelling lessons and marshaled most of his pedagogic efforts toward introducing a national "standard of pronunciation." "Such a standard," Webster claimed, "universally used in schools, would in time, demolish those odious distinctions of provincial dialects, which are the objects of reciprocal ridicule in the United States." Webster, a staunch Federalist and ardent proponent of the union, hoped to mitigate political tensions by erasing local linguistic differences. Indeed, the expressed hope of the *Grammatical Institute* was that standardized pronunciation, not so much alphabetic orthography, would mediate among a regionally and socially differentiated people. If Americans would only adopt his reformed speller, Webster believed, "all persons, of every rank, would speak with some degree of precision and uniformity. Such a uniformity in these states is very desirable; it would remove prejudice, and conciliate mutual affection and respect."[9]

8. Noah Webster, *A Grammatical Institute of the English Language,* part 1 (Hartford, Conn., [1783]), 28, 29, 36, 113. Webster explains: "The syllables of words are divided as they are pronounced; and for this obvious reason, that children learn the language by the ear, rules are of no consequence but to Printers and adults. In Spelling Books they embarrass children, and double the labour of the teacher. The whole design of dividing words into syllables at all, is to lead the pupil to the true pronunciation; and the *easiest* method to effect this purpose will forever be the best." See *The American Spelling Book: Containing, An Easy Standard of Pronunciation, Being the First Part of a Grammatical Institute of the English Language* (Boston, 1794), ix (expanded and restructured from 1783 *Grammatical Institute*).

For the reconstruction of post-Revolutionary reading lessons, see William J. Gilmore, *Reading Becomes a Necessity of Life: Material and Cultural Life in Rural New England, 1780–1835* (Knoxville, Tenn., 1989), 34–42; David D. Hall, "The Uses of Literacy in New England, 1600–1850," in William L. Joyce et al., eds., *Printing and Society in Early America* (Worcester, Mass., 1983), 12–27; E. Jennifer Monaghan, "Literacy Instruction and Gender in Colonial New England," in Cathy N. Davidson, ed., *Reading in America: Literature and Social History* (Baltimore, 1989), 53–80; Monaghan, *A Common Heritage: Noah Webster's Blue-Back Speller* (Hamden, Conn., 1983). On Webster's influence in general, see Harry R. Warfel, *Noah Webster: Schoolmaster to America* (New York, 1936); Henry Steele Commager, "Schoolmaster to America," in *Noah Webster's American Spelling Book* (New York, 1962).

9. Noah Webster, *Grammatical Institute,* 6; Webster, *Dissertations on the English Language . . .* (Boston, 1789), 396–397. See also Kenneth Cmiel, *Democratic Eloquence: The*

By concentrating on pronunciation rather than orthography, Webster sidestepped the fact that he was still using the English language to create the proposed American variant. He acknowledged that English was a fickle instrument for creating a national community. He predicted that, even if there were an American English language, the new citizen "will claim a right to pronounce most agreably to his own fancy, and the language will be exposed to perpetual fluctuation." Webster's reform plan seemed already defeated, for he must negotiate the inherent flexibility underlying all languages, the fact that linguistic forms do not always follow rules but evolve constantly and are shaped by individual oral applications, local habits, and social settings.[10]

Webster resolved this dilemma by turning to the discourse of geography, in particular the spelling of place-names. He assured his readers that a geographical lexicon could overcome local differences. Commenting in the *Grammatical Institute,* Webster writes that "the advantage of publishing, in a work of this kind, the names of the United States, the counties in each, etc. will not be disputed by any American." Thus, while the opacity surrounding the English language was fueling the regionally motivated debates over the proper wording of the Republic's basic document, Webster imagined that the "undisputed" pronunciation of geographical words could provide a sense of clarity and a practical code when imagining a unified community.[11]

The assertion that the consensual pronunciation of geographic place-names was the nation's neutral linguistic ground provided Webster with a formula through which he simultaneously decolonized and nationalized his speller. Webster's self-assigned challenge was to displace the British schoolbook *A New Guide to the English Language,* by Thomas Dilworth, a speller that had dominated the classrooms and homes of British Ameri-

---

Fight over Popular Speech in Nineteenth-Century America (New York, 1990), 53. Cmiel suggests that Webster's linguistic theory was driven by the search for an egalitarian, analogous language in order to defuse social and regional tensions, an observation that corresponds with my reading of Webster's use of geography.

10. Webster, *Grammatical Institute,* 5.

11. Ibid., 11. Webster's use of American toponyms has been commented on but with altogether different conclusions by Simpson, *Politics of American English,* 56–80; Kramer, *Imagining Language,* 38–49. Joseph J. Ellis comes closest to my analysis when he perceptively describes the use of place-names as "a secular catechism to the nation state" but leaves it at that. *After the Revolution: Profiles of Early American Culture* (New York, 1979), 175.

cans since the 1740s. On first sight, Webster's book hardly differed from his imperial predecessor. Both were written in the English language; both endorsed the alphabetic pronouncing-form method. But by focusing on Dilworth's textbook, Webster chose to compete against one of the more popular spellers that promoted geographical literacy. Dilworth's speller emphasized place-names as the literary context through which his British reading subjects would facilitate communication in the British common-wealth as well as uphold its imperial economy on a global scale; or, as Dil-worth put it, it is only "by this means a Briton holds correspondence with his friend in America or Japan, and manages all his business." Webster targets this section, offering, instead of "twelve or fifteen pages devoted to names of English, Scotch and Irish towns and boroughs," eight pages of "the names of the United States, the counties in each, etc." Whereas Dilworth had been rehearsing primarily the place-names found in En-gland, Webster now offered those of the new American nation-state.[12]

Indeed, in transforming his speller into an agent of national unifica-tion, Webster incorporated a spelling exercise that anticipated the found-ers' signing ritual. As if projecting the visual form of the United States map of 1783, he introduced the students to the proper spelling of Ameri-can toponyms by including district and city names of all thirteen states. In print the alphabetic assembly of the national map looked like this:

The United States of America

States	Capital Towns
New Hamp-shire	Ports mouth
Mas sa chu setts	Bos ton
Rhode-Island	New port
Con nect i cut	Hart ford
New-York	New-York
New-Jersey	Tren ton
Pen syl va ni a	Phil a del phi a
Del a ware	New-Cas tle
Ma ry land	Bal ti more
Vir gin i a	Rich mond
North-Car o li na	New bern
South-Car o li na	Charles ton
Ge or gi a	Sa van nah

12. Thomas Dilworth, *A New Guide to the English Tongue* (Boston, 1783), x; Webster, *Grammatical Institute,* 10–11. Geographic place-names are generally absent in spelling

The effect of this spelling table was to establish the geographical order of the national map as an alternative to the alphabetical order of English. Names of states and cities were organized according to their geographical coordinates from north to south rather than from *A* to *Z*.[13]

Given the table's role in securing a "standard of pronunciation," it meshed the textual structure of the national map with the practice of oral alphabet lessons. The pronunciation of American place-names imitated the typographic hyperextension of place-names on maps. Just as the written word "Massachusetts" implied a larger territorial unit by being stretched across the face of a map, so too did the pronunciation of "Mas-sa-chu'-setts" imitate the territorial form of the geographic referent. Being sounded aloud, the place-name now signaled spatial demands, invoking territorial rights and borderlines for both readers and listeners. Moreover, as the chorus of students rehearsed its lines of geographic location, its tonal scale subordinated regional differences to the largest common territorial denominator. In Webster's lineup, pupils voiced the words "The United States of America" before those of the states. For the duration of these pronunciation exercises, as place-names wafted through American classrooms or parlors, students learning to spell also learned how to noisily claim the national map as the soundscape encompassing a common linguistic identity.

Having folded the pronunciation of the national map into his alphabetic spelling book, Webster uses geographical literacy as the touchstone of his language reform. Initially, his *Grammatical Institute* warned the reader that the American community was not so much threatened by the flexibility of the English language per se, but that the English variants and dialects were infinitely more debilitating to the project of unifying the national reader through one linguistic standard. Yet, toward the end of his introduction to the *Grammatical Institute* Webster concludes that spellers and grammars were not in need of improvement, but that language reformers needed better geographical primers. "The accounts from several states, are yet imperfect," he writes, "but care will be taken to collect, by the best means of information, such accurate accounts from

---

books found on early American bookshelves; for example, [Ralph] Harrison, *Institutes of English Grammar* (London, 1777); John Fell, *An Essay towards an English Grammar . . .* (London, 1784); or Thomas Sheridan, *Elements of English: Being a New Method of Teaching the Whole Art of Reading, Both with Regard to Pronunciation and Spelling* (London, 1786).

13. Webster, *Grammatical Institute*, 92.

the several states, as to correct any errours and supply any defects, that the present imperfect and fluctuating state of geography in this country may unavoidably occasion."[14]

Describing the state of geographic literacy becomes Webster's way of describing the state of literacy instruction in America. During the first three decades of nationhood, as his spelling books rapidly replaced those of a colonial make, lessons in geographic literacy seeped into spelling exercises. For example, new editions of former colonial classics such as George Fisher's handbook *The Instructor; or, Young Man's Best Companion* (1794) appended their chapters on language instruction with a rehearsal of American place-names. For Enos Weed, the alphabetization of the map became the principal method of spelling instructions; his *American Orthographer,* part 2, *The Geographical Spelling-Book* (1798) had students practice their alphabetic skills in tables containing lists of place-names that, broken down into their syllabic components, imitated the stress and pauses of speech and also used the hyperextended printing of letters to demarcate geopolitical and cultural spaces on the map. With the emergence of schoolbooks like these, Webster's mapping gambit had succeeded beyond merely instituting place-names as a methodology of language instruction. As a result of his spellers and reading books, an entire generation of American citizens studied the English language through the geographer's lexicon and the cartographer's mode of projection.[15]

PRIMERS AND JEDIDIAH MORSE'S EXPERIMENTAL WORD MAPS

As much as the initial reading lessons of the early Republic revolved around Webster's oral approach, language instructions also depended on the visual pedagogy of the picture primer. In order to achieve an unmediated, transparent relationship between words and the material world, or between signifiers and their signifieds, proponents of English language reforms embraced and emphasized pictorial instruction schemes. In fact, after the Revolution the programmatic dissemination of dozens of newly conceived illustrated primers became the disciplinary site through which

14. Ibid., 10.

15. George Fisher, *The Instructor; or, American Young Man's Best Companion* . . . (Walpole, N.H., 1794), 259–282. See also Donald Fraser, *The Young Gentleman and Lady's Assistant* . . . (New York, 1791), 30–38.

the new citizens sought to train students into models of republican virtue and self-discipline. For such reformed primers, it was not only questionable orthography or slippery grammatical systems that rendered language inherently volatile and therefore open to factious appropriation, but the very nature of written language itself. Pictures, instead of serving as supplements to written text, became a second language. Authors repeatedly engaged a visual code to reimagine language and hoped to forge the new nation through this new language.[16]

By taking the pictorial turn, American educators worked in the tradition of revolutionary linguistic movements dating back to the mid-seventeenth century. Following the Thirty Years' War and the English Revolution, European linguists and political theorists blamed much of the social violence on miscommunications resulting from the variety and ambiguity of national languages. After decades of political instability and the related loss of meaningful forms of signification, Europeans searched for an ideally prelapsarian or Adamic universal language. As the idea of a universal language became the common goal of linguistic reform, pictures in particular were tapped for their ability to transmit meaning concretely, unambiguously, and free from verbal interferences.[17]

In the context of the post-Revolutionary United States it was thus not a surprise that American educators rediscovered the seventeenth-century philosopher Johann Amos Comenius, who created pedagogic schemes that first anchored the political order in the pictorial and only then turned to the written word. In his primer *Orbis Sensualium Pictus: Visible World; or, A Picture and Nomenclature of All the Chief Things That Are in the World* (originally published in 1659 and reissued in the United States as late as 1810), difficult abstract subjects, such as "Philosophy" and "Humanity" as well as geopolitical constructs like "Kingdom" and "Region," were represented through illustrations of material objects. "The Kingdom and the Region," for example, was established in a concrete and stable form through a woodcut with a neatly modeled landscape depicting the various elements of the early modern state (Figure 27). Through the picture, the student learned to read and comprehend the social order. The corresponding text is in the service of this image:

16. Patricia Crain, *The Story of A: The Alphabetization of America from "The New England Primer" to "The Scarlet Letter"* (Stanford, Calif., 2000), 55–95.

17. On universal language schemes, see Murray Cohen, *Sensible Words: Linguistic Practice in England, 1640–1785* (Baltimore, 1977); James Knowlson, *Universal Language Schemes in England and France, 1600–1800* (Toronto, 1975).

The Kingdom and
the Region.

Regnum & Regio.

Many Cities *and* Villages	Multæ *Urbes* & *Pagi*
make a Region	faciunt *Regionem*
and a Kingdom.	& *Regnum.*
The King *or* Prince	*Rex* aut *Princeps*
refideth in the chief City, 1.	fedet in *Metropoli*, 1.
the Noblemen, Lords,	*Nobiles, Barones,*
and Earls *dwell*	& *Comites* habitant
in the Caftles, 2.	in *Arcibus*, 2.
that lie round about it ;	circumjacentibus ;
the Country People	*Ruftici*
dwell in Villages, 3.	in *Pagis*, 3.

H₃

Figure 27. "The Kingdom and the Region." From Orbis Sensualium Pictus: Visible
World . . . , *by Johann Amos Comenius. 1777.* Courtesy, University of Delaware Library

Many Cities and Villages make a Region and a Kingdom. The King, or Prince, resideth in the chief-City; 1. the Noblemen, Lords, and Earls, dwell in the Castles 2. that lye round about it, the Countrey-people dwell in Villages. 3. He hath his toll-places upon navigable Rivers 4. and High-Roads, 5. where Portage and Tollage is exacted of them that Sayl, or Travell.

The picture thus functions not only as a mnemonic device for learning a basic political vocabulary but also like a map, illustrating the spatial organization of the state. The messy realities of human existence and complexities of political order vanish in the tidy graphic simplicity of the landscape overview.[18]

In American hands, picture primers assumed a dual function. First, just as in their European context, primers carried forth a latent ideology of universal language schemes. Second, and more particular to the post-Revolutionary order, pictorial primers worked to negotiate the representational tensions spurred by the Federalist debate; the picture, more powerfully than the word, was able to reconcile the political concepts of "union" and "states." But, while the pictorial primers like Comenius's were adopted because of their availability and status of promoting a universal language, these primers' European heritage entailed historic and practical limitations. Although picture primers paved the way for the entrance of the visual into America's language handbooks, the primer's traditional representation of words and images relating geopolitical spaces like the "kingdom" was no longer applicable. The invention of a new type of nation-state with a precarious and experimental relationship of the parts to the whole could not, many feared, be given proper expression through the pictorially mediated letters of the English language. Moreover, federalist educators feared that the sustainability of this new political form depended not so much on written decrees and charters and international treaties as it did on citizens' absorbing and comprehending the social relationships of this political hybrid.

Maps, themselves a hybrid form of word and image, provided primers with this language. Map images were not new to picture primers; after all, Comenius's *Visible World* contained maps showing the world as a

---

18. Johann Amos Comenius, *Orbis Sensualium Pictus: Visible World; or, A Picture and Nomenclature of All the Chief Things That Are in the World* (1659; rpt. Menston, Eng., 1970), 278–279. On American imports and editions of Comenius's and other picture primers, see Crain, *The Story of A*, 26–27, 55–95, 230–231.

Figure 28. "A Globe." From
The Child's Museum. *1804.*
Courtesy, American
Antiquarian Society

"Terrestrial Sphere . . . divided into 5 Zones" and Europe, containing "the chief Kingdoms." Eighteenth-century American primers and ABC books, following in Comenius's footsteps, incorporated the textual materials of the geographer into the display of alphabetized objects. For instance, primers such as *The Child's Museum, Containing a Description of One Hundred and Eight Interesting Subjects,* following the schoolbook definition that "a Map is a picture of the earth," included the picture of a globe (and the written subtitle, "A Globe") in the array of alphabetized objects (Figure 28). The seemingly arbitrary inclusion of the globe into the primer is a first comment on the materiality and availability of cartographic texts in the early American linguistic stock.[19]

More than simply illustrating the alphabet, the figure of the map worked conceptually to teach abstract principles of literacy. This is suggested by the primer *The Mother's Gift; or, Remarks on a Set of Cuts for Children* (Figure 29). This primer presents the student reader with a picture of a map, a subtitle spelling out the words, "A Map," and a narrative description: "MAP. As you get forward in the study of geography you will find great entertainment in maps. How pleasant is it to trace the progress

19. Comenius, *Orbis Sensualium Pictus,* 218–221; "A Globe," in *The Child's Museum, Containing a Description of One Hundred and Eight Interesting Subjects* (Philadelphia, 1804), table III, fig. 13; David N. Livingstone, *The Geographical Tradition: Episodes in the History of a Contested Enterprise* (Oxford, 1992), 98–100.

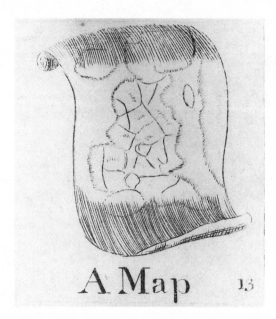

Figure 29. "A Map." From The Mother's Gift. 1809. Courtesy, American Antiquarian Society

A Map 13

of a traveller of whom we read; and still more interesting where a friend is on a voyage or journey." Here, map literacy is taught as a reading skill and a life skill: maps are understood to inform the student's future geography lessons; they are considered textual companions of the leisured reader who consumes travel narratives and novels; maps provide the material link through which friends and families communicate with each other. As the titles of primers like *The Mother's Gift* suggest, alphabetic literacy was the product of a domestic ideology in which the child was the focus of alphabetic instructions provided by the ideal republican mother; in this context the map was introduced to the child reader by the most intimate member and designated disciplinarian of the early national household.[20]

But the alphabetic lesson surrounding the map was not only the pedagogic means of embedding the student inside a social network. The picture primer's rationale also created a visual narrative in which individual bodies were circumscribed by cartographic signs. In *The Uncle's Present: A New Battledoor* (1809) the letter *Z* is depicted by a street peddler who is carrying different sized maps while calling "Zealand, or England, and a

20. "A Map," in *The Mother's Gift; or, Remarks on a Set of Cuts for Children* (Philadelphia, 1809), 14. The map is thus another proscriptive tool in the process of identity formation that Richard H. Brodhead calls "disciplinary intimacy." See *Cultures of Letters: Scenes of Reading and Writing in Nineteenth-Century America* (Chicago, 1993), 13–47; for a discussion of this model in relation to alphabetic instruction see Crain, *The Story of A,* 103–142.

Figure 30. "Z [for] Zealand, or England, and a Map of the World." From The Uncle's Present. 1814. Courtesy, American Antiquarian Society

Map of the World" (Figure 30). While in this picture alphabet the map appears in the form of a consumer article, the map also ties the market economy to the anthropomorphized ABCs. As the human figure associates maps with the alphabetic sign, it establishes a somatic link between the reader's body, the alphabetic reading material, and cartographic writings. Like the human alphabet, which instituted the notion that the body was subject to the authority and discipline of the written sign, in this example the alphabetized individual becomes intrinsically part of a largely commercial cartographic archive and expanded notion of geographic literacy.[21]

While American primers were establishing a deep structural nexus between alphabetic and map literacy, one of the more influential geography books consciously developed this nexus into a national form of print language. In the best-selling textbook *Geography Made Easy* (1784), the Federalist minister and geographer Jedidiah Morse tested the relationship between alphabetic and cartographic literacy. He pursued the question of how maps could aid the literary process of making the idea of

---

21. "Z," in *The Uncle's Present: A New Battledoor* (Philadelphia, 1810), appendix; also in the primer *The Cries of London* (Hartford, Conn., 1807).

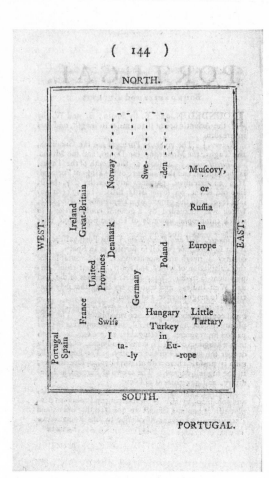

(144)

NORTH.

WEST.

EAST.

Norway

Swe- -den

Muſcovy,
or
Ruſſia
in
Europe

Ireland
Great-Britain

Denmark

Poland

France
United
Provinces

Germany

Portugal
Spain

Swiſs
I
ta-
-ly

Hungary
Turkey
in
Eu-
-rope

Little
Tartary

SOUTH.

PORTUGAL.

Figure 31. Word Map. From Geography Made Easy, *by Jedidiah Morse. 1784.* By Permission of the Houghton Library, Harvard University

nation a permanent inscription in the minds of American students. "Calculated particularly for the Use and Improvement of SCHOOLS in the United States," the textbook was the first in a series of books whose intended goal was explicit: "That our youth of both sexes, at the same time that they are learning to read, might imbibe an acquaintance with their own country, and an attachment to its interests." To demonstrate a possible means for attaching youngsters to a national imaginary, Morse inserted two kinds of maps in his first edition of *Geography Made Easy,* experimental word maps and a conventional national map.[22]

22. Jedidiah Morse, *Geography Made Easy* . . . (New Haven, Conn., 1784), iv; and *Geography Made Easy* . . . , 3d ed. (Boston, 1791), vi. For a detailed account of Morse's publishing activities and his selection of maps and mapmakers, see Ralph H. Brown, "The American Geographies of Jedidiah Morse," *Annals of the Association of American Geographers,* XXXI

The word maps, advertised as "newly constructed Maps, adapted to the Capacities and Understanding of Children," demonstrate how Federalists like Morse imagined the geographic process of national unification as purely alphabetic (Figure 31). Each of these four maps, representing South America, Europe, Africa, and Asia, consists of a blank rectangular frame. Into this spatially delimited tabula rasa Morse spells out the names of existing nation-states, arranging the printed letters to indicate their geographic dimensions and relations. Having thus jettisoned the usual elements of map reading necessary for one's orientation and self-location—the geographic grid, local place names, and pictographic symbols—Morse represents each continent as the verbal approximation of political rather than geographical locales. In each continental map, the elaborately printed names of nations appear as synecdochic figures of actual places. Conversely, the geographical order of the world is upheld by the alphabetic construction of nations. More specifically, the word map subordinates the implied cartographic image to the machine-made appearance of the printed text, and the representation of continents and geopolitical entities to the conventions of print typography. With these word maps, Morse's geography imitated a spatial order derived from print technology, an order according to which "typographic control typically impresses more by its tidiness and inevitability: the lines perfectly regular, justified on the right side, everything coming out even visually."[23]

Yet—and this is the dilemma that Morse's experimental maps demonstrate—for the nation to become the perfectly regular alphabetic environment, the word maps had to reconcile a strain that lies at the heart of all cartographic representation: their formal arrangement had to negotiate the reader's imaginary freedom of movement offered by the hybrid textuality of the map. By reading the map as a quasi-blank and verbally

---

(1941), 145–217. For material on Morse's use of maps, see also John Rennie Short, *Representing the Republic: Mapping the United States, 1600–1900* (London, 2001), chap. 6; Richard J. Moss, *The Life of Jedidiah Morse* (Knoxville, Tenn., 1995), 38–51.

23. Morse, *Georgraphy Made Easy*, iv; Walter J. Ong, *Orality and Literacy: The Technologizing of the Word* (New York, 1982), 122. As with most geography books that were published from the seventeenth through the nineteenth centuries, collaboration and plagiarism went often hand in hand. Morse modeled his word maps and most of *Geography Made Easy* on a relatively unknown textbook by R[ichard] Turner, *A New and Easy Introduction to Universal Geography* (London, 1780). I am grateful to Barbara McCorkle for this reference.

elastic text, the apprentice map reader was able to create a space of his or her own. Just as the alphabet enabled politicians to organize the world into political spaces, the unorthodox arrangement of Morse's letters undercut the fantasy of territorial control. The word maps established national alignment as a ludic activity; just as the printer's apprentice shuffled the typeface inside the letterbox, Morse's students learned how to playfully scramble the verbal markers of political territories. Through a random shuffle, nations vanish or become reconstituted as a different word.

In order to better control the reader's alphabetic literacy, Morse exploited the pedagogic (and political) authority by which the mapmaker shaped the signification and interpretation of political geography. It is telling that at the historical moment of 1784, when language threatened to upend the new nation, the alphabet and alphabetic maps seemed to be insufficient tools for stabilizing the new American nation. Instead of adding a fifth word map that spelled out the constitutive names of the United States, Morse turns to the conventional map and the iconic outline of the new federal state as the dominant lesson signifying the union. Upon opening the textbook, the student readers were greeted with the first picture of the nation, *A Map of the United States of America* (1784) (Figure 32). This map by Amos Doolittle was one of the first national maps published in the United States immediately following the Peace of Paris. The map is thus designed to show exclusively the territory of the nation-state, tracing its international borders from the Atlantic Ocean in the east to the Mississippi River in the west, and from British Canada to the north and Spanish Florida to the south.[24]

To the lower right of the map, a cartouche introduces through its visual

24. Domestic productions included Abel Buell's large-sheet map, titled *New and Correct Map of the United States* . . . (1784) and William McMurray's wall map, *The United States according to the Definitive Peace Treaty Signed at Paris* . . . (1784). Following the publishing success of Morse's school geography, Doolittle's map reached thousands of students for several generations. On the history of specifically "national maps," see Walter W. Ristow, *American Maps and Map-Makers: Commercial Cartography in the Nineteenth Century* (Detroit, Mich., 1985); Seymour I. Schwartz and Ralph E. Ehrenberg, *The Mapping of America* (New York, 1980). On the economics of mapmaking in the early Republic, see David Bosse, " 'To Promote Useful Knowledge': *An Accurate Map of the Four New England States* by John Norman and John Coles," *Imago Mundi,* LII (2000), 138–154; Bosse, "The Boston Map Trade of the Eighteenth Century," in Alex Krieger and David Cobb, eds., *Mapping Boston* (Cambridge, Mass., 1999), 36–55; also see Susan L. Danforth, "The First Official Maps of Maine and Massachusetts," *Imago Mundi,* XXXV (1983), 37–57.

Figure 32. A Map of the United States of America. *By Amos Doolittle. 1784.*
By Permission of the Houghton Library, Harvard University

narrative the relationship between map and alphabetic literacy. Hovering in a swirl of billowing clouds, the female figure of Liberty (or perhaps Columbia), together with the American eagle, lifts a banner inscribed "Per Aspera ad Astra" in order to unveil the new nation's name (in bold print) while the land is strategically placed underneath (in a rough sketch). When considered in juxtaposition to the map image, the cartouche suggests that as long as they are viewed separately the two discursive modes of either word or image foster imaginings that are easily clouded and distorted. If used jointly, however—as the dual gesture of unveiling the geographic name of the nation and by analogy of the map image itself indicates—the cartouche celebrates the mixed language of geography as the ideal literary means for representing the nation in clear and unambiguous terms.

The map bears out the cartouche's invitation to conceive map reading as a hybrid product of print literacy. Inside the map image, cartographic symbols compete with the letters of the alphabet for the reader's attention. While pictographic dots, lines, and mountain symbols describe the nation's topography, an array of alphabetic names identify places from the locally specific ("Philadelphia") to the larger geopolitical unit ("Pennsylvania"). These toponyms are typographically differentiated according to political significance: the names of states appear in large capitals, the names of cities in roman characters, and those of villages in a running hand. The map, however, contains the typographic tension between regional and local places through the structural evenness of the geographic grid and borderlines. While the written names of concrete places and abstract political territories are located within the grid, the map orients its east-west, north-south base lines along the "Meridian of Philadelphia." As cartographic and alphabetic signs become thus aligned with the nation's capital, the map's diversified symbolic code becomes a grammatical construct: it expresses American independence from England (and the meridian of Greenwich) by providing a new baseline for imagining the nation's geographic framework.[25]

At the same time, it was the map's small-scale projection (it shows a relatively large area without attention to local detail) that invited readers to view the nation as a picture rather than a product of writing systems. Thick washes of watercolor marked the territorial outline of the nation's constitutive states, creating schematic images of the various states similar to today's didactic map puzzles in which color and shape rather than geographic content and location guide the student's memory. Some copies of the book map even included a thick trace of color marking the nation's external border line, thus presenting the image of the nation-

25. The typographic differentiation of place-names in writing and print goes back to Gerard Mercator. On the history and application of graded fonts, see Eileen Reeves, "Reading Maps," *Word and Image*, IX (1993), 52; James R. Akerman, "The Structuring of Political Territory in Early Printed Atlases," *Imago Mundi*, XLVII (1995), 144. On the role of the "zero" meridian on a later date, see Matthew Edney, "Cartographic Culture and Nationalism in the Early United States: Benjamin Vaughan and the Choice for a Prime Meridian, 1811," *Journal of Historical Geography*, XX (1994), 384–395.

state in the form of an iconographic symbol or hieroglyph, similar to modern cookie-cutter shapes or commercial logos.[26]

It was precisely the cartographic design of the nation's official borderline by which Morse imagined he could inscribe the student's visual memory and verbal literacy with the idea of the nation. Contemporaneous formulations of national ideologies, especially those by the German Johann Gottlieb Fichte, looked to the borderline rhetoric of the national map in order to unite a fragmented society under the rubric of a collective imaginary. Writing at a time when Germany (even under Napoleonic rule) looked like a puzzle on the political map, Fichte argued in his *Reden an die deutsche Nation* (1808) that for a people to become a nation the "external frontiers" of the state (however loosely defined, as body politic, civic union, or bureaucratic institution) must become the "internal frontiers" of the citizen. According to this formulation, the nation-state always began and ended with the cartographic line demarcating political boundaries. Through a self-fulfilling logic of dialectic reasoning, these boundary lines—once they were established—were deemed to be natural boundaries dividing traditionally established political territories. With the stroke of a mapmaker's pen, the line became a cognitive and disciplinary tool transposing local into national identities.[27]

Like the Federalist language reformer Noah Webster, Morse sought to achieve a degree of national identity by aligning the overall practices of alphabetic training with geographical knowledge. Given the programmatic rethinking of elementary literacy instruction, the map became a product of alphabetic learning. Indeed, as the basic principles of literacy (the alphabet, representational sign systems, phonetics) became imbricated with basic principles of geography (notions of place, systems of measurement, taxonomic organization), the conventional words and verbal text were perceived through a geographic consciousness. By prefacing

26. For a quick example of an overdetermined tracing of the national outline, see the Readex copy of the 1784 edition of *Geography Made Easy,* Early American Imprints, 1st Ser., 18615.

27. See Etienne Balibar's discussion, "Fichte and the Internal Border: On *Addresses to the German Nation,*" in Balibar, *Masses, Classes, Ideas: Studies on Politics and Philosophy before and after Marx,* trans. James Swenson (New York, 1993), 61–84. The words of Fichte are echoed by Emile Benveniste, who, in tracing the etymology of the word "region," writes that through the act of "tracing out the limits by straight lines" the author delimits "the interior and the exterior, the realm of the sacred and the realm of the profane, the national territory and foreign territory." See *Indo-European Language and Society,* trans. Elizabeth Palmer (London, 1973), 311–312.

his textbook with a map of the new nation-state, Morse invariably coupled the map reader's desire for visual self-location to the textbook's otherwise verbal representation of political identities. Students following the reading protocol of the textbook map, then, learned not only to privilege the geographic dimension of the nation-state over representations of local places but also to superimpose the cartographic signs representing the union over the textbook's alphabetic notations describing the states. Thus, while Webster relied on the national map to Americanize the spelling and pronunciation of English words, Morse's map-reading lesson transformed the study of geography into a nationalistic spelling bee.[28]

MAPS, ATLASES, AND THE MATERIAL RHETORIC OF UNION

Federalists like Webster and Morse who used the rhetoric of the national map operated inside an established cartographic tradition in which maps had historically accompanied the creation of national ideologies. Ever since Abraham Ortelius and Gerard Mercator published their world maps and atlases in the sixteenth century, single-sheet maps had presented the sovereign states as visually and territorially unified constructs. During the eighteenth century, the wealthier European nation-states had sponsored or were about to initiate the production of national maps. Developing out of the discourses of property surveys and regional mapping projects, the national map served a dual function. First, in the map-making process, surveyors left visible markers on the land (such as boundary markers and border crossings). Second, the map image as a material artifact provided a visual proxy and reproducible evidence of the nation's territorial, optically organic, and demonstrably material existence.[29]

28. Morse's choice of map here reflects the way in which child psychologists describe the cultural construction of national identity. In their study "The Transition from Ego-centricity to Reciprocity," Jean Piaget and Anne Marie Weil seek to establish "the development in children of the idea of the Homeland and the Relations with other Countries." While they approach their test subjects from the positions of the cognitive (when does the notion of country become reality?) and the affective (when do evaluative attributes such as loyalty and patriotism emerge?), both authors presuppose the knowledge of geographic images like school maps. See Sarah F. Campbell, ed., *Piaget Sampler: An Introduction to Jean Piaget through His Own Words* (New York, 1976), 37–58.

29. On the mapping projects in eighteenth- and nineteenth-century absolutist European nation-states, see James C. Scott, *Seeing Like a State: How Certain Schemes to Improve the Human Condition Have Failed* (New Haven, Conn., 1998); Norman J. W. Thrower, *Maps and Civilization: Cartography in Culture and Society* (Chicago, 1996), 91–124; Josef W. Kon-

In the first decades of the United States' existence, the image of the national map was one of the few visual artifacts demonstrating what many perceived to be either an abstract or even untenable fiction, namely that there could be a national union between disjointed regions and politically disparate people. Unlike in Europe, where governments controlled the output of national maps, in the United States the national map quickly became the dual product of the federal government and the private economic sector. On the one hand, the federal government sponsored the production of national maps on two occasions. The passage of the Land Ordinance Acts of 1785 and 1787 anticipated a burst of mapmaking activities as it launched a national survey. The copyright law of 1790, which was advertised on the inside of every book printed in the United States as "an Act . . . securing the copies of Maps, Charts, and Books," protected maps by giving them the status of a preferred commodity.

On the other hand, the appearance of a state-regulated distribution of national maps would be misleading because the majority of maps and other geographical writings were produced by private individuals and small commercial publishers. The new citizens were most likely to encounter the image of the nation by reading inexpensive, small-scale maps, like the one inserted in Morse's school geography. The map image of the United States proliferated significantly when publishers like Mathew Carey of Philadelphia included national maps in various book genres and through multiple packaging reduced significantly the average price per map. According to Carey's sales catalog of 1795, single-sheet maps sold for as little as twelve and a half cents (by comparison, the folio edition of the *American Atlas,* containing twenty-one maps, was priced at five dollars—six if "coloured"). These numbers show that single-sheet maps rather than map collections were affordable texts and as such quickly absorbed into the nation's cultural landscape.[30]

---

vitz, *Cartography in France, 1660–1848: Science, Engineering, and Statecraft* (Chicago, 1987); Monique Pelletier, *Les cartes des Cassini: La science au service de l'état et des régions* (Paris, 2002). On the history of borders in relation to nation-states, see Anthony Giddens, *A Contemporary Critique of Historical Materialism,* II, *The Nation-State and Violence* (Berkeley, Calif., 1985), 4, 49–51; Akerman, "The Structuring of Political Territory," *Imago Mundi,* LXVII (1995), 139–144.

30. Walter W. Ristow explains: "Most non-official compilers of state maps were not professional surveyors or cartographers. For the most part, they earned their livelihood from other vocations, and the maps they produced were generally one-time efforts." See *American Maps,* 20.

On atlas prices, see Mathew Carey, *Catalogue of Books, Pamphlets, Maps, and Prints*

Figure 33. Mrs. Noah Smith and Her Children. *By Ralph Earl. 1798.* Permission of The Metropolitan Museum of Art, Gift of Edgar William and Bernice Chrysler Garbisch, 1964. (64.309.1)

Indeed, the national map permeated American material culture in many and unexpected places. For example, after the Revolution families like that of Mrs. Noah Smith not only displayed their material belongings (and thus good taste) when they posed for portraits but opted to have the

---

(Philadelphia, 1795). To give a later price comparison, *Mathew Carey's Exchange Catalogue* (Philadelphia, 1798) advertised Jefferson's *Notes on the State of Virginia* at $1.75 and a student's copy of the *Drawing Book for Human Figures* at $.25. The pricing of the national map was in large part the result of market forces. Carey had to negotiate negative reader responses when his traveling salesman, Parson Mason Locke Weems, reported complaints about the high cost of the school atlas (which in 1798 Carey offered at $9.00, or $16.00 if bought with Guthrie's school geography). This has led to the speculation that Carey's multiple repackaging of the same kind of maps into different atlas editions and books was a sign of a print investment gone awry and that, unable to sell his first print run, he kept hawking his maps in new venues. Here I would like to thank James Green of the Library Company of Philadelphia for his helpful comments. For a less skeptical interpretation, see John Brian Harley, "Atlas Maker for Independent America," *Geographical Magazine,* XLIX (1977), 766–771.

Figure 34. Dining Room of Dr. Whitridge's as It Was in the Winter of 1814–15: Breakfast Time (Pot-Apple-Pie). *By Joseph Shoemaker Russell. Circa 1850.* Courtesy of the New Bedford Whaling Museum. ©New Bedford Whaling Museum

map of the United States close to the portrait's center to better demonstrate their new Americanness (Figure 33). Considering the domestic habit of putting maps on display inside private settings, the national map in all likelihood decorated the walls of American homes (Figure 34). The nation's map image certainly became·a pedagogic piece of furniture in schools. It was a fundamental part of textbooks, globes, and wall decorations. Teachers and parents even experimented with the cognitive function of the national map by integrating it into didactic puzzles (Figure 35). Once we leave the domestic and institutional spaces of the home and the school, we discover that the nation's cartographic shape hung on rollers or under glass in public places. Wall maps were displayed in public offices and coffeehouses; as the genre painting *Barroom Dancing* by John Lewis Krimmel shows, the national map was displayed in taverns, where it functioned as decoration, conversation piece, and metaphoric touchstone of communal identity (Figure 36).[31]

31. On the presence of national maps in paintings, see Milo M. Naeve, *John Lewis Krimmel: An Artist in Federal America* (Newark, Del., 1987); Marshall B. Davidson, *Life in America,* I (Boston, 1974); Jane C. Nylander, *Our Own Snug Fireside: Images of the New England Home, 1760–1860* (New York, 1993); Elisabeth Donaghy Garrett, *At Home: The*

A spate of American-made atlases greatly popularized the image of the nation-state. Beginning with the publication of Mathew Carey's *American Atlas* (1795), four more national atlases almost simultaneously captured the public eye: Carey's *General Atlas* (1796), *Carey's American Pocket Atlas* (1796), Joseph T. Scott's *Atlas of the United States* (1796), and John Reid's *American Atlas* (1796). Each of these atlases privileged the national map. While the atlas as a printed form imitated the generic design of a book, the map showing the territory of the United States often functioned like a table of contents or prefatory chapter. Placed in this position, the national map more than introduced the states; in most cases it emphasized national unity over state autonomy.

The map of the "United States" by Samuel Lewis from Carey's *General Atlas* illustrates the way in which the image of the nation graphically subsumed images of the states. Lewis's national map was the twenty-fourth of forty-eight maps and served as the preface to the subsequent set of seventeen maps of the states and Maine (Figure 37). Located as the atlas's middle and turning point, this map separated international maps from those delineating the new nation-state. Designed for pedagogic uses (it was intended to supplement William Guthrie's schoolbook, *A New System of Modern Geography* [1794]), the Lewis map creates the nation as a self-contained entity. Lewis limits his workmanship to meticulously inscribing the graphic space of the United States; he leaves virtually uninscribed the surrounding spaces (thus making it difficult for the inexperienced map reader to tell land from water). With the name of the United States being visibly absent from the actual map image (it appears in the map margin inside an unembellished cartouche), Lewis downplays the alphabetic element used for hailing national identities in cartographic writing. Instead, he emphasizes the map's geographical aspect. Using the border line and topographic symbols, Lewis limns the nation in almost corporeal

---

American Family, 1750–1870 (New York, 1990). On probate records, see Abbott Lowell Cummings, "Inside the Massachusetts Home," in Dell Upton and John Michael Vlach, eds., *Common Places: Readings in American Vernacular Architecture* (Athens, Ga., 1986); Kym S. Rice, *Early American Taverns: For the Entertainment of Friends and Strangers* (Chicago, 1983).

Francis Hopkinson wrote in "An Improved Plan of Education" for the *Pennsylvania Magazine* about the usefulness of the map puzzle, suggesting the efficacy of "teaching geography by maps pasted on thin boards, and cut into pieces, according to the divisions of counties or kingdoms." See Hopkinson, *The Miscellaneous Essays and Occasional Writings* (Philadelphia, 1792), I, 13.

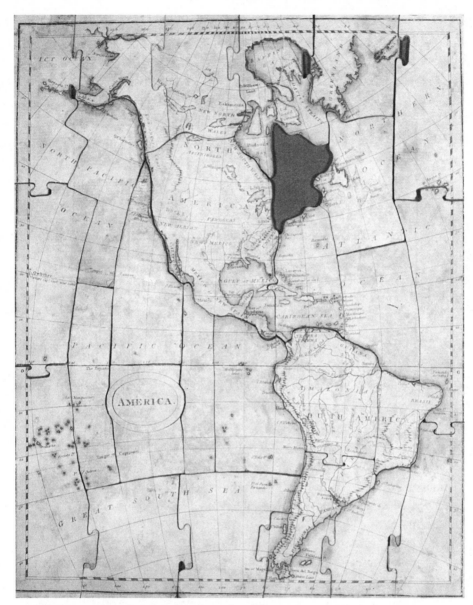

Figure 35. Map Puzzle, A New Map of America. *1809?*
Courtesy, American Antiquarian Society

Figure 36. Barroom Dancing. *By John Lewis Krimmel. Circa 1820.*
Courtesy, The Library of Congress

terms. Similar to images describing the human anatomy in contemporary magazines and handbooks, the thickly shaded lines tracing the coastal and national boundaries in the east, north, and south resemble the epidermal layer visually protecting the land against the encroachment of oceans and neighboring territories. At the same time, the double-lined course of the Mississippi River invokes not only the nation's western border but also the anatomical imagery of a skeleton's spine or a body's vascular system. The constitutive parts of the national body, the states, recede inside the image of the nation-state. Their thinly drafted boundary lines collapse inside the map's corporealized gestalt of the nation's territory.

When considering the political conflict between the Federalist ideology and sectionalist interest groups that raged during the first two decades of independent nationhood, the rhetorical effect of the atlases' national maps by and large supported the Federalist cause. Each atlas promoted a cartographic system of checks and balances. While the national map was often afforded additional space in the form of foldouts, none of the state maps published in the early atlases were allowed to dominate optically. Each state map was cut to a uniform size, projecting the idea of equal

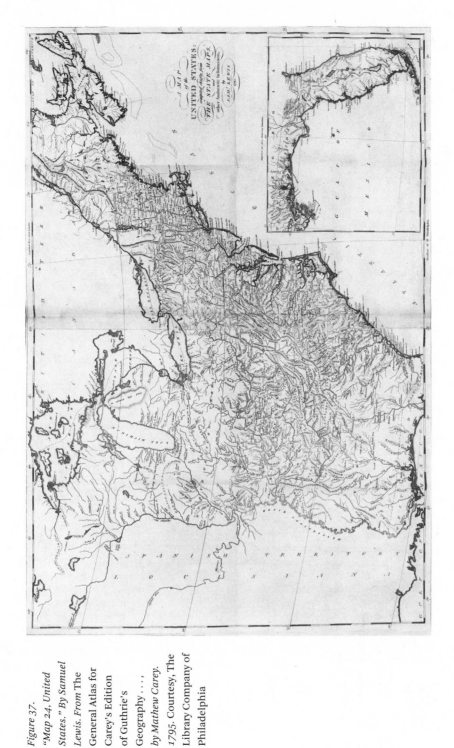

Figure 37.
"Map 24, United
States." By Samuel
Lewis. From The
General Atlas for
Carey's Edition
of Guthrie's
Geography . . . ,
by Mathew Carey.
1795. Courtesy, The
Library Company of
Philadelphia

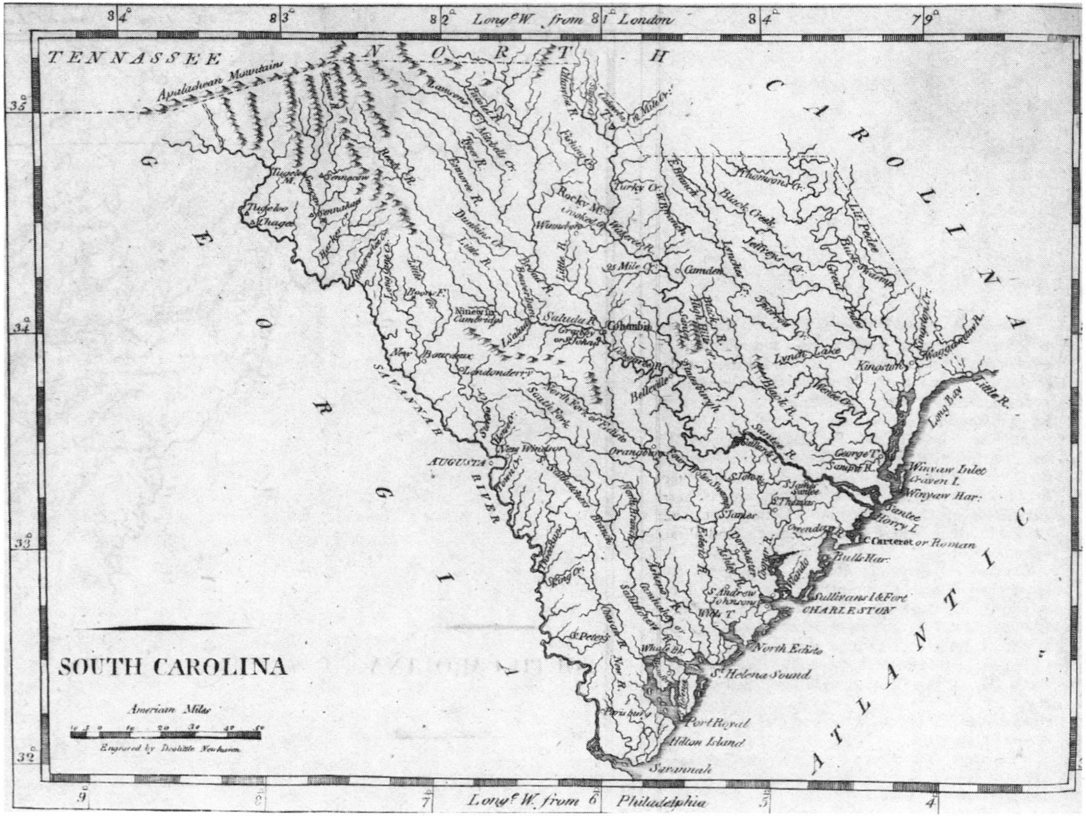

Figure 38.
*"South Carolina." By Samuel
Lewis. From Carey's American
Pocket Atlas. 1796.* Courtesy,
The Library Company of
Philadelphia

representation under one nation. When viewed in the context of the atlas maps' overt emphasis on boundary lines and visual unity, the national map functioned as the archival container and frame of reference for the smaller state maps. By virtue of its cartographic design the national map adumbrated the Federalist notion that there is "unity in diversity," a unity that is predicated on a national cartographic network that assumes authority over its local constitutive parts.[32]

What is significant, however, is that, at the same time as the first United States atlas maps seemed to provide a material palimpsest upon which readers could trace out nationalistic fantasies of interstate unity, it was precisely the unique material context of the atlas that deanatomized the nation's cartographic image. Early American atlas maps conceptualized the individual states not as dismembered parts of a larger corporate body but as miniature copies imitating the symbolic form of a larger nation-state. For example, in *Carey's American Pocket Atlas* the map of South Carolina (1796), also drawn by Samuel Lewis, appeared not only as a self-contained unit but was drawn to look like a geographically separate nation-state unrelated to either the United States or the North American continent (Figure 38). Its graphic presentation creates the geographical illusion that the state hinged between two oceans rather than between the states of North Carolina and Georgia. The impression that each state could be a separate nation was further enhanced by the use of map scale. States were depicted, not in relative proportion to their geographical size, but in maximal proportion to the textual space they were to fill on the

---

32. Early national mapmakers like Doolittle above and Lewis here anticipate the nineteenth-century theory proposed by the German geographer Carl Ritter, according to which regional geographies and particular topographies were simultaneously expressions of a divine creation and a national will. Arguing from this position, Ritter's book *Erdkunde* (1819) proposes that, as a kind of disinterested creation, geography rather than a people engenders specific historical events. Ritter applied this principle in a series of regional geographic studies. Each study bore out the nationalistic principle of a local a priori unity *(Zusammenhang)*, concluding that specific regions "naturally" match the territorial claims made by modern nation-states. In the end, Ritter argued for the total congruity of place and people as a predestined national locale by applying the holistic and inherently aesthetic concept of "unity in diversity." See Richard Hartshorne and Klaus D. Gurgel, "Zu Carl Ritters Einfluss auf die Entwicklung der Geographie in den Vereinigten Staaten von Amerika," in Manfred Büttner, ed., *Carl Ritter: Zur europäisch-amerikanischen Geographie an der Wende vom 18. zum 19. Jahrhundert* (Paderborn, Germany, 1980), 201–219; Preston E. James and Geoffrey J. Martin, *All Possible Worlds: History of Geographical Ideas,* 2d ed. (New York, 1981), 126–131.

page. The maps of Delaware and Rhode Island covered as much paper space as did the maps of Maine and Pennsylvania. Optically, then, the state maps repeated the same cartographic designs that initially had been reserved for the national map. Like the national map, the state map turned on a binary structure of territorial representation, privileging the state's visual outline over its verbal identification, its geographical over its political anatomy, its interior over its exterior relations.

United States atlas maps here seem to confirm the Federalist and Antifederalist fear that even those writing systems that ceased to subordinate the reading experience to an exclusively alphabetical order were still incapable of representing the idea of a new nation-state in immediate and unambiguous terms. While the image of the national map seemed to uphold the constitutional principle of checks and balances (maps represented states optically in equal terms), the state map appeared to undercut the Federalist ideal of national unity by projecting the thirteen (or more) states as separate nations and unrelated to the larger union. The pictorial rhetoric of the national map failed to offer a design that established a hierarchical relationship between the union and state. Unable to give precedence to either unit, the medium of the map potentially undercuts its symbolic power by signifying opposite values: even as its visual rhetoric could serve as a tool of national integration, it also could promote the union's disintegration.

The ambiguity surrounding the image of the national map grew out of the post-Revolutionary debates over the issue of statehood. Federalists, Antifederalists, and local patriots like Thomas Jefferson were equally invested in the rhetorical trope of the national map, but for very different reasons. If we turn to the constitutional debate first, the national map appeared in the two opposing literatures—John Jay's Federalist No. 2 and the *Agrippa Letters* by James Winthrop—that were influencing both public opinion and the text of the Constitution itself. Jay invoked the map as a metaphor in order to persuade his audience of the Republic's natural predisposition to unity. As if he were reading one of the schoolbook maps, Jay traces out the geographical body of the new nation-state:

> It has often given me pleasure to observe, that independent America was not composed of detached and distant territories, but that one connected, fertile, wide-spreading country was the portion of our western sons of liberty. Providence has in a particular manner blessed it with a variety of soils and productions, and watered it with innumer-

able streams, for the delight and accommodation of its inhabitants. A succession of navigable waters forms a kind of chain round its borders, as if to bind it together.

In Jay's word map, natural boundaries become indistinguishable from the artificially imposed political ones. In a move that anticipates Fichte's call for the "external frontiers" of the state to become the "internal frontiers" of the citizen, Jay transforms his cartographic vision of connectedness into a vision of cultural uniformity: "With equal pleasure I have as often taken notice, that Providence has been pleased to give this one connected country to one united people—a people descended from the same ancestors, speaking the same language, professing the same religion, attached to the same principles of government, very similar in their manners and customs." Implicit in his word map is the dialectical assumption that, by mapping the territory of the nation, the latter's inventory consisting of language, religion, and custom becomes inflected by the terms of the national map. Just as the word map upholds the imaginary fusion of "one connected country to one united people," Jay suggests that in order for Americans to imagine the United States they would have to interweave two different linguistic systems: if English was the language spoken by the "people," the word map emerged as the second language of "the country."[33]

The motive of Jay's deferral to geographical literacy is his desire to shorten the enormous distance separating many of the new Republic's constitutive parts. Jay's word map seeks to deflect the Antifederalist argument that, as a federal union that models itself upon the classical republic, the United States would be ungovernable because of its overextended size. Geographical dimension was the standard argument made by Antifederalists like James Winthrop, who invoked the image of the national map to dismantle the Federalist argument of unity. "The idea of an uncompounded republick, on an average, one thousand miles in length, and eight hundred in breadth, and containing six millions of white inhabitants all reduced to the same standard of morals, or habits,

---

33. John Jay, Federalist No. 2, in Brock, ed., *The Federalist,* 5–6. Jay's passage on "one united people" has been discussed differently by William Boelhower, "Nation-Building and Ethnogenesis: The Map as Witness and Maker," in Steve Ickringill, ed., *The Early Republic: The Making of a Nation—The Making of a Culture* (Amsterdam, 1988), 108–112. See also Ferguson, " 'We Hold These Truths,' " in Sacvan Bercovitch, ed., *Reconstructing American Literary History* (Cambridge, Mass., 1986), 5–6.

and of laws, is in itself an absurdity, and contrary to the whole experience of mankind." For Winthrop, the new nation's geography was politically debilitating, and the national map was the proof demonstrating the flaw in the Federalists' argument. It illustrated in certain terms how the geographical or, rather, natural dimensions of the United States would undermine the union's political structure and seriously impede the formation of a republican government. Because large distances separated the states from each other, it would prohibit political participation inside the union; looking at the national map revealed that distance would prevent the equal application of federal power, hindering the union's task to supervise the new citizens or to reconcile federal and state interests.[34]

But, while both Jay and Winthrop cited the national map in the forensic sense as proof of the feasibility or unfeasibility of a greater continental polity, the map's rhetorical clout had already become seriously defused in the writings of local patriots like Thomas Jefferson. His *Notes on the State of Virginia* (1785) reveals how, through the practice of cartographic writing, the state of Virginia emerged as a geopolitical construct sharing the identical symbolic and discursive attributes that Webster, Morse, and the authors of the Federalist papers ascribed to the national map.

From the start, Jefferson locates the *Notes* inside the map image of Virginia; he opens his first query with the verbal recitation of the "Boundaries of Virginia," which corresponded to a manuscript map that had accompanied the original draft. Acknowledging that both his own notes and map drawings might be compromised, Jefferson grounds the authority of his *Notes* in two specific cartographic texts. When he states in his fourth query, "For the particular geography of our mountains I must refer to Fry and Jefferson's map of Virginia; and to Evans's analysis of his map of America for a more philosophical view of them," Jefferson refers the reader to his father's *Map of the Most Inhabited Part of Virginia* (1753) and the mapmaker's manual *Geographical, Historical, Political, Philosophical, and Mechanical Essays* (1755) by Lewis Evans.[35]

---

34. James Winthrop, "Letters of Agrippa," in Storing, ed., *The Complete Anti-Federalist,* IV, 77; also discussed by Benjamin R. Barber, "The Compromised Republic: Public Purposelessness in America," in Robert H. Horwitz, ed., *The Moral Foundations of the American Republic* (Charlottesville, Va., 1986), 45.

For a study examining how distance and territorial size affected early national politics, see Rosemarie Zagarri, *The Politics of Size: Representation in the United States, 1776–1850* (Ithaca, N.Y., 1987), chap. 4.

35. Thomas Jefferson, *Notes on the State of Virginia,* ed. William Peden (Chapel Hill,

In the chapter "On Rivers" Jefferson presents yet another argument for the way in which post-Revolutionary Americans embraced the map as a writing system superior to the English language and conventional literary forms, in this case the practice of note-taking and verbal description. Before describing the rivers of Virginia, Jefferson deliberately cautions the reader against his verbal efforts, because "an inspection of a map of Virginia, will give a better idea of the geography of its rivers, than any description in writing." Jefferson encourages readers to consult maps rather than his own text because, unlike any other form of "description in writing," only maps are capable of communicating the idea of rivers in ways that normal language could not—immediately and yet mediated, undistorted and yet artificially represented. Ever wary of language as a means of communication, Jefferson indicates that in order to ensure the proper representation of the state of Virginia he must defer his own writing to the signs and script of cartographic writing.[36]

While the map thus answered Jefferson's authorial scruples in much the same vein as it did for the framers of the Constitution a few years later, it also enabled Jefferson to appropriate the greater discourse of cartography as the foundation of state representation. In Query 13, writing on "the constitution of the state, and its several charters," Jefferson invokes the figure of the map as the state's original text. By citing the cartographically represented space of Virginia rather than history as the state's genealogical source of origin, he points to the language of cartography as the ideal agent of political mediation and representation. Moreover, when Jefferson concedes that the state's founding document was written at a time when "we were new and unexperienced in the science of government," he is quick to add that it was due to cartographic writing that Virginians discovered "very capital defects" in the constitution.[37]

N.C., 1954), 18. While the Evans manual was written to analyze the author's own map called *A General Map of the Middle British Colonies, in America* (1755), it acknowledged its debt to the Fry-Jefferson map. Both references illustrate the persistence with which older, outdated maps and geographic records informed colonial and postcolonial thinking.

36. Jefferson, *Notes,* ed. Peden, 5.

37. Ibid., 110, 118. During the debates surrounding the first state constitution of Virginia (1776), Jefferson used boundary maps as the rhetorical device exposing not only the potential for territorial misrepresentation but for lodging the demand that Virginia's territory should be defined according to the original colonial charters—meaning, its territory would extend indefinitely westward. For a discussion of territorial rights and the rhetoric of boundaries, see Peter S. Onuf, *Jefferson's Empire: The Language of American Nationhood* (Charlottesville, Va., 2000), 66–68.

By the end of this query, the implied map image of Virginia, though invisible throughout the *Notes* as such, has fulfilled the demand of eighteenth-century national ideologies. Jefferson's rhetorical use of the map facilitated the narrative fusion of the state's external boundaries with those of the individual citizen. The implied map image had succeeded in dividing the state into local working units (counties); its writing system implicitly was preventing "injury" among the state's citizens; and, more important, it had laid the groundwork for depicting Virginia as a homogenous culture working the land collectively (a point Jefferson further elaborated in Query 19). Jefferson's *Notes* thus illustrates how during the early decades the very terms surrounding the idea of nation were flexible. For Jefferson, the semantic application of "nation" was as dynamic and constitutive a concept as that of "state." Cartographic writing allowed Jefferson to keep alive this definitional uncertainty. As the word map of Virginia furthered Jefferson's sectionalist argument, it also prepared the argument for one of Jefferson's future political goals: the guarantee of autonomy for the individual state inside the proposed unified superstate.[38]

THE NATIONAL MAP AS LOGO AND CONSTITUTIVE LOGOS

What neither Jay, Winthrop, nor Jefferson had foreseen was the fact that the national map as a specialized print form controlled its potential for divisiveness; it functioned like a proleptic device, asserting the primacy of the union while anticipating and containing the local desire for self-definition. During the period marked by the constitutional debate and the tumult over states' rights, commercial mapmakers as well as ordinary map readers developed the nation's cartographic image into a hieroglyphic sign consisting exclusively of the nation's territorial outline. Indeed, as I will show below, in the hands of American statesmen and students alike the national map became what Benedict Anderson has identified as an avatar of modern nationalism, the "map-as-logo."[39]

38. On the flexibility of the term "nation" and focus on Virginia in Jefferson's writings, see Peter S. Onuf, *Jefferson's Empire*. On the arguments of state-union relations, see also Matson and Onuf, *A Union of Interests;* Onuf, *The Origins of the Federal Republic: Jurisdictional Controversies in the United States, 1775–1787* (Philadelphia, 1983).

39. Benedict Anderson, *Imagined Communities: Reflections on the Origin and Spread of Nationalism* (London, 1991), 175. Although Anderson is discussing the postcolonial conditions of twentieth-century Southeast Asia, the discursive dynamic he traces can be just as easily recognized in the decade immediately following the Peace of Paris. "In [the map's]

In the United States, one of the first examples showing the nation as a pure sign and logo appeared in William McMurray's wall map, *The United States according to the Definitive Treaty of Peace Signed at Paris* (1784) (Figure 39). In this map the nation's topographic image enters into a comparative dialogue with an inset map (on the lower right) showing the North American continent and its division into geopolitical units. The inset map distinguishes the new political nation-state from the continent by outlining its territory as a blank space bearing the bold print label "UNITED STATES." While the inset map thus announces the map title in lieu of a cartouche, when placed in relation to the larger national map the dialogue shifts the reader's attention from the comparatively locative stance (how do I find myself on the map?) to the more competitive and possessive stance (this map shows my country!). Its blankness erases local knowledge, regional claims, and above all the fact that the national space was not fully under federal control (west of the Allegheny Mountains, Native American nations were still officially masters of their domains). Through the map's metanarrative between the geographic and the inset parts, McMurray illustrates the way in which the nation's bare, skeletal outline functioned in the sphere of politics as a signifier of reconciliation and containment: the map simultaneously maintained and closed the gap between the nation and the states.[40]

While McMurray's map reached only a limited audience, the material proliferation of the national map vastly aided the dissemination of the United States map as a logo. In particular, the image of the logo map pervaded the self-representational culture of the educated middle class. Examining Ralph Earl's portrait of Mrs. Noah Smith and her family, a closer look reveals that the nation's outline becomes the direct prop of the young man holding the geography book (Figure 40). The pervasiveness of

---

final form all explanatory glosses could be summarily removed: lines of longitude and latitude, place names, signs for rivers, seas, and mountains, *neighbours*. Pure sign, no longer compass to the world. . . . Instantly recognizable, everywhere visible, the logo-map penetrated deep into the popular imagination, forming a powerful emblem for the anticolonial nationalisms being born." While Anderson's argument about how print culture facilitated the construction of national ideologies has held our attention, it is easily overlooked that the widespread diffusion of typographical images during the formation of national communities prompted him to speculate toward the end of his study that, generally speaking, neither the technology of print nor languages as such but the visual quality of printed signs and materials invented nationalism.

40. For a different reading of the map as logo, see Boelhower, "Nation-Building," in Ickringill, ed., *The Early Republic,* 109.

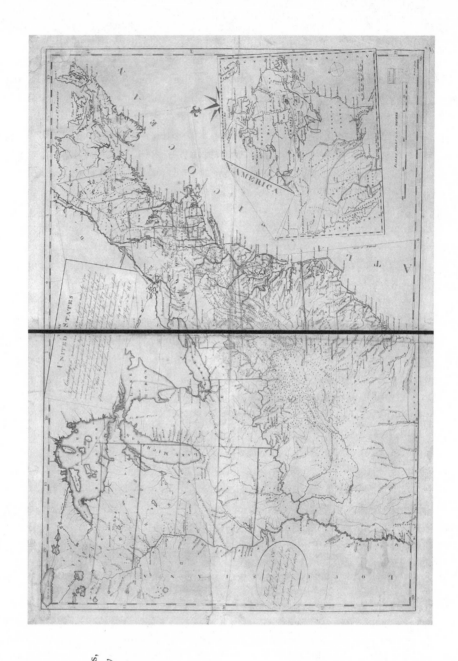

Figure 39.
The United States
according to the
Definitive Treaty of
Peace Signed at Paris,
Sept. Third, 1783. *By
W[illia]m McMurray.
1784.* Courtesy, The
Library of Congress

Figure 40. Detail from Mrs. Noah Smith and Her Children. *By Ralph Earl. 1798.*
Permission of The Metropolitan Museum of Art, Gift of Edgar William and Bernice
Chrysler Garbisch, 1964. (64.309.1)

the logo map, with its simultaneous integration into alphabetic and geographic training, is vividly exemplified in the needlework samplers created by American schoolgirls. Throughout the eighteenth century, formal
alphabet lessons had been accompanied by needlework samplers repro-
ducing the letters of the alphabet and didactic quotations. By the 1790s,
however, as American literacy lessons were increasingly taking a geo-

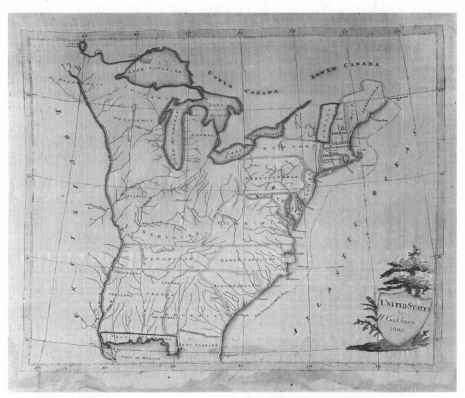

Figure 41. Map Sampler, Eastern United States. By H[annah] Cockburn. 1808. Photograph ©
Worcester Art Museum. Permission of the Worcester Art Museum, Worcester, Massachusetts

graphic turn, the samplers' thematic range was expanded to include the
reproduction of maps. While pupils continued to embroider the alphabet, they also took up pen, brush, and needles to draw, paint, and stitch
the United States map outline and place-names on paper and on silk.

Hannah Cockburn's sampler, for example, displays both her needlework and her geographic knowledge as she faithfully imitates Morse's
map-reading lesson by showing the border lines and names of the union
and its states, including the "Twenty League Line" separating national
from international waters (Figure 41). Mary Franklin's sampler, while depicting both the North and South American continents, nonetheless advertises the national form as the heavily traced border line of the nation-
state distinguishes the political territory from its larger geographic context (Figure 42).[41]

41. These samplers are representative of an arts-and-crafts movement in education in
the early Republic. For further examples, see Betty Ring, *Girlhood Embroidery: American*

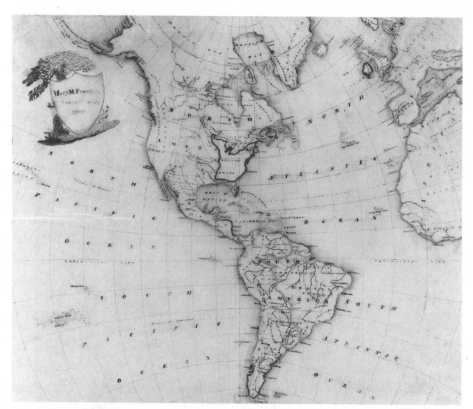

Figure 42. Needlework. By Mary M. Franklin. 1808. Courtesy, Winterthur Museum

Both samplers demonstrate that, because the national map shaped the methodologies of formal literacy instruction, the nation's outline had become internalized and was now shaping practices of self-representation and political identification. The samplers' representation of the national territory—using blazes of color, thicker thread, or wider brush strokes—privileged the outline map as the recognizable sign through which young Americans were taught to express their national identity. The samplers' materiality even suggested that the text of the national map was beginning to be understood quite literally as the nation's material texture.

Indeed, the logo functioned like a universal signifier when it was mass-produced and valorized as a sentimental object. As early as 1792, Ameri-

Samplers and Pictorial Needlework, 1650–1850 (New York, 1993); also see Judith Tyner, "The World in Silk: Embroidered Globes of Westtown School," *Map Collector,* LXXIV (1996), 11–14.

Figure 43. Pitcher. 1792–1810. Courtesy, Winterthur Museum

cans imported milk jugs on which enterprising Englishmen had printed the map-as-logo, surrounding it with the likenesses of two founders, George Washington and Benjamin Franklin (Figure 43). Americans thus appear to have viewed the cartographic image of the nation as more than a desirable consumer object. Considering the widespread circulation of national maps, citizens endowed the logo image with the kind of political-aesthetic value of "Americanness," which significantly would retain and generate its sacred aura despite the fact that the logo was mass-produced.[42]

Central to this aura is that, emerging from within the postcolonial culture, the map logo assumed the very communicative properties so eagerly sought after by the proponents of a new American language scheme. But while language reformers concentrated on the alphabetic construction of a newly nationalized English, it was through the everyday popular use of the national map that its territorial outline became an emblem rivaling the letters displayed in the ABC books. Instead of redefining the alphabet so that "A stands for America," mapmakers and pupils discovered in the map logo the ideal sign representing the nation unambiguously and in diverse textual contexts: the national outline literally became a legible sign, a ready-made icon that was easily transported into the process of mediation and national identification.

Reduced to the shape of a logo, the map became the communicative agent through which a multitude of individuals were taught not only to imagine but to "read" themselves as parts of a national whole. Every time citizens recited "American" letters in spellers or drew or stitched the map image of the nation, they contemplated themselves as a local representation contingent upon a national geography. If the outline map established the nation as a material artifact, then during the 1780s and 1790s it functioned as a sign that American citizens were trained to recognize as we today are trained to recognize the logo of McDonald's golden arches. The most compelling description of a realized and representative model of an American linguistic community derives from the fact that people as different as John Jay and Hannah Cockburn simultaneously "read" the vernacular of the map logo. If nationalism invented the American people, it was common readers who inaugurated the nation by poring over geographic texts that produced and reproduced their cultural community as a geographic reality, as a recognizable American sign.

42. The images framing the logo were recycled materials taken from the cartouche decorating the map by John Wallis, *The United States of America* (London, 1784).

chapter four

GEOGRAPHY TEXTBOOKS AND READING NATIONAL CHARACTER

In his essay *On the Education of Youth* (1788), Noah Webster proclaims, "Every child in America should be acquainted with his own country. He should read books that furnish him with ideas that will be useful to him in life and practice. As soon as he opens his lips, he should rehearse the history of his own country; he should lisp the praise of liberty and of those illustrious heroes and statesmen who have wrought a revolution in her favor." This passage manifests the overlapping imperatives and agendas that Webster and other educational reformers ascribed to reading in the new Republic. Webster's thesis initially appears to be that reading should serve a pragmatic, utilitarian function, putting "ideas" in the service of "practice." As he elaborates his vision, however, Webster's description becomes more imaginative: books provide a historical narrative that is to be repeatedly and dramatically "rehearsed," and history itself is quickly transformed into a patriotic story of "America," replete with heroes and the personified feminine character of "liberty."[1]

The entry into American history, though, comes from an acquaintance with the "country." As his subsequent commentary demonstrates, Webster is thinking of "country" less as historical artifact—here the new nation-state—than in its geographical representation. Webster demands books that will "call home the minds of youth and fix them upon the interests of their own country, and . . . assist in forming attachments to it"; to that end, the ideal book begins with "a selection of essays respecting the settlement and geography of America." This geographical essay is required to combat what Webster sees as a dismaying national shortcoming. "The people in this country, even the higher classes, have no correct

1. Noah Webster, "On the Education of Youth in America" (1788), in Frederick Rudolph, ed., *Essays on Education in the Early Republic* (Cambridge, Mass., 1965), 64–65.

information respecting the United States." "Such ignorance," Webster fears, "is not only disgraceful but is materially prejudicial to our political friendship and federal operations." In order to address this ignorance, Webster proposes that "a tour through the United States ought now to be considered as a necessary part of a liberal education."[2]

For American educators intent on nationalizing liberal education, an actual tour of the nation was not the ideal pedagogic solution. A grand tour was not a financial or logistical possibility for most American students. But, if they were unable to physically pack their bags, they were able to take an imaginative trip via an abundant literature of travels and natural histories. Through these two genres, Anglo-American culture had long negotiated the question of geographical identity, fusing the literary survey of the country to the didactic process of character formation. However, if the agenda was to "call home the minds of youth and fix them upon the interests of their own country," these two genres offered a geographical tour with potentially counterproductive results: popular travel narratives of the 1780s and 1790s tended to promote an unmistakable English national identity while natural histories promoted an overdetermined local and antinational sense of identity.[3]

Travel narratives like Andrew Burnaby's *Travels through the Middle Settlements in North-America, in the Years 1759 and 1760* (1775) or Jonathan Carver's *Travels through the Interior Parts of North America, in the Years 1766, 1767, and 1768* (1778) created characters out of geographical writing. For both Burnaby and Carver the educational tour and the traveler's mobility were self-consciously modeled upon and contained by well-advertised maps. Burnaby acknowledges Lewis Evans's map of the middle colonies; Carver inserted a map of North America that was made by the royal geographer Emmanuel Bowen. Their respective tours further linked the traveler to the geographical essay by imitating the organizational

2. Ibid., 65, 77.

3. On the relationship of educating "character" through literatures imitating the effect of journeys (which are not necessarily identical with travel narratives) in the early Anglo-American context, see the various generic approaches delineated by Michael McKeon, *The Origins of the English Novel, 1600–1740* (Baltimore, 1987); Percy G. Adams, *Travel Literature and the Evolution of the Novel* (Lexington, Ky., 1983); Wayne Franklin, *Discoverers, Explorers, Settlers: The Diligent Writers of Early America* (Chicago, 1979); Charles L. Batton, Jr., *Pleasurable Instruction: Form and Convention in Eighteenth-Century Travel Literature* (Berkeley, Calif., 1978); Richard Slotkin, *Regeneration through Violence: The Mythology of the American Frontier, 1600–1860* (Middletown, Conn., 1971).

structure used by geography books and gazetteers. The narrative of Burnaby's *Travels* follows strategically placed (and often typographically italicized) place-names, like *"Virginia"* or *"Williamsburg."* While these terms allow readers to navigate the text like a map, they also function as keywords prefacing the encyclopedic narrative of geography books. In the case of Burnaby, they become entry headers for narrative segments that incorporate the factual (he reports on climatic conditions), the anecdotal (personal meditations on lightning), and the cultural (Burnaby notes that the Virginia character is marked by indolence). Two narrative patterns are the result. On the one hand, as they recount local characters, they assert differences in cultural habits and customs in order to separate the English from the non-English. On the other hand, the travelers' Englishness itself was confirmed by their ability to place and interpret both the story and the persona of the traveler within an imperial British geographical archive. In the end, these geographical tours helped to construct English identities rather than American national identities.[4]

By comparison, the genre of natural history privileges neither English nor American national identities but invents local characters. Like the travel narrative, natural histories, such as John Filson's *Discovery, Settlement, and Present State of Kentucke* (1784), Jeremy Belknap's *History of New Hampshire* (1784), and Thomas Jefferson's *Notes on the State of Virginia* (1785), also operated inside a narrative framework that begins with a map image (or its verbal approximation) and ends with the assertion of character types. Written in response to a questionnaire by a natural historian, the *Notes on the State of Virginia* was organized in accordance with the literary protocol of geography books. The table of contents practically copies that of the early modern geography book, moving from boundaries, rivers, seaports, mountains, and cascades to productions, climate, and population. When viewed in its entirety, Jefferson's *Notes* imitated the dual structure of geographies, which traditionally allotted one half of the text to the information about the state's natural geography, and the other half to its social customs and civic institutions. In Jefferson's discussion of the state's population, the narrative logic of natural history anticipates the creation of two literary constructions: the ideal country

4. Andrew Burnaby, *Travels through the Middle Settlements in North-America, in the Years 1759 and 1760, with Observations upon the State of the Colonies* (London, 1775), 4–22. For a general survey of early American travel writing, see Myra Jehlen, "The Literature of Colonization," in Sacvan Bercovitch, ed., *The Cambridge History of American Literature*, I, *1590–1820* (Cambridge, 1994), 59–168.

of Virginia and the ideal character of the Virginia planter, the yeoman farmer. Filson's natural history of Kentucky follows this narrative trajectory even more closely: the encyclopedic rehearsal of the state's history, boundaries, air, soil, and so on is appended by the memoir of the region's emblematic character, Daniel Boone.[5]

These books—travels and natural histories—hardly answered Webster's call for appropriate reading materials educating the young. Not only did they not supply the requisite geographical information covering the whole nation, but they were also constructed so as to deflect rather than "assist in the forming [of] attachments" to the fledgling country as a whole. Geography textbooks, a genre that conditioned the literary sensibilities of early American readers, answered Webster's call most closely. Aiming to educate as well as entertain, the first generation of United States school geographies exploited textual strategies that infused geography with ideas of setting and character; just as the traveler's and natural historian's own prose, self-consciously or not, mingled utilitarian, narrative, and affective priorities, so did geography books. But with one difference: by privileging the geography of the nation-state, they grounded the reader inside a national ideology of education.

Early national geography textbooks are at the very heart of the geographical literatures so prominent in the new Republic; these widely published books created and informed the geographical consciousness that

5. On the history and structural organization of geography books, see David N. Livingstone, *The Geographical Tradition: Episodes in the History of a Contested Enterprise* (Oxford, 1992); Margarita Bowen, *Empiricism and Geographical Thought: From Francis Bacon to Alexander von Humboldt* (Cambridge, 1981). This dual structure coincides with Robert A. Ferguson's observation, whereby he distinguishes Jefferson's *Notes on the State of Virginia* from other regional or natural histories because it maintained the "elementary structural separation . . . between natural phenomenon and social event." See Ferguson, *Law and Letters in American Culture* (Cambridge, Mass., 1984), 46.

My understanding of natural history as literary convention in the early United States is informed by Christopher Looby, "The Constitution of Nature: Taxonomy as Politics in Jefferson, Peale, and Bartram," *Early American Literature*, XXII (1987), 252–273; Mary Louise Pratt, *Imperial Eyes: Travel Writing and Transculturation* (London, 1992); James Clifford and George E. Marcus, eds., *Writing Culture: The Poetics and Politics of Ethnography* (Berkeley, Calif., 1986); James Larson, "Not without a Plan: Geography and Natural History in the Late Eighteenth Century," *Journal of the History of Biology*, XIX (1986), 447–488; Clifford Geertz, *The Interpretation of Cultures: Selected Essays* (London, 1973), chap. 9. For other approaches, see Christoph Irmscher, *The Poetics of Natural History: From John Bartram to William James* (New Brunswick, N.J., 1999); Pamela Regis, *Describing Early America: Bartram, Jefferson, Crèvecoeur, and the Rhetoric of Natural History* (DeKalb, Ill., 1992).

pervaded American social, political, and personal identities. Geography textbooks shaped American reading practices and expectations; since textbook authors emphatically insisted upon the genre's function in promoting literacy, geography books taught as much about the process of reading (and writing) as they did about the subject of geographical nomenclature. The geography textbook was also a valid literary form with its own generic and aesthetic conventions. Just as writers like Jedidiah Morse claimed that their textbooks had a role in promoting reading, so too they perceived themselves as literary authors. Geography textbooks were deliberately fashioned as didactic pleasure reading. Underlying these dual impulses of geography textbooks—the promotion of literacy and the self-identification as entertainment—is a profound and overt nationalistic ideology. More than any other genre in early American literature, the geography textbook epitomized geography's role in shaping literary consciousness and its attendant construction of fictional characters. In the fiction created by early national geographies, the narrative setting of the nation would promulgate national character types.

TOWARD A MORPHOLOGY OF NATIONAL GEOGRAPHY BOOKS

Webster's call for new geography textbooks was echoed by many. The American political leadership and intellectual elite, including Thomas Jefferson, John Adams, Benjamin Rush, and Benjamin Franklin, endorsed geographical instruction in the post-Revolutionary curriculum. Calling on John Locke—"*Youth* ought to begin with this Science [geography] as an introduction to their future studies"—clergymen, teachers, and politicians advocated geography as a subject promoting national education and good citizenship. This advocacy spurred authors and booksellers to supply the growing demand for geography books. Between 1784 and 1800, major and minor printing centers—including Boston and Philadelphia as well as Bennington in Vermont, Wilmington in Delaware, and Charleston in South Carolina—inundated coastal towns and the countryside with school geographies. Local geographers copyrighted nearly three dozen textbooks, to which we must add at least the same if not a larger number of pirated editions, not to mention foreign imports.[6]

6. For proposals on geographic education in the early Republic, see Thomas Jefferson, *Notes on the State of Virginia,* ed. William Peden (Chapel Hill, N.C., 1954), 146; and the essays by Benjamin Rush, Noah Webster, and others collected in Rudolph, ed., *Essays on Education.* As David G. McCullough has shown, John Adams deemed geography "abso-

The demand for geography textbooks was so high that nearly a dozen of the reported school geographies survived beyond their second and third editions. Jedidiah Morse's best-selling textbook series—consisting of *Geography Made Easy* (1784), *The American Geography* (1789), *The American Universal Geography* (1793), and *Elements of Geography* (1795)—lasted for several decades and reached more than twenty editions. Other best-sellers of significant longevity included William Guthrie's Americanized version of *A New System of Modern Geography; or, A Geographical, Historical, and Commercial Grammar* (1794); Benjamin Workman's *Elements of Geography* (1795); Nathaniel Dwight's *Short but Comprehensive System of the Geography of the World; by Way of Question and Answer* (1795); and Caleb Bingham's *Astronomical and Geographical Catechism* (1795).[7]

Writing geography textbooks quickly evolved into a lucrative business, enabling male and female writers to make a living as quasi-professional authors. When in 1784, for example, the textbook *Geography Made Easy* became an instant best-seller, its financial success came as such a surprise to the author Jedidiah Morse that he nearly quit his theological studies in order to become a professional geographer. Morse did become a minister, but geography books provided a significant if not primary income for the rest of his life.[8] Far from being idiosyncratic, Morse's vocation as a

---

lutely necessary to every person of public character." "Really there ought not to be a state, a city, a promontory, a river, a harbor, an inlet or a mountain in all America, but what should be intimately known to every youth who has any pretensions to liberal education." See McCullough, *John Adams* (New York, 2002), 149.

Geographers regularly invoked John Locke's treatise on education, in which he sang the merits of geographic knowledge. This quote is from Jedidiah Morse, *Elements of Geography . . .* (Boston, 1795), iv. For the original text, see John Locke, *Some Thoughts concerning Education,* ed. John W. Yolton and Jean S. Yolton (Oxford, 1989), par. 178, 234–235.

7. *Geography Made Easy,* originally published in 1784, reached its twenty-second edition in 1820. For comprehensive surveys of early American school geographies, see William Warntz, *Geography Now and Then: Some Notes on the History of Academic Geography in the United States* (New York, 1964); Charles Carpenter, *History of American Schoolbooks* (Philadelphia, 1963); John A. Nietz, *Old Textbooks . . .* (Pittsburgh, Pa., 1961); Clifton Johnson, *Old-Time Schools and School-Books* (1904; rpt. New York, 1963).

8. Studies on the profession of authorship in early America tend to gloss over the geographic venue. A large number of American authors wrote geography books on commission for local schools. For example, Susanna Rowson wrote geographies for the female academy she managed in Boston. Authors like Morse, Guthrie, Dwight, and Bingham survived in the print marketplace for several decades by reissuing, updating, and repackaging continually their various products.

As the popularity of his geographies grew, Morse found himself surrounded by com-

minister-geographer reflected the pervasive overlap of geography books and devotional literature. Geography was located between sacred and secular literacy, positioning it among the ultimate best-sellers in the early Republic. In the rural as well as the urban northern United States, records indicate that, for more than three decades, only the Bible and Noah Webster's spelling books were more popular than geographies.[9]

Geographic schooling in the United States turned upon the textuality of geography books. The textual forms presenting geographic knowledge ranged from pasteboard flash cards and pamphlet-sized catechisms to schoolbooks and leatherbound display editions—all made available by the local stationer, bookseller, lending library, and chapbook peddler. Geographers like Morse took great promotional pains to include an unusually diverse audience by explicitly addressing American readers of all ages, classes, and genders. His *Geography Made Easy* addressed "the Young Gentleman and Ladies, throughout the United States," advertising his books as "[in]expensive for the purchase, of by far the greater part of the inhabitants of the United States." A decade later Morse was able to announce the completion of a textbook series appropriate for children, college students, and families.[10]

------

petitors and critics who regularly embroiled him in legal battles over issues of plagiarism and regional politics. In particular, Morse's blatant proselytizing on behalf of the "New England way" regularly incurred the scorn of southern textbook authors. For general materials on Morse, his publishing interests, and his critics, see John Rennie Short, *Representing the Republic: Mapping the United States, 1600–1900* (London, 2001), 120–126; Richard J. Moss, *The Life of Jedidiah Morse: A Station of Peculiar Exposure* (Knoxville, Tenn., 1995), 25–26, 103–112. On Morse's business acumen, see Conrad Wright, "The Controversial Career of Jedidiah Morse," *Harvard Library Bulletin,* XXXI (1983), 64–87.

9. For a discussion of Morse's deterministic geography in relation to eighteenth-century theology, see David N. Livingstone, "Geographical Inquiry, Rational Religion, and Moral Philosophy: Enlightenment Discourses on the Human Condition," in Livingstone and Charles W. J. Withers, eds., *Geography and Enlightenment* (Chicago, 1999), 93–119. On the privileged role of geography in eighteenth-century Protestant theology, see Manfred Büttner, "Geographie und Theologie im 18. Jahrhundert," in Büttner, ed., *Religion/Umwelt-Forschung,* II (Bochum, 1989), 6–16; and for its seventeenth-century antecedents, see Rienk H. Vermij, "The Beginnings of Physico-Theology: England, Holland, Germany," in Heyno Kattenstedt, ed., *Abhandlungen zur Geschichte der Geowissenschaften und Religion/Umwelt-Forschung,* IX (Bochum, 1993), 173–184.

On the popularity of geography books, see William J. Gilmore, *Reading Becomes a Necessity of Life: Material and Cultural Life in Rural New England, 1780–1835* (Knoxville, Tenn., 1989), 64.

10. Jedidiah Morse, *Geography Made Easy: Being a Short, but Comprehensive System of*

Geography textbooks fall into three subgenres: the geographic catechism, the geographic writing manual, and the geographic encyclopedia.

Geographic Catechism. The catechism was designed for memorization and oral recitation. Geographies such as Nathaniel Dwight's *Short but Comprehensive System of the Geography of the World* (1795) rehearsed the country's geography in a question-and-answer format, thus duplicating the long-established formal method of knowledge acquisition. For example, in the exercise "Of North America," Dwight writes:

> Q. What is the situation and extent of North America?
>
> A. It is situated between 8 and 80 degrees of north latitude, and between 54 and 131 degrees of west longitude. It is about 5,000 miles long, from north to south, and . . . 3,700 miles broad, from east to west.
>
> Q. How is North America bounded?
>
> A. It is bounded on the north by the Northern Ocean; on the east by the Atlantic Ocean; on the south by South America; and on the west by the Pacific Ocean.

This interrogatory form was preferred for the young. In Morse's description of his own series of geography books, the catechism is "for the use of children under 8 years of age." The geographical catechism echoes the sacred history of literacy instruction. But where alphabetic literacy was the key to sacred knowledge, it here becomes secularized and is made worldly by the geography book's substitution of biblical history with geographical knowledge.[11]

In its minimal format the catechism emphasized the modern political geography of nations, kingdoms, and empires. Many catechisms were

---

That Very Useful and Agreeable Science (New Haven, Conn., 1784), iv, v. Morse's series consisted of "a small 'Astronomical and Geographical Catechism' for the use of children under 8 years of age. . . . The *second* is the work before us, adapted to children from 8 to 14 years old, . . . The *third* is *Geography made Easy,* which . . . is now in use in many of the Schools and Academies in the United States, . . . The *fourth* is *The American Universal Geography,* . . . for higher classes in Academies, for Colleges, and private families." *Elements of Geography,* vi–vii.

11. Nathaniel Dwight, *A Short but Comprehensive System of the Geography of the World; by Way of Question and Answer* . . . (Philadelphia, 1795), 135; Morse, *Elements of Geography,* vii. Also see [Caleb Bingham], *An Astronomical and Geographical Catechism* (Boston, 1795); *A Small Collection of Questions and Answers, from Various Authors* (Litchfield, Conn., 1799); Samuel Litch, *An Astronomical and Geografical Catechism* . . . (Jaffrey, N.H., 1814); Jedidiah Morse, *Questions Adapted to the Use of Morse's Geography Carefully Arranged for the Use of Mrs. Wetmore's Seminary for Young Ladies* (Baltimore, 1818).

brief, cheaply made pamphlets; the form was even appropriated by flash cards. A set of cards, titled *Geography, an Amusement; or, Complete Set of Geographical Cards* (1805), consisted of seventy-six cards made of thick cardboard. These cards were numbered, color-coded (red for America, black for Europe, blue for Asia, and yellow for Africa), and often signed and hand-numbered by the owner ("Miss Eliza Strong"). These cards represented a set of questions pertaining to one particular nation-state or political unit: for example, card no. 9, "Massachusetts," began the catechism with the header "BOUNDARIES," which was followed by the list "N. New-Hampshire and Vermont; S. Connecticut, Rhode-Island, and the Ocean; E. the Atlantic; W. New-York." The list of topics continued, eliciting questions on dimension, counties, chief towns, universities, productions, manufactures, mountains, rivers, and bays. Having completed a round of these cards dealing with Europe, Africa, and Asia, the student had rehearsed a geography lesson that privileged the natural geography of continents over the artificial constructs of nation-states; in a parallel lesson, the cards asserted the various nation-states, downplaying their constitutive geopolitical components such as provinces or principalities. The exception to the rule was the color-coded deck of cards dealing with America: the questions pertaining to the North American continent and the United States result in answers that in general undo geographical hierarchies. Through the random method of asking questions, the catechism blurs local distinctions. Regions, states, and counties appear to be equal entities, albeit set inside the territorial setting of the United States' territory.[12]

Another type of catechism was offered to the more advanced student when authors like Robert Davidson cast the oral repetition of geographic knowledge in rhyming couplets. Following the idea that "instructions conveyed in any tolerable kind of *verse,* are much more easily remembered, than when delivered in the most elegant and harmonious *prose,"* the student reciting the geography of *"The United States of North America"* would begin on cue:

(The Boundary Line.)
From the source of *St. Croix,* these *States* to define,
Due *north* to the *Highlands,* first, draw a right line.

12. See *Geography, an Amusement; or, A Complete Set of Geographical Cards* (Burlington, N.J., 1805); *A New Set of Geographical Cards, for the Agreeable Improvement of Gentlemen and Ladies, in the Necessary and Pleasing Study of Geography, Taken from the Latest and Best Authorities* (Philadelphia, 1786).

Then *westward* along the said Highlands extend it,

To south of what Streams with St. Lawrence are blended.

Thus let it proceed, 'till it meet in its course,

Connecticut River's north-westernmost source.

Then down the said river, until it arrive,

At degrees of north latitude *forty and five*.

Memorizing a geography lesson in verse required a working vocabulary of geographic terms. It was common for many geographers to advise tutors to assert that "a Vocabulary of Proper Names . . . may be very usefully committed to memory, after the rate of six or eight words per day." Committing geographic knowledge to memory required the repetition of a vocabulary consisting of words like "situation" and "extent," "latitude" and "longitude," "north" and "south," "lines," "miles," and "boundary." The catechism rehearsed the basic elements of the national map in the same way that spelling books recited basic phonetic or grammatical principles of language. Because they generally lacked visual aids such as maps, tables, or pictures, these geographic catechisms reproduced the nation-state as an inherently antivisual memory, as a verbal construct grounded in the names as they appear in alphabetic form on a two-dimensional sheet of paper.[13]

The Geographic Writing Manual. The eighteenth-century students' literacy lessons concentrated on ciphering and how to read before or in lieu of writing. By contrast, geographies in many instances reinforced oral internalization by pairing reading with the exercise of writing in designated copybooks. To that end, geographic writing manuals frequently contained blank lined pages in which the reader could practice writing. Jedidiah Morse bluntly claimed, "Geography is a speceies *[sic]* of composition." In the case of Joseph Goldsmith's *Easy Grammar of Geography* (1804), the author posits a series of questions that serve as essay topics ("to be answered in writing by the young Student in Geography"); he asks, "For what are the United States of America celebrated?" followed by questions on the states, principal cities, lakes, and so forth. Writing exercises like this one engaged students in two forms of composition. By writing

13. [Robert Davidson], *Geography Epitomized; or, A Tour round the World: Being a Short but Comprehensive Description of the Terraqueous Globe: Attempted in Verse, (for the Sake of the Memory;) and Principally Designed for the Use of Schools* (Philadelphia, 1784), iii, 54–55; J[oseph] Goldsmith, *An Easy Grammar of Geography for the Use of Schools* (Philadelphia, 1804), 109.

out orally rehearsed textbook passages they transposed geographic memory into a material form, giving it the appearance of durability, stability, and, above all, order. Following an overtly patriotic line of questioning, however, the students were forced to engage in an ideological writing process, incorporating the most recent narratives about national boundaries and territorial dimension into the story about the country's immediate history.[14]

The compositional exercises of geographic memory were physically reinforced by handwriting exercises. An integral part of literacy instruction, handwriting lessons rounded off the student's initiation into alphabetic literacy. The study of writing was considered the physical expression of the writer's social status and possible professional competence. In this context, the scriveners of the early Republic were asked to practice the "geographical running hand," which essentially was a generic round-hand style that was used for writing place-names in copy books. Manuals such as *Milns's Geographical Running Hand* (1797) specialized in these exercises; the student is required to write out the specifics of European locations ("Amsterdam, Holland, Netherlands. Europe. 52• North"), the boundaries of the continent ("Hudson's Bay. Coast of Labrador. North America"), and definitions of geographic principles ("Latitude, the distance of Places from the Equator").[15]

Geography textbooks closely modeled their writing exercises on the eighteenth-century definition of "textbook" offered by the *Oxford English Dictionary,* according to which a *"text-book . . .* is a Classick Author written very wide by the Students, to give Room for an Interpretation dictated by the Master, etc. to be inserted in the Interlines." Learning to write took place in the space between the lines of a master text, just as the "Inter-

14. Morse, *Geography Made Easy,* 215; Goldsmith, *An Easy Grammar of Geography,* 92–93, 101–102. On reading lessons in colonial America, see Jennifer Monaghan, "Literacy Instruction and Gender in Colonial New England," in Cathy N. Davidson, ed., *Reading in America: Literature and Social History* (Baltimore, 1989), 53–80; Davidson, *Revolution and the Word: The Rise of the Novel in America* (New York, 1986), 55–74. For a detailed history of literary education in the early Republic, see the transnational study by Harvey J. Graff, *The Legacies of Literacy* (Bloomington, Ind., 1987), 248–257, 340–343.

15. William Milns, *Milns's Geographical Running Hand Copies for the Use of Commercial Schools* (Boston, 1797), 3. For a comprehensive discussion of early national writing instruction, see Tamara Plakins Thornton, *Handwriting in America: A Cultural History* (New Haven, Conn., 1996), esp. chap. 2.

pretation" was dictated by a schoolmaster. While other geographic forms prepared the student for independent movement and even a degree of creative thought, writing manuals emphasized an orthographic absolutism. Moreover, these texts were decidedly "manuals." The geographical hand suggested mechanical labor and thus conformed to the popular idea that the standardized script of the running hand imitated print. Ideally, the work of handwriting belonged to the realm of technological reproduction; it was unaffected by human error and fundamentally denied human agency. In the context of the geographical writing manuals, however, these exercises reasserted the individual author through the manuscript's spatial agency; just as surveying allowed individuals to inscribe themselves directly on the map, geographic handwriting—along with the map, the grid, or other narrative devices—became one more literary technique through which early citizens practiced their hands at self-emplacement.[16]

The Geographic Encyclopedia. Geographic encyclopedias were notorious for presenting the verbal translations of information in cramped fonts and for swelling the number of pages (in some cases to more than nine hundred) so that textbooks had often to be sold as two- or even three-volume sets. They ranged from basic, inexpensive editions to more costly volumes embellished with color and prints. The geographic encyclopedias were nearly always supplemented with foldout maps, engravings, and statistical tables and were often accompanied by separately published atlases. Not unlike the universal encyclopedias of Denis Diderot or Thomas Dobson, geographic encyclopedias were a mixed medium in two ways. On the one hand, they joined different modes of representing information, letting maps interact with prose, statistical tables with words, and so forth. On the other hand, the representation of geography was subjected to the organizational structures of alphabetic literacy.[17]

16. This definition of "textbook" was brought to my attention by D. F. McKenzie, *Bibliography and the Sociology of Texts* (London, 1986), 50.

17. On encyclopedic form, see Elizabeth L. Eisenstein, *The Printing Press as an Agent of Change: Communications and Cultural Transformations in Early-Modern Europe*, 2 vols. (Cambridge, 1979); Roger Chartier, *The Order of Books: Readers, Authors, and Libraries in Europe between the Fourteenth and Eighteenth Centuries* (Stanford, Calif., 1994). On the first American example of an encyclopedia, see Robert Arner, *Dobson's Encyclopaedia: The Publisher, Text, and Publication of America's First "Britannica," 1789–1803* (Philadelphia, 1991). Dobson's encyclopedia contained a large geographical section with contributions by Morse.

The most prominent example of the geographical encyclopedia was Jedidiah Morse's 1797 compendium, and here I cite the title in full:

The American Gazetteer, Exhibiting, in Alphabetical Order, a Much More Full and Accurate Account, Than Has Been Given, of the

States,	Towns,	Harbours,	Mountains,
Provinces,	Villages	Gulfs,	Forts,
Counties,	Rivers,	Sounds,	Indian Tribes, and
Cities,	Bays,	Capes,	New Discoveries,

on the American Continent, also of the West-India Islands, and Other Islands Appendant to the Continent, and Those Newly Discovered in the *Pacific Ocean:* Describing the Extent, Boundaries, Population, Government, Productions, Commerce, Manufactures, Curiosities, etc. of the Several Countries, and Their Important Civil Divisions;—and the Longitude and Latitude, the Bearings and Distances, from Noted Places, of the Cities, Towns, and Villages,—with A Particular Description of *the Georgia Western Territory.* The Whole Comprising Upwards of Seven Thousand Distinct Articles.

The American Gazetteer thus reflected the Enlightenment's "encyclopedic mentality," which idealized geographic knowledge as "a corpus of data, continually growing and correcting itself, its ultimate purpose [being] to encompass and to replicate the real world." Morse's *Gazetteer* stored geographical names and verbal descriptions as an early national linguist stored letters, *"Exhibiting, in Alphabetical Order"* the nation by using the alphabet's sequential *(a, b, c)* and hierarchical order (*A* is first, *B* second, and so forth) to delineate the "seven thousand Articles" of geographical entries.[18]

Morse and many of his fellow geographers advertised the proximity of their encyclopedic projects to literacy instruction. Advertised by various title headers such as "easy," "system," and "grammar," geography encyclopedias were framed in terms of literary research: in *Geography Made Easy* Morse "assures the public, that he has been assiduous in collecting every thing necessary to complete a book of this kind; for which purpose he has had recourse to a great variety of authors, miscellaneous papers,

18. Jedidiah Morse, *The American Gazetteer* . . . (Boston, 1797), i; Matthew H. Edney, "Reconsidering Enlightenment Geography and Map Making: Reconnaissance, Mapping, Archive," in Livingstone and Withers, eds., *Geography and Enlightenment,* 170.

and verbal information." Or they were framed in terms of reading. According to Morse's *Elements of Geography,* students "will be pleased and entertained, and their curiosity gratified, at the same time that they are making progress in the art of reading, and in the science of Geography." Morse, like many of the American textbook authors of the first generation, thus purposefully integrated geography into the pedagogic domain of language acquisition, asserting bibliographic and linguistic properties as the taxonomic tool for creating literary sense and order out of spatial information.[19]

Geographic reading begins with the most essential, basic element of alphabetic comprehension. Indeed, the ABCs figure prominently in geography textbooks; topographic shapes are likened to the letters of the alphabet, so that students literally learn to "read" the landscape. In *Geography; or, A Description of the World* (1814), Daniel Adams compares geographic knowledge to alphabetic literacy: "The natural and artificial divisions of the earth, the courses of rivers, and the relative position of cities and towns, are mechanical in their nature, as much as the letters of the alphabet." In Goldsmith's *Easy Grammar of Geography,* orthographic competence is integrated into the acquisition of geographic knowledge; he informs his audience of the need for "a Vocabulary of Proper Names of Places, divided and accented in the way in which they are usually pronounced . . . [and that] the letters are understood to possess the ordinary powers of the English language." A geographic education is presented as the result of learning to read and pronounce words from a dictionary. Indeed, as Goldsmith's title indicates, in a larger sense geography is presumed to be structured like a language.[20]

The study of geography thus followed the same progression as literacy training; the student made his or her way from the alphabet to grammatical structures to reading competence. This development is made explicit in Adams's text. Dividing the study of geography into sections, Adams distinguishes three types of categories: *geographical orthography* ("In the *first part* the pupil acquires the spelling and the pronunciation of the names of those kingdoms, countries, mountains, rivers, seas, lakes, islands, etc."); *grammar of geography* ("The *second part* contains the prin-

19. Morse, *Geography Made Easy,* 1; Morse, *Elements of Geography,* vi.

20. Daniel Adams, *Geography; or, A Description of the World* (Boston, 1814), 3; Goldsmith, *An Easy Grammar of Geography,* 109.

ciples of Geography . . . and is that part *designed to be committed to memory*"); and, finally, *geography* ("The *third part* is a further illustration of the same subjects, together with a particular account of the climate, soil, productions . . . *designed for reading in private, or by classes in schools*").[21]

The pedagogy of geography was thus directly fashioned after the pedagogy of letters. In this, the American textbook authors distinguished themselves from their European counterparts. European texts followed the dictum that "geography is the eye and key of history," an idea that privileged the visual over the textual, the map over the word. In contrast, American textbooks emphatically gave primacy to the textual over the visual, the word over the map. Nathaniel Carter argued in *A Geographical Vocabulary* (1813) for subordinating the map image to that of a geographer's dictionary. While he supports the pedagogic method "that maps must be studied by themselves, and not merely turned to occasionally while the scholar is reading," he also argues: "Methods of teaching the maps . . . [are] imperfect . . . for the want of a Vocabulary. . . . After becoming perfect in this Vocabulary, he is prepared for reading GEOGRAPHY." Calling upon the art of reading and writing (Carter's "vocabulary"), American geographers conceived their subject matter in logocentric terms; the fallible, ambiguous, and unpronounceable form of the map is inferior to the security and stability of the written word.[22]

By privileging the word, United States textbook authors reacted against the primacy of the map, in particular the map logo and its promise to reduce the complexity of geographical knowledge to a didactic shorthand. Indeed, fearing the loss of control over the message and the medium of the textbooks, Morse even goes so far as to nearly write the map out of his book. The visual memorization of place-names on a map is sup-

21. Adams, *Geography*, 3–4.

22. Nathaniel Carter, *A Geographical Vocabulary, Designed as a Guide to a Topographical Knowledge of the Whole Surface of the Globe, by Maps* (Portland, Maine, 1813), iv, v. Geography as eye: cited in *The Young Woman's Companion, in Grammar, Writing, Arithmetic, Geography, Bee-Keeping* (Manchester, Eng., 1806), 258. European geographers had been praising the eye as the principal means of communicating geographical knowledge at least since Isaac Watts wrote, "How can our Meditations follow the Blessed Apostles in their laborious Journies thro' Europe and Asia . . . unless we are instructed by Maps and Tables, wherein those Regions are copied out in a narrow Compass, and exhibited in one View to the Eye?" *The Knowledge of the Heavens and the Earth Made Easy* . . .(London, 1736), vi-vii.

planted by the mnemonic strategies afforded by the alphabet; geographical data are best recalled through words, not cartographic forms. Morse writes that while

> geographical facts may be arranged . . . to assist the memory . . . [a] mode of assisting the memory is by an ingenious combination of the initials of names. The word VIBGYOR [violet, indigo(?), blue, green, yellow, orange, red] contains the initials of seven primary colors, in the order in which they appear in the rainbow. This method may in some instances be successfully applied to Geography. For example: the three large towns, Boston, Albany, and Detroit, are near the same parallel of latitude, and the initials spell BAD. Montreal, Albany, and New York are near the same meridian, and the initials spell MAN.

In his enthusiasm and urgency to replace the function of the map, Morse seems un–self-conscious about the ideational complications of associating his preferred northern climes with BAD MAN (not to mention the elocutionary challenges of VIBGYOR).[23]

And yet, *Elements of Geography* ends with a teacher's classroom fantasy, in which discipline becomes meshed with patriotism. The author demands that the student repeat after him: "I am truly delighted, Sir, with the account you have given of my country, and I am sure I shall love it more than I ever did before. I hope I shall always be disposed to respect and obey my rulers." While the closing is a way to exhort the proper credit and respect due to the teacher, it also returns the text to its original and most fundamental aim: the teaching of geography is intended to breed patriotism. Webster's initial request for books that will "call home the minds of youth and fix them upon the interests of their own country, and . . . assist in forming attachments to it" is met in Morse's textbooks, designed so that "at the same time that [students] are learning to read, [they] might imbibe an acquaintance with their country, and an attachment to its interests." The gargantuan tomes of intricate taxonomic geographical information were geared toward creating a strong affective bond between reader and the fragile new nation. This goal of creating an emotional response, one of "love" and "attachment," was utterly crucial to the success of the geographic agenda. Judging by self-depictions in diaries and portraits, the agenda succeeded, aided in part by the descriptive, encyclo-

23. Jedidiah Morse, *Geography Made Easy* . . . (Boston, 1820), iii–iv.

pedic, and, above all, comparative narrative practices of many geography textbooks.[24]

GEOGRAPHIC READERS

How did readers of geography respond to these books? Evidentiary traces of cultural practices give us an indication of how geographic texts operated in personal, institutional, and familial settings. By the 1790s, at a time when book ownership was becoming the rule of middle-class respectability, the Connecticut farmer and local politician Sherman Boardman made a point of having his portrait painted while tracing a map in an open geography book (Figure 44). This staged self-representation was corroborated by his family's observation that he was generally "celebrated for his attainments in geography." Just as Sherman Boardman prided himself in owning geographic knowledge, so too did the literary acquisition of geography lessons play a decisive role in the life of the schoolgirl Sally Ripley of Greenfield, Massachusetts. In 1800, at the age of fifteen, she entered into her diary on Monday, February 23, "This day I attended school . . . and recited a lesson in Geography." According to other entries she practiced her geography on several days of the week and throughout the school year. Ripley's diary also lists her extracurricular reading activities, including poems and the occasional popular didactic novel. But at the end of the year, when she takes stock of her readings, she fails to mention these novels. Instead, Ripley proudly notes, "During this year I have been engaged in the following studies, Reading, Spelling, Writing, Arithmetic, Grammar, Geography and Speaking." Reflecting the success of the textbook ideology, Ripley locates geography primarily in the company of other linguistic skills. Ripley's self-monitored reading history dwindled rapidly after she left school and ended abruptly shortly after her marriage. Of course, that she stopped recording her reading does not mean that she stopped reading altogether. But, while she kept notes on her reading activities, Sally Ripley's diary points us to the protocols of geographic education and how these informed the construction of the early national reader.[25]

24. Ibid. (Boston, 1800), iv, 65, 121.

25. Elizabeth Mankin Kornhauser et al., *Ralph Earl: The Face of the Young Republic* (Hartford, Conn., 1991), 216; "The Diary of Sally Ripley," 41, MS, American Antiquarian Society, Worcester, Mass.

Figure 44. Sherman Boardman. *By Ralph Earl. 1796.* Courtesy, The New Milfrod Historical Society, Connecticut

These cameos of personal reading histories suggest that, in the early Republic, geography constituted a broad literary movement of symbolic educational value rather than the self-advertised practical use. Sherman Boardman's portrait celebrates the reading as well as the ownership of geography books. The significance of geography books becomes even more apparent when we return to other early national portraits. There we see patrons frequently holding a book, and in those cases where they are legible we see Americans pose either with the Bible, account books, or geographies marked by foldout maps (see Chapter 3 and Figure 33). As noted earlier, national maps became an icon injecting national identity into many attempts at self-representation in the early Republic. In the case of these portraits, however, the map is a book insert, a material supplement and synecdochic extension of the main body of the geography book. The book becomes a primary focal point inside the domestic setting, and thus inside the pedagogic space of elementary education and socialization. In this spatial scenario it is not a coincidence that the geography books on display are textbooks. In the Smith family portrait by Ralph Earl it is the school-age son who holds the geography book while showing off its foldout map of America.

Early national schoolbook illustrations show how elementary geo-

GEOGRAPHY

graphic instructions brought children into contact with maps, globes, and textbooks at an early age. As suggested by some frontispieces, the pedagogic arrangement of geography followed the heuristic or Rousseauean principle of personal guidance by showing a schoolmaster intimately conversing with his pupil while explaining the geographic concepts of spatial cognition and the organization of local knowledge (Figure 45). At the same time, others showed that geographic education also closely followed a more disciplinarian model, depicting ferule-wielding teachers dominating a classroom full of boys who, standing up like choristers, recite aloud the geography lessons learned (Figure 46).

As an extension of these images, Sally Ripley's diary is significant in that she records the programmatic diffusion of geographic instruction as a valued subject that testified to her intellectual competence. As Ripley's

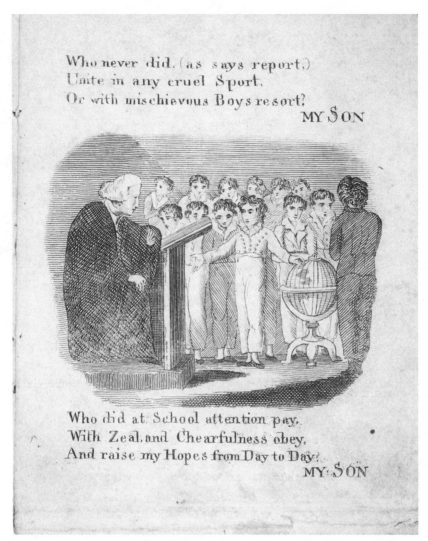

Figure 46. Boy Standing before Schoolmaster. From My Son, *by Richard Gregory. 1816.*
Courtesy, American Antiquarian Society

diary illustrates, geographic instruction was central to the education of girls as well as of boys. Diary entries like hers document the much-noted increase in female literacy following the Revolution. They further indicate that, among the growing cohort of newly alphabetized citizens, geography books had emerged as a literary form that supplemented as well as informed advanced reading and writing lessons. In this context, Sally's education in geography anticipates that of Catharine Beecher, who, as a

Figure 47. Detail from Miniature Panorama: Scenes from a Seminary for Young Ladies. *Circa 1810–1820.* Courtesy, The Saint Louis Art Museum

student at Litchfield Female Academy in 1810, "found grammar, arithmetic, geography, history, and the 'accomplishments' of map-drawing, painting, embroidery, and piano available." In a time when women's education expanded significantly and female literacy was increasingly perceived as socially useful, all-female schools (including Susanna Rowson's Boston academy) differentiated between geography "book" lessons and "map-drawing." Privileging book learning over the decorative arts, geography became the educational status symbol for American daughters and idealized future mothers (Figure 47).[26]

Indeed, for both genders geography became one of the subjects representative of official education. On public examination days, both boys' and girls' schools demanded the extensive recitation and even written reproduction of geographic knowledge. For example, in 1785 the *Pennsylvania Gazette* reported, "Friday last the students of the Trenton Academy were

26. On women and literacy, see Monaghan, "Literacy Instruction," in Davidson, ed., *Reading in America,* 70–74; William J. Gilmore, *Elementary Literacy on the Eve of the Industrial Revolution: Trends in Rural New England, 1760–1830* (Worcester, Mass., 1982); Gilmore, *Reading Becomes a Necessity,* chap. 3; Mary Kelley, "Reading Women/Women Reading: The Making of Learned Women in Antebellum America," *Journal of American History,* LXXXIII (1996–1997), 401–424. On Catharine Beecher, see Nancy F. Cott, *The Bonds of Womanhood: "Woman's Sphere" in New England, 1780–1835* (New Haven, Conn., 1977), 115.

publicly examined in Latin and English Grammar, in Geography, and in the other branches of Education taught in this seminary." In 1788, the same newspaper reported how in Philadelphia "on Monday the 3d inst. and on Tuesday the 4th, was held the Quarterly Examination of the YOUNG LADIES belonging to Mr. POOR's Academy . . . in reading, writing, arithmetic, grammar, geography, etc." Within the institutional setting of the school, geography figured as one of the first intensive and extensive reading activities; within the setting of the new nation-state geographical literacy became one more cultural passport identifying the individual citizen.[27]

THE TEXTBOOK AS NOVEL:
GEOGRAPHIC SETTINGS AND LITERARY CHARACTERS

I return to Morse's dictum that "geography is a speceies of composition." The compositional nature of geography textbooks was particularly obvious within geographic writing manuals, as the reader is also to become the writer, practicing the paleography and orthography required for good geography. More generally, the entire enterprise of writing a geography book was cast not only as a compositional exercise but as a literary undertaking. Introducing *A New System of Modern Geography* (1794) to his American audience, the Englishman William Guthrie confessed, "Upon close examination, he [the author] very soon discovered, that the grammar, which had been so long, and so loudly celebrated, united, in many passages, almost every fault, that can disgrace a literary composition." In castigating the success of British school geographies, Guthrie discreetly praises the literary merits of his own text. Geography books were often self-conscious of their literary qualities. When Robert Davidson decided to write a geographic textbook in rhymed couplets, for example, he was clearly transforming geographic information into a distinctly literary form. In other instances, the literary influence is more subtle. Such is the case with Morse's influential textbooks. Through extensive descriptive passages, Morse's textbooks begin to assume a seminovelistic form. In creating a narrative depth to his litany of place-names, Morse creates settings and characters that are charged with a novelistic aesthetic.[28]

Morse's successful books, in particular his magisterial *American Uni-*

27. See *Pennsylvania Gazette,* Apr. 13, 1785, Mar. 12, 1788.

28. William Guthrie, *A New System of Modern Geography; or, A Geographical, Historical, and Commercial Grammar; and Present State of the Several Nations of the World* (Philadelphia, 1794), I, 3.

versal Geography, illustrate the way in which textbooks not only shaped a geographic reading protocol but, by obeying the textbook's structural organization, engendered a narrative pattern consisting of national reduction and reproduction. In order to launch the process of reduction, Morse radically inverted the European standard for representing the world. Like his transatlantic competitors, Morse followed the traditional two-part textbook structure that for centuries had divided the world into the geography of Europe and the geography of colonial possessions on the remaining continents. However, for the first time in Western print history, Morse imposed a New World order by starting with the description of North America—in particular the United States—*before* delineating the rest of the Americas, Europe, Africa, and Asia. Through this geographic recomposition of the traditional geographer's narrative space, Morse at once forced his audience to assume an overtly nationalist and competitive perspective.

Morse's *American Universal Geography* reproduced the figure of the nation by strategically replacing maps or other geographic images with word compositions that were at once encylopedic and novelistic. On a practical level, each of his textbooks demands that the reader shuttle back and forth between the book's foldout maps and its encyclopedic textbook entries. Of the few illustrations that Morse allowed to be bound into his *American Universal Geography,* the foldout image of the world map was prominently located at the beginning. Two types of world maps, the equatorial map and the Mercator map, functioned to situate the reader's perspective before organizing the book's textual materials. These maps presented the world geography in its most basic skeletal framework, as a relatively uninscribed and hence strategically emptied space. In each map type, the United States appears as a blank space, bound by geographic coordinates, political boundaries, and a few place-names. It became the task of the geography book to flesh out this frame by linking boundary lines and place-names to detailed descriptive accounts, always moving from the more general region and geopolitical unit to the more particular local settings. In the case of the United States, the reader moves from the map to the book section called "America," to the section entitled "United States," until reaching, for example, the more particular geopolitical entity of the state of "New York."[29]

29. Jedidiah Morse, *The American Universal Geography* . . . (Boston, 1793), is the expanded version of his *American Geography* . . . (Elizabethtown, N.J., 1789), subsequently referred to as *AUG.*

In the course of the encyclopedic reading exercise, Morse transforms the mapping of the state into geographic settings; as the reader progresses deeper and deeper into the book, the description becomes thicker and thicker. "New York," for example, gains shape and a differentiated identity when Morse lists specific geographic landmarks. Moving through the state's natural properties, Morse describes in succession the "Rivers and Canals," followed by the "Face of the Country, Mountains, Soil and Productions." Moving from the natural to the cultural habitats of the state, Morse concentrates on the "Chief Towns." In the case of New York City, he first sketches out its plan before taking the reader to the various neighborhoods, which in later editions comprised a tour of the "Battery," "Broadstreet," "Churches," the "Almshouse," the "state prison," and the "hospital." By the end of the chapter (this is the standard pattern among early American textbooks) Morse has provided the reader with a descriptive tour of the state's physical and cultural geography. As his textbook repeats this tour for each and every state, Morse fills out the frame of the nation's body politic, giving it the spatial appearance of a thickly described text whose inclusive reading protocol is metonymically bound to and contained by the geography book itself.[30]

Morse's taxonomic description also functions selectively, reducing the geographic horizon to a handful of stereotypical settings that are as much geographic as they are literary types. Early national geography textbooks applied the ideas of environmental determinism that, on the one hand, sought to codify moral-ethnic valences between geographic places and their inhabitants while, on the other hand, propagating a narrative that polarized the sociological landscape, moving along meridional lines from north to south. For Morse, the textbook entries labeled as the "Face of the Country" became the narrative space in which he converted and encoded the sprawling space of national geography into a few memorable generic settings. Beginning in the north, the geography student discovers a physical setting whose lack of natural resources (there are no precious metals to be mined or cash crops to be raised) becomes valuable for its aesthetic potential. For example, New Hampshire is described as a rocky, hilly, and generally infertile environment. But, having said that, Morse writes in the section "New Hampshire—Face of the Country":

These vast and irregular heights, being copiously replenished with water, exhibit a great variety of beautiful cascades; some of which, fall in a

30. *AUG*, 419–427, 458–459; 4th ed. (Boston, 1802), 472–476.

perpendicular sheet or spout, others are winding and sloping, others spread, and form a bason in the rock, and then gush in a cataract over its edge. A poetic fancy may find full gratification amidst these wild and rugged scenes, if its ardor be not checked by the fatigue of the approach. Almost every thing in nature, which can be supposed capable of inspiring ideas of the sublime and beautiful, is here realized. Aged mountains, stupendous elevations, rolling clouds, impending rocks, verdant woods, chrystal streams, the gentle rill, and the roaring torrent, all conspire to amaze, to soothe and to enrapture.

In comparison to this aesthetic setting of the north, Morse defines the mid-Atlantic region in purely functional terms, as the nation's quintessential workshop. In the case of Pennsylvania, the topographic description of the country recedes behind the verbal image of an industrial map showing, for example, the homogeneous distribution of mill sites:

Among the natural advantages of Pennsylvania, her almost innumerable mill seats ought not to be omitted. They are conveniently distributed by Providence throughout the state, and afford the means of establishing every species of mill work and labour-saving machines, to meet the produce and raw materials almost at the farmers doors.

Aside from mills, the typical mid-Atlantic landscape includes the detailed listings of travel roads and routes, time and distance markers, specific statistical information regarding the flow of goods and money, and the more prominent sites of commercial exchange.[31]

In contrast to these two northern scenes, Morse composes two settings intended to be representative of the southern states. Looking up the state of North Carolina, the reader is given two geographic landscapes, one being a veritable death zone and the other a Lubberland, an imaginary land of plenty without labor. Thus, under the header of "North Carolina—Face of the Country, Soil and Production," we read about the coastal region:

North Carolina, in its whole width, for 60 miles from the sea, is a dead level. A great proportion of this tract lies in forest, and is barren. . . . [Climate, Diseases, etc.] In the flat country, near the sea coast, the inhabitants, during the summer and autumn, are subject to intermitting fevers, which often prove fatal, as bilious or nervous symptoms

31. *AUG*, 333, 476.

prevail . . . if suffered to continue for any length of time, [the fevers] bring on other disorders, which greatly impair the natural vigor of the mind, debilitate the constitution, and terminate in death.

This fatal setting is offset by that of the mountainous "Backcountry" ("Sixty or eighty miles from the sea, the country rises into hills and mountains"), in which Morse observes a constant increase in population.

To explain this we must observe that the human species, and all other animals, are found to increase in proportion to the comforts of life, and the ease with which they can support their progeny. Remove the rigors of an inhospitable climate, and the more uniform dissuasive to matrimony, the *apprehended* difficulty of supporting a family, and the human species would double, not in 20 but in 15 years. In North Carolina, neither the cold of winter, nor the heat of summer, are in the back country, at all disagreeable; land continues to be plenty and cheap; grain is raised with so much ease, and the trouble of providing for cattle in winter so trifling, that a man supports his family with half the labour that is required in the cold climates.

Textbook entries like these not only imitate and reify what were essentially literary settings; they also cloak these settings under the authoritative mantle of scientific objectivity.[32]

According to the logic of geography books, each setting is representative of a material reality that the geography books reproduce according to the code of empirical enumeration and scientific observation. Places are described, not idiosyncratically and spontaneously, but according to the principle of the modern experiment and deductive reasoning. Ideally each setting comprised a limited set of elements that were static, easily discernible, and infinitely reproducible. Or, in other words, Morse's settings became the programmatic apparatus ascribing, like a scale of weights or a water gauge, descriptive differences that were deemed quantifiable and universal. Morse's textbooks, like those of many of his peers, expand the taxonomic protocol of Enlightenment sciences and apply the method of inductive modeling. The textbook entries simply assert the absolute value of a place through a set of descriptive binaries (north-south, cold-hot, rocks-swamps, fertile-barren, empty-full, moral-immoral). As each binary purports to consist of essentially quantifiable information (we can measure the temperature—so why not measure morality?), Morse's descrip-

32. *AUG*, 576–577, 580.

tion transforms physical geography into a moral geography. His cultural geography builds upon the stadial theory of civilization as proposed by eighteenth- and nineteenth-century European philosophers from Giambattista Vico to Georg Wilhelm Hegel. According to this dialectical theory, society moves from the barbaric to the civilized over the course of history, or—as the favorite interpretation of eighteenth-century geographers would have it—according to a society's geographic location.[33]

In American geography books, this stadial theory of civilization creates a dialectic pitting the narrative structure of the nation's geography against other modes of narrative, in particular, history. Ideally, visitors traveling in New Hampshire, Pennsylvania, or North Carolina would record the same geographic elements and thus deliver descriptions that were identical with the textbook entries. In the case of Morse's textbooks, however, the narrative elements prepared the reader, as he or she would have memorized the setting *before* visiting the actual place. Thus Morse's textbooks walk the reader through a thick geographic description that builds the nation's history as a chapter in a quasi-novelistic account. While moving through a landscape marked by local difference, the geographic reader occupies settings marked by a sense of timelessness and sameness that was the hallmark of fiction.

A similar narrative logic informs the representation of the American character. If the world map engendered the notion of comparative horizontal inclusion (the multitude of nation-states are equally discrete units on the map), then Morse's description of the United States' "Character and Manners" places individual citizens on a playing field marked by cultural differences. "Federal Americans," Morse writes, "collected together from various countries, of different habits, formed under different governments, have yet to form their national character." If we turn to the example of New York, Morse turns the sociological landscape into one defined by demography and linguistics. Under the rubric "Population and Character," Morse cites statistical records, in particular the first census report of 1790, to which he adds cultural attributes in order to define the people of New York. Morse concentrates on the state's dominant

33. Historians of geography have emphasized that from the times of Ptolemy and Strabo geography has functioned as a text differentiating the status of cultures; already then geographic "klimata"—or coordinates—served to locate, identify, and control newly formed communities, and geographic descriptions determined and transfixed the subject's position within a national frame of reference.

language and observes that "the English language is generally spoken throughout the state," but that at the same time "the manners of the people differ as well as their language." Morse here identifies New York as a polyglot community consisting of a more locally defined people who, on the one hand, are loosely united by the English language, but on the other fail to present a unified character because of the pervasive profusion of linguistic variants.[34]

But, unlike Noah Webster, who sought to overcome difference by eradicating local dialects, Morse's strategy for nationalizing the collective body of "Federal Americans" does not so much resist the practice of regional dialects as supersede local differences by invoking the literary authority of his textbook settings. Morse stabilizes the linguistic diversity and character of the imagined people by sidestepping the conceptual link between social manners and the New Yorkers' dialects. Instead, he locates the speakers' linguistic identities inside their respective geographic settings, invoking geographic location and environmental difference. Thus, under the entry header "New Hampshire—Population and Character," the reader finds the statement: "The inhabitants of New Hampshire, like the settlers in all new countries, are in general, a hardy, robust, active, brave people." For "the Pennsylvanian character," which is diagnosed as hopelessly slippery because polyglot, Morse determines, "As the leading traits in this character, thus constituted, we may venture to mention industry, frugality, bordering in some instances on parsimony, enterprize, a taste and ability for improvements in mechanics, in manufactures."[35]

The slightly critical inflection of the Pennsylvania character, which was farther south than New Hampshire, here testifies to Morse's northern, New England bias. According to this bias only the New Englanders were described as "a hardy race of free, independent republicans," who, famous for industry, lived without any "temptations to luxury" in a state of "happy mediocrity." Farther south, the people of Maryland "appear to live very retired and unsocial lives. The effects of this comparative solitude are visible in the countenances, as well as in the manners and dress of many of the country people. . . . As the negroes perform all the manual labour, their masters are left to saunter away life in sloth, and too often in ig-

34. *AUG,* 208–209, 426.
35. *AUG,* 341, 481.

norance." The entry following "North Carolina—Population, Character, Manners and Customs" reports this:

> They appear to have little taste for the sciences. . . . Less attention and respect are paid to the women here. . . . Temperance and industry are not to be reckoned among the virtues of the North Carolinians. The time which they waste in drinking, idling and gambling, leaves them very little opportunity to improve their plantations or their minds. . . . The citizens of North Carolina . . . spend their time in drinking, or gaming at cards and dice, in cock fighting or horse racing . . . [and] a strange and very barbarous practice . . . called gouging . . . when boxing, putting out the eye of his antagonist with his thumb.

Chapter for chapter, state after state, Morse here consolidates the multitude of local characters into a few regional geographic types. As the art historian Elizabeth Johns has observed when discussing early republican genre paintings: "Regional differences in the citizenry promoted stereotyping. . . . Reifying these several kinds of differences, citizens began as early as the 1780s to categorize the social body . . . by inventing types that were singularly American: the Yankee, the Kentuckian, the black, the domestic woman, and the urban street child." In the same way, Morse's textbooks began the rehearsal of fictional character types—today identified by readers as the thrifty New Englander, the lazy Virginia Gentleman, the Vanishing Indian, and the Docile Slave or Female—which became ultimately subordinated to the geographically constructed idea of the nation (that is, the image of the national map and the printed textbook header, "The United States"). As the practice of geographic typing moved with the student reader in and out of classrooms and schooling in general, the geoliterate constructions of local types became a basic part of the reader's everyday perception. Such typing configured en masse the reader's expectation of what constituted the national space and its generalized occupants, the regional characters.[36]

Morse presented his national survey of American characters—couching local character traits within the narrative of the national map image or geography book—at the same time as many of his peers were invested in the figuration of national character. During the 1780s and 1790s, "the discourse of character and national character informed changing rela-

36. *AUG*, 311, 314, 352, 581. On regional genre painting, see Elizabeth Johns, *American Genre Painting: The Politics of Everyday Life* (New Haven, Conn., 1991), 11–12.

tionships between citizens and structures of power." Significantly, American writers summoned with great regularity the national character as a dual pedagogic trope vacillating between fantasies of discipline and fictional identity. At the height of the Federalist debate, James Madison discerns in *The Federalist* that nothing harmed American interests more, abroad and at home, than the "want of a due sense of national character." He seems to cringe when asking, "What has not America lost by her want of character with foreign nations; and how many errors and follies would she not have avoided?" Similarly, Noah Webster concludes in his *American Magazine,* "Every engine should be employed to render the people of this country national, to call their attachments home to their own country, and to inspire them with the pride of national character."[37]

The focus on the figure of the "national character" was more than a timely rhetorical ploy; it resonated with the various eighteenth-century definitions of the term "character." Samuel Johnson's *Dictionary* defines the term "national" unequivocally, as something "publick; general; not private; not particular." But the term "character" proves to be more elastic. By the 1780s, according to the *Oxford English Dictionary,* "character" could denote, first, a graphic symbol; second, an aggregate of distinctive features, in particular the sum of the moral and mental qualities that presumably distinguished an individual or a race (or a nation); and, third, a distinctive personality, in particular the emergent novelistic form of the fictional character. The idea of a national character is thus inherently paradoxical, or, rather, imagined; it requires the constant suspension of disbelief because it is at once defined as general and as a distinctive concept of identity. Further, "character" at once denotes innate personal traits and the mechanical, abstracted form of alphabetic letters, the true nature of an individual as well as artificial construct. The national character is at once a function of literacy (alphabetic characters), regional traits, and a fictional persona.[38]

37. David Waldstreicher, *In the Midst of Perpetual Fetes: The Making of American Nationalism, 1776–1820* (Chapel Hill, N.C., 1997), 124–125; James Madison, Federalist No. 63, in William R. Brock, ed., *The Federalist; or, The New Constitution* (London, 1992), 322; Webster, *American Magazine,* in Hans Kohn, *The Idea of Nationalism: A Study of Its Origins and Background* (New York, 1944), 305.

38. The discourse of character is often viewed in context of state power. See Pierre Bourdieu, "Identity and Representation: Elements for a Critical Reflection on the Idea of Region," in Bourdieu, *Language and Symbolic Power,* ed. John B. Thompson, trans. Gino Raymond and Matthew Adamson (Cambridge, Mass., 1991), 220–228.

Geography books naturalized the idea of national character precisely by their strategic merger of graphic symbols (national map), verbal representation (encyclopedic delineation of the nation-state), and geographical personification (types). These books modeled character types for a generation of readers that was unsure about the relationship between local and national identities. The textbooks' characters provided fictional models introducing a sense of regional identity. Through the constant invocation of the national map and geography, many geographies further essentialized the characters by stripping their regional connotation until they became representatives of an "American" national character. When taken to its logical conclusion, the textbook-induced typology of regional stereotypes promulgated the idea that locally defined acts of geographic reading could be nothing but part and parcel of a collectively enacted memory. This memory, though established inside the disciplinary context of education, was not a function of institutional or state power. Rather, it was the product of a participatory culture in which geographical literacy became fused to the standards of self-cultivation and literary taste. As geography books thus informed and formed individual authors, readers, and publishing conventions, at least during the early decades after Independence they performed the kind of cultural work that is often attributed to the nineteenth-century literary classic. Through geographic reading lessons the idea of national identity was made immediately obvious and became diffused to the point that it became permanently integrated into the consciousness of the popular reader.[39]

39. I refer to Philip Fisher's discussion of cultural work in *Hard Facts: Setting and Form in the American Novel* (New York, 1987), 3–5.

chapter five

NOVEL GEOGRAPHIES

OF THE REPUBLIC

We have seen how geography textbooks ultimately assumed novelistic properties. At the same time, early American novels incorporated and responded to geographic reading practices. Geography textbooks ranked with Bibles and spellers as best-sellers in the late eighteenth century. However, many people believed that novels dominated their neighbors' reading habits. Either to promote or castigate novel reading, authors both praised and damned this genre. For example, in 1797 the editor of the *New-York Magazine* confidently proclaimed, "This is a novel-reading age." In the same year, the novelist Royall Tyler observed in *The Algerine Captive,* "Country booksellers, fostering the new-born taste of the people, [have] filled the whole land with modern travels and novels." By contrast, outspoken critics of the form, such as the Reverend Samuel Miller, diagnosed a Republic caught up in a novel frenzy: "All classes of persons in society, from the dignified professional character to the lowest grades of labouring indigence, seek and devour novels."[1]

In assessing early American novels, literary surveys have emphasized, as has Michael T. Gilmore, that "the founding of the American polity and the creation of the native novel occurred at virtually the same moment." For citizens of the early Republic, "works of fiction facilitate[d] the abstract conceptualization necessary to nationalism by dramatizing a bounded human community," a process that was inextricably bound up in the novel. Carroll Smith-Rosenberg summarizes the larger critical consensus: "From the mid-eighteenth century on, much of the work of in-

1. *New-York Magazine,* n.s., II (1797), 398, cited in Robert B. Winans, "The Growth of a Novel-Reading Public in Late-Eighteenth-Century America," *Early American Literature,* IX (1975), 272; Royall Tyler, *The Algerine Captive,* ed. Don L. Cook (1797; rpt. Albany, N.Y., 1970), 27; Samuel Miller, *A Brief Retrospect of the Eighteenth Century,* I (1803; rpt. New York, 1970), 172.

stituting a *Homo Americanus* took place upon the pages of the new nation's popular press—its newspapers, urban magazines, popular fiction." The works of authors such as Susanna Rowson and Charles Brockden Brown became the representative sites upon which "the new American subject was elaborated, problematized, and interpellated."[2]

The rise of nation-states and national ideologies was tied to novelistic characters, and the design and propagation of an American subjectivity was systemically linked to the novelistic construction of national communities. "It was the *novel*," as Timothy Brennan writes, "that historically accompanied the rise of nations by objectifying the 'one, yet many' of national life, and by mimicking the structure of the nation, a clearly bordered jumble of languages and styles." As a communicative form, the novel is usually defined by its capacity to incorporate other genres and its ability to organize the cacophonous diversity of extraliterary languages, social speech types, and so forth. Or, as Benedict Anderson has argued, it was the novel form that served to fold the individual subjects into the larger textuality of the nation by depicting "the movement of a solitary hero through a sociological landscape of a fixity that fuses the world inside the novel with the world outside."[3]

While not disputing these readings of the form and function of the

2. Michael T. Gilmore, "The Literature of the Revolutionary and Early National Periods," in Sacvan Bercovitch, ed., *The Cambridge History of American Literature*, I, *1590–1820* (Cambridge, 1994), 549; Carroll Smith-Rosenberg, "Subject Female: Authorizing American Identity," *American Literary History*, V (1993), 482. For materials exploring the relationship of national subjectivity to the novel, see the range of fascinating studies inspired by Cathy N. Davidson's *Revolution and the Word: The Rise of the Novel in America* (New York, 1986). For example, Michelle Burnham, *Captivity and Sentiment: Cultural Exchange in American Literature, 1682–1861* (Dartmouth, N.H., 1997); Jared Gardner, *Master Plots: Race and the Founding of an American Literature, 1787–1845* (Baltimore, 1998); Teresa A. Goddu, *Gothic America: Narrative, History, and Nation* (New York, 1997); Dana D. Nelson, *National Manhood: Capitalist Citizenship and the Imagined Fraternity of White Men* (Durham, N.C., 1998); Shirley Samuels, *Romances of the Republic: Women, the Family, and Violence in the Literature of the Early American Nation* (New York, 1996).

3. Timothy Brennan, "The National Longing for Form," in Homi K. Bhabha, ed., *Nation and Narration* (London, 1990), 49; Benedict Anderson, *Imagined Communities: Reflections on the Origin and Spread of Nationalism* (London, 1991), 24–25, 30. See also Michael McKeon, *The Origins of the English Novel, 1600–1740* (Baltimore, 1987); Ian Watt, *The Rise of the Novel: Studies in Defoe, Richardson, and Fielding* (Berkeley, Calif., 1957). This definition of the novel follows M. M. Bakhtin's definition of the novel as a heteroglot site of communication. See *The Dialogic Imagination: Four Essays,* ed. Michael Holquist, trans. Caryl Emerson and Michael Holquist (Austin, Tex., 1981), 6–7, 262–263.

novel, I want to focus on a phenomenon that complicates this nation-novel nexus in the early Republic. Several of the very novelists celebrated today for exploring the construction of the American subject ceased to publish novels in favor of writing geography schoolbooks. In 1800, after publishing *The Algerine Captive,* Royall Tyler proposed as his next book project a "Cosmography" for children. Two years earlier, Susanna Rowson had used her last novel, *Reuben and Rachel,* to announce, "As a novelist . . . I have made my last essay." Rowson then proceeded to write four schoolbooks, two of which were geography textbooks, *An Abridgment of Universal Geography* (1805) and *Youth's First Steps in Geography* (1818). And Charles Brockden Brown, upon completing his last novel, *Jane Talbot,* in 1801, took an equally profound geographic turn. Brown forsook writing his own novels in order to translate C. F. Volney's geographical treatise, *A View of the Soil and Climate of the United States* (1804). During the last years of his life, Brown worked on an ambitious two-volume geography book, *A System of General Geography,* which he advertised in a prospectus shortly before his death in 1810.[4]

In part, the interpenetration of geographic and novelistic genres was a natural function of the new spatialization of the evolving eighteenth-century novel. Anderson's invocation of the idea of "landscape" and the merging of "the world inside of the novel with the world outside" reflects not only the novel's capacious sense of setting but also the active dynamic of genres. The novel became an increasingly spatialized form. For Mikhail M. Bakhtin, the modern character emerged no longer "against

4. G. Thomas Tanselle, "Author and Publisher in 1800: Letters of Royall Tyler and Joseph Nancrede," *Harvard Library Bulletin,* XV (1967), 129; Susanna Rowson, *Reuben and Rachel; or, Tales of Old Times* (Boston, 1798), iv. This nation-novel nexus has historically been a bone of contention among scholars. Two schools of literary and cultural criticism have examined the burgeoning of nationalistic rhetoric that emerged in public speech and print in the early Republic. In the older school of criticism it was taken as token evidence of what I would call the "expressive literary nationalism"; see Benjamin T. Spencer, *The Quest for Nationality: An American Literary Campaign* (Syracuse, N.Y., 1957); Emory Elliott, *Revolutionary Writers: Literature and Authority in the New Republic, 1725–1810* (New York, 1982). For critical reexaminations of nationalism and literary production, see Jane Tompkins, *Sensational Designs: The Cultural Work of American Fiction, 1790–1860* (New York, 1985); Larzer Ziff, *Writing in the New Nation: Prose, Print, and Politics in the Early United States* (New Haven, Conn., 1991). For a skeptical examination of the meaning of the "national" in the early Republic, see Michael Warner, *The Letters of the Republic: Publication and the Public Sphere in Eighteenth-Century America* (Cambridge, Mass., 1990), 118–150.

the immobile background of the world, ready-made and basically quite stable" but was engendered by receiving through "the novel's plot . . . new and realistically productive points for viewing the world . . . and [thus] enters into a completely new, *spatial* sphere of historical existence." Franco Moretti likewise specifies the genre's spatial production of the modern self in national geographic terms. Discussing the bildungsroman and its construction of the modern self, he writes, "Just as in space it is essential to build a 'homeland' for the individual."[5]

American geography textbooks and novels, as much as they initially appear to be worlds apart, in fact share similar aims. Both endeavor through layered description of places and spaces to create a distinct sense of homeland. Through this geographic sense of plot or narrative the individual American subject is endowed with agency and national identity. Further, both genres work to create a feeling of homeland through the discourse of the passions. That the novel seeks to evoke an affective response in the reader is inherent in the eighteenth century's preoccupation with the subject of sentimental feeling. Sentimental response is also a fundamental goal of geography textbooks: Noah Webster specifies that their aim should be "to assist in forming attachments" to the reader's own country; Jedediah Morse follows these dictates, proclaiming that the purpose of his books is for readers to "imbibe an acquaintance with their country and [form] an attachment to its interests." The interpolation of geography textbooks and the novel thus becomes not merely a function of adapting structure and content (although early American novels *do* adapt the structure and content of popular geographic genres). Rather, by incorporating geographic elements, these novels also import the specific geographic discourse of nationalistic affect. The combined discourses of geographic feeling and novelistic sentimentality result in an affective surfeit that can stabilize as well as threaten the form of the novel and national ideology itself.[6]

---

5. M. M. Bakhtin, "The *Bildungsroman* and Its Significance in the History of Realism (Toward a Historical Typology of the Novel)," in Bakhtin, *Speech Genres and Other Late Essays,* ed. Caryl Emerson and Michael Holquist, trans. Vern W. McGee (Austin, Tex., 1986), 23–24; Franco Moretti, *The Way of the World: The "Bildungsroman" in European Culture* (London, 1987), 26. For Bakhtin the bildungsroman is the culmination of the novel's historical development, refining the travel novel, novel of ordeal, and biographical novel. While in the latter, geographic "setting" was a static device, it accretes meaning and even a lifelike function of its own in the former.

6. Noah Webster, "On the Education of Youth in America" (1788), in Frederick

Examining early American novels, geographic feelings prove to fulfill a stabilizing function in picaresque novels such as Tyler's *Algerine Captive,* the anonymous *History of Constantius and Pulchera* (1795), and James Butler's *Fortune's Football* (1798). Ostensibly extending the narrative formula of the early modern travelogue—for example, it inserts the first person pronoun or the narrative "I" into the catalog of events and objects described—the American picaresque novel has the generically prescribed journey into the greater world inadvertently morph, through the adaptation of geographic reading materials, into a sentimental journey home. While all three texts enacted the novelistic fantasy of the curious, transgressive, and ultimately expansionary individual whose geographic mobility allowed a world of external representation to become fused to an increasingly self-reflective subjectivity, it was their narrative fusion of the personal with the textualities of modern national geography that rendered the movement toward interiority incomplete. Two novels by Charles Brockden Brown further illustrate the vexed relationship between the early novel, geography books, and geographical literacy; *Jane Talbot* and *Edgar Huntly* exemplify two different responses to the tensions intrinsic to geography textbooks and their reading protocols in an era of national consolidation. These two novels, combined with Brown's obsession with geographic writing, present a paradox unique to Brown's career: even as he gave priority to writing geographies to the point of forsaking writing novels, his novels provide an extended critique examining the virtues and limitations of a culture trained to develop geographic feeling.

READING GEOGRAPHIC NOVELS

Given the extreme popularity of geography textbooks, it is no surprise to discover that early American novels become immersed in this genre, either because authors were themselves a product of an educational system in which geography predominated or because authors calculated that inflecting their novels with geographic discourse would increase their public appeal. In *The Algerine Captive,* geography shapes the novel's formal structure and presentation of national character types. The author

---

Rudolph, ed., *Essays on Education in the Early Republic* (Cambridge, Mass., 1965), 65; Jedidiah Morse, *Geography Made Easy: Being an Abridgement of the American Universal Geography* (Boston, 1800), iv.

imitates the conceptual structure of the early national textbooks, which create a division between America and the rest of the world. In the first part of *The Algerine Captive,* the solitary hero Captain Updike Underhill traverses the United States from north to south, rehearsing many of the local stereotypes made popular by Morse's school geographies, including the Yankee, the southern gentleman, and the slave. Moreover, in accordance with school geographies, Tyler gives the reader a tour of the territorially bounded sociological environment of the United States. The tour takes the reader through familiar scenes gleaned from various schoolbooks, including elementary literacy instruction ("read a lesson in Dilworth's spelling book, which I recited as loud as I could speak") and the fatal application of the narrator's literary education ("I killed a fat heifer . . . the process, notwithstanding I followed closely the directions in the *Georgics,* some how or other failed"). In the progress from north to south, Underhill, seeking employment as a recently apprenticed physician, visits the American city spaces of Boston, Philadelphia, and "the town of F—, in Virginia" and records several regional characters already stereotyped by Morse's moral geography: Virginians "hastened to the horse race" and "a game at cards or billiards," and New Englanders, "habituated to the social but respectful intercourse customary in the northern states," were applying themselves to "local business."[7]

Having thus treated the subject of North America, the second volume, like the second part of an American geography book, directs the reader to other global spaces. The second volume contrasts the American settings with North Africa. Underhill, describing his misfortune of becoming enslaved by Algerian pirates, offers a lengthy, encyclopedic description of Algeria's geography. As if copying the entries of contemporary textbooks, he informs the reader about the country's language, religion, and history, describing its "Infirmary," "the City of Algiers," "Government," "Reve-

7. Tyler, *Algerine Captive,* 45, 50, 94–97. The novel's publication also coincided with that of James Wilson Steven's textbook, *An Historical and Geographical Account of Algiers . . .* (Philadelphia, 1797). The tour of the first volume of *The Algerine Captive* ends with the narrator's taking his search for employment abroad. On his way to becoming a ship surgeon on a slave trader, he briefly visits London, where he sees the English as the historical prototype of the American national character, "a motley race in whose mongrel veins runs the blood of all nations" (99), thus adding the character figure of the "mongrel" (as did Crèvecoeur in his *Letters from an American Farmer* [1782]) to the already densely populated cast of American characters.

nue," "The Dey's Forces," and finally "Notices of the Habits, Customs, etc. of the Algerines."[8]

Tyler's *Algerine Captive* here imitates the metanarrative design of school geographies. Like these, the novel rapidly moves its hero and the reader through a series of descriptive geographic settings, and, like a geography textbook, the descriptions serve not only to educate the reader about the land but to instill a sense of regional difference and northern American cultural superiority. Indeed, the novel turns upon differential settings; throughout the story the reader coinhabits in rapid sequence two oppositional metasettings, New England and the southern states, the United States and North Africa. Inside these settings the spatial distribution of characters presents dialogues of cultural comparison, confirming geodeterministic types that are essential to the Western invention of the category of orientalism.[9]

In this context, it hardly comes as a surprise that the novel deploys its comparative geographical settings in order to translate the occidental narrative of Western homogeneity into one of national stability. As with the geography textbooks, Tyler's novel reveals that geographic reading, for all its pretense of mobilizing the reader, is a stationary progress that is predicated on the idea of national territoriality. Just as Morse's textbooks construct the United States (and not the home or the family) as the reader's primary setting, so too *The Algerine Captive* emphasizes the character's return to his native country rather than local community. Thus, having first depicted the United States as a nation sundered by the habit of regionalist typing, Tyler's novel ends on a unifying nationalistic note. After an absence of seven years, the traveling hero sentimentally discovers that there's no place like home outside the new American states. He uses his homecoming to cap the novel's nationalistic narrative arc by proclaiming the Federalist call of unity, "By uniting we stand, by dividing we fall."[10]

Two other picaresque novels, *The History of Constantius and Pulchera* (1795) and Butler's *Fortune's Football,* largely unfamiliar today but popular during the early decades of the nineteenth century, illustrate the

8. Tyler, *Algerine Captive,* 152–175.

9. On antebellum adaptations of geographical writings, see Bruce A. Harvey, *American Geographics: U.S. National Narratives and the Representation of the Non-European World, 1830–1865* (Stanford, Calif., 2001). On the European invention and intellectual history of the Orient, see Edward W. Said, *Orientalism* (New York, 1978).

10. Tyler, *Algerine Captive,* 224.

generic affinity between geography books, literacy instruction, and conceptions of national identity. Like Tyler's *Algerine Captive,* these novels also take the reader on a whirlwind journey, in the course of which they present inexhaustible genealogies of events and family histories. Additionally, they reconstruct countless geographic sites familiar to the experienced textbook reader, using a geographic signpost such as a place-name or prominent landmark in order to evoke the matching, carefully memorized textbook entries. In *The History of Constantius and Pulchera* the reader's horizon expands from Philadelphia to encompass geographic sites along the North Atlantic rim (Essex, Massachusetts, Bordeaux, Lisbon), only to return in the end to the capital of the United States. In *Fortune's Football,* the hero (and reader) also occupies in quick succession a series of geographic locales: London, Venice, Malta, Algiers, London, Quebec, Florence, Esfahan, Baghdad, Moscow, and again London.[11]

The History of Constantius and Pulchera and *Fortune's Football* are not simply geographic in the sense that characters travel and see the world. These novels are shaped by the reading practices taught in geography textbooks. The act of reading *The History of Constantius and Pulchera* takes place in the textual setting of the spelling book. The school-age character Pulchera moves through a verbal landscape consisting of rote word exercises in which both she and the reader practice, in the spirit of Dilworth and Webster, a polysyllabic vocabulary. This vocabulary "call[s] upon the reader's ready imagination to fill in the lacunae in the notably undelineated plot." Words like "bountiful," "inexhaustible," and "benevolent" operate as semantic proxies signifying educational capital and social status; the academic recital of complex words we are thus to imagine operates as a bridge, allowing the reader to insert personal experiences into the fictionalized representation of social intercourse. The mastery of a geographic vocabulary was also a central element of geography textbooks. Thus, the perceived lacunae are supplied with the nomenclature of a geographic vocabulary where words such as "Philadelphia," "Essex," "Quebeck," and "Bourdeaux" are linguistic as well as narrative placeholders, inserting into the novel not just geographical knowledge but the pedagogic practices surrounding the acquisition of geographical literacy.[12]

A similar kind of geographic determination informs the reading expe-

11. *The History of Constantius and Pulchera; or, Constancy Rewarded* . . . (Salem, Mass., 1795); James Butler, *Fortune's Football; or, The Adventures of Mercutio: Founded on Matters of Fact* (Harrisburg, Pa., 1797–1798).

12. Davidson, *Revolution and the Word,* 185.

rience of Butler's two-part novel *Fortune's Football*. Here the reader again enters a stylized selection of metasettings and national character types similar to those conveyed by geography textbooks. Driven by the novel's romance plot of a young couple's love lost and found, the protagonist Mercutio becomes the novelized geographer. Like a textbook reader, he tours the world as if it were a geographical dictionary. But instead of using the alphabet to enter the text of the world or to organize the narrative sequence, he recites, as if on command and at random, geographical knowledge gained by rote memorization. Using city names as narrative place markers, he rehearses encyclopedic vignettes of topographic and sociological landscapes, because as a habit he "attended all public places of recreation." Next to the physical geography he reports on the civic one, on the forms of government, military strength, and the "customs and manners" such as the costumes of the Spanish nobleman or the marriage ritual of the Persian "Sophi" culture. The novel's apparent irregularity in plot and character description is modeled after the late-eighteenth-century genre of narrative geographies, an English genre of illustrated anthologies that became increasingly popular in the United States beginning in the 1790s. These books were illustrated reader's digests. Their anthologized narrative excerpts and abridged textbook entries described national cultures, and the books' plates reified them as types by depicting settings and costumes that were considered representative of, say, North Africans or Native Americans. Furthermore, these narratives and character types were read in tandem with world maps, such as Thomas Jefferys's board game map (Figure 48), in which the reader, by advancing from numbered place to numbered place, not only practiced geography through textbook excerpts written in the map margins but learned how to identify the pictorial representation of characters as a narrative function of geographic reading.[13]

The novel *Fortune's Football* illustrates geographic reading practices in that its kaleidoscopic array of settings and characters becomes a sort of

---

13. Butler, *Fortune's Football*, I, 35, 104, II, 99. Cathy Davidson has pointed to the generic link between the picaresque novel and geographies, though without further discussing it; see *Revolution and the Word*, 171. For examples of narrativized geographies, see *The World Displayed; or, A Curious Collection of Voyages and Travels . . .*, 8 vols. (Philadelphia, 1795); or Isaac Taylor, *Scenes in Europe: For the Amusement and Instruction of Little Tarry-at-Home Travellers* (Philadelphia, 1822 [1st Am. ed. from 3d London ed.]). For an example of a map game, see Thomas Jefferys, *The Royal Geographical Pastime: Exhibiting a Complete Tour round the World* (London, 1770).

Figure 48. The Royal Geographical Pastime: Exhibiting a Complete Tour round the World. *By Thomas Jefferys. 1770.* Permission, Colonial Williamsburg Foundation

geographic primer designed to facilitate the basic lesson of romance novels: upon his return to London, Mercutio submits to the authority of his father and concludes the marriage plot demanded by a patriarchal system (while his own marital status remains ambiguous, he gives the hand of his sister to his best friend). Furthermore, he returns to the everyday life of bourgeois normalcy, marked by a plodding calendar ("the next day") and its mundane daily rituals ("breakfast," "dinner," and so on). In this anticlimactic conclusion, the novel not only solves loose narrative ends but shows Mercutio to be unaffected by his adventures; or as Cathy Davidson observes: "The novel [cannot] be read as a kind of *bildungsroman*. Mercutio apparently learns nothing from his trials, and we as readers learn little about him. Nor is the ending any clearer from the beginning (or the middle either)."[14]

This lack of transformation, though, is precisely the point of the novel. Through having Mercutio return to the domestic table of everyday meals unchanged, Butler indicates that, if there were any lessons to be learned, they were to be learned by the reader, not Mercutio. The lessons were purely pedagogic, a reflection of mechanical reading habits: Mercutio's unchanged state of mind and social status indicate that, in spite of his extensive travels, at least ideologically he never left home. His journey from and to London was strictly imaginary, spurred by a geographical imagination that imitated the reader's familiarity with a world map and a geography book. Thus, the lessons are supplied instead by the reader who rehearses his or her geographical knowledge in the form of a geographical conversation. The novel in a way repeats the domestic conclusion offered by *The Algerine Captive*. As the ideal geographic reader, Mercutio is a stationary figure bound to the geographic reading culture that informed his hometown (and that of a larger English reading culture); that is, he is bound to the geographic types (and in so doing becomes the quintessential English character) that textbooks prescribed as emblematic of his nationality. At the same time, because Mercutio fails to develop, Butler's novel becomes a politically useful tool; it contains the desire for geographic and social mobility, thus preempting critics like the Reverend Samuel Miller who saw the novel as one of the engines responsible for frivolous behavior, social upheavals, and the nation's political instability.[15]

14. Davidson, *Revolution and the Word*, 166.

15. On the antinovel discourse, see G. Harrison Orians, "Censure of Fiction in American Romances and Magazines, 1789–1810," *PMLA*, LII (1937), 195–214.

The textbook, and not the world, was the epistemological habitat in which the fictional characters of the early national period were supposed to make themselves comfortable. Underhill, Constantius and Pulchera, and Mercutio link personal happiness with a sentimental attachment to national space. In this they become idealized national characters whose stationary progress is a testament to the nation's gravitational pull. While the position of the armchair geographer might seem passive and escapist, the stationary progress is in fact the effect of a highly active and proscribed geographic reading practice. This reading practice, generated by text-books and appropriated by American novels, consists of uniform charac-ters and revolves around a strictly territorial imaginary that is aesthetically calculated and political, intent on having the American subject occupy both real and imaginative spaces that nurture nationalistic sentiment.[16]

THE CONFLICTED GEOGRAPHIES OF CHARLES BROCKDEN BROWN

In William Dunlap's memoirs of Charles Brockden Brown (1815), the author recalls a visit he paid to the Brown family when Charles was still a child. Dunlap describes seeing the precocious schoolboy "at the hour of dinner in the parlour, where, having slipped off his shoes, he was mounted on a table and deeply engaged in the consultation of a map suspended on the side of the wall." Dunlap further recounts how "at the age of ten" Brown "was so intimately acquainted with the science of geography, that he became a sort of gazetteer to his father, and would point out to him on the map or chart almost any part of the world . . . and [he] could generally give some account of the place." The young Brown, Dunlap implies, was an avid reader of his school geographies.[17]

Brown's childhood fascination with geography continued into adult-hood. It is a much-overlooked facet of Brown's literary career that while working as a journalist and editor he regularly discussed issues relating to the techniques of geographic representation. The pattern begins in 1798 (and thus coincides with the publication of his first novels) when he inter-

16. Here I depart from phenomenological, structuralist, and new historicist analyses of reading—and I am measuring a trajectory of attitudes that is at work in reader response theories by Wolfgang Iser and Michel de Certeau, or in book histories by Robert Darnton and Cathy Davidson—that tend to associate the stationary fantasies of readers with the function of escapism.

17. William Dunlap, *The Life of Charles Brockden Brown* . . . (Philadelphia, 1815), 7, 12–13.

preted geographic and demographic data for the *Weekly Magazine* in a two-part essay called "Facts and Calculations Respecting the Population and Territory of the United States." A year later, now the editor of the *Monthly Magazine, and American Review,* Brown edited (and perhaps co-authored) a comparative geographic analysis called a "Parallel between New-England and Great-Britain." Modeled on textbook protocols (dimension, latitude and longitude, climate, population, and character), the essay explores the "moral and political condition of the two nations," concluding that "virtue and happiness of a people depend chiefly upon two things, the quantity and the equal distribution of knowledge and property." Although the comparison between New England and Old England becomes a mock-academic exercise ridiculing the quest for the origins of true English, it reiterates Morse's bias favoring the northern states, but with a twist. Having equated "happiness" with "knowledge" (literacy) and "landed property" (geography), Brown claims Americans were on the whole more virtuous and happier because "every native of New-England, of mature age, can read and write. This cannot be said of the natives of Britain." Moreover, it was safe to "venture . . . that among fifty families, forty-nine are in the enjoyment of house and land . . . in Great-Britain not more than one in fifty is in possession of this blessing." Underlying this article is the assumption not only that knowledge begets property (and vice versa) but that both literacy and geographic competence are equally applicable indexes of the psychological health of the American nation.[18]

The range of Brown's geographic writings increased after the publication of his final novel, *Jane Talbot.* Brown's various technical interests in geography became manifest in the editorial comments of his last book publication, the translation of C. F. Volney's *View of the Soil and Climate of the United States* (1804). But his geographical interests were more explicitly discussed in articles published during Brown's tenure as the editor of

18. [Charles Brockden Brown], "Parallel between New-England and Great-Britain," *Monthly Magazine, and American Review,* I (1799), 12–15. The article is signed by the pseudonym "Francisco," which is not listed in the otherwise immensely useful anthology and annotated bibliography on Brown's magazine work edited by Alfred Weber and Wolfgang Schäfer, *Charles Brockden Brown: Literary Essays and Reviews* (Frankfurt, 1992), 209–212. It was not coincidental that this article was printed back-to-back with the essay "On the State of American Literature." I discuss "Parallel" at length in "Sense, Census, and the 'Statistical View' of the Modern Subject in *The Literary Magazine* and *Jane Talbot,*" in Philip Barnard, Mark Kamrath, Stephen Shapiro, eds., *Revising Charles Brockden Brown: Culture, Politics, and Sexuality in the Early Republic* (Knoxville, Tenn., 2004), 281–309.

the *Literary Magazine* (1803–1807). In this magazine, for example, Brown assessed the demographic survey of the second census through the lens of a geographer. In the same issue, Brown also published an essay, "The American Character," a showcase study of regional typing as modeled by geography textbooks; for example, "The states of New Hampshire, Massachusetts, Rhode Island, and Connecticut, retain more of their primitive manners . . . the inhabitants are brave, enterprizing, and industrious." The characterization becomes increasingly negative as Brown's descriptions wander farther south: "Virginia excels Maryland in luxury and indolence. . . . Passing over North Carolina, which has emerged very little from its original state of barbarity, the same description, as has been given of Virginia, will serve for South Carolina and Georgia." The most technical article was "Improvement of Geography, Topography, etc.," in which the reader learns about the cartographic practice of isomorphic mapping. The most literary application of geography appeared a month later and was called "Literary Blunders." Brown opens with the line, "Geographical errors are more common in books than any other kind of errors." As an example, Brown cites how geographic records were distorted by the poetic license of writer-physicians explaining the origins of the 1793 yellow fever epidemic. Quoting Racine, he comments, "Strange that the poet should not have looked at a map before he ventured to describe." Writing, editing, and compiling geographic information were central to Brown's last official employment before his death. Working as the editor of the *American Register; or, General Repository of History, Politics, and Science* (1807–1810), he devoted his final literary energies to the tabulation, classification, and interpretation of literary and scientific news, in particular reports on the nation's geography.[19]

This technical discussion of geography was more than an editorial task; it became Brown's scholarly obsession. While working for the *American Register,* Brown was simultaneously writing a substantial manuscript (alleged to be a thousand pages long), which was advertised shortly before his death as *A System of General Geography* (1809). (Sadly, this manuscript went missing after his death.) According to the "Prospectus," the pub-

19. Brown's contributions to *Literary Magazine, and American Register:* "A Statistical View of the United States of America," II (1804), 179–180; "The American Character," II (1804), 252–257; "Improvement of Geography, Topography, Etc.," III (1805), 99–101; "Literary Blunders," III (1805), 188. For an assessment (albeit negative) of Brown's work in the *American Register,* see Steven Watts, *The Romance of Real Life: Charles Brockden Brown and the Origins of American Culture* (Baltimore, 1994).

lished précis of *A System of General Geography,* his book was intended to supplement and revise the existing geographical canon. Brown acknowledges the popular craving for a nationalized geography and the dominance of Morse's books. He lauds Morse, "whose labours have supplied an indispensable demand of American curiosity. He has fulfilled the first and most reasonable expectation of his countrymen, in giving them that knowledge of their country which they would seek in vain in any foreign publication." Viewed in this tradition of textbooks, Brown's *System of General Geography* would have been familiar and conventional: it consisted of two volumes, "the first containing the geography of America, the second containing the geography of the Eastern Hemisphere"; it differentiated between "physical" and "political" geography; and it entailed the conceit of touring the world by leisurely reading geographies ("mak[ing] excursions, in almost any direction, over the world of man and nature").[20]

But, if Brown's geography appears to be properly classified and organized according to conventional divisions and taxonomies, elsewhere his vision of geography becomes expansive, totalizing, and even chaotic in its undiscriminating appropriation of nearly all forms of knowledge. At the scripted moment, in keeping with the tradition of textbook authors who define "Geography" as "a description of the earth," Brown inserts his definition of authorship and readership. This definition begins conventionally enough with the fundamentals of the geographer's work: "Geography will . . . confer her name upon our labours, if we consider the earth as composed of solid inert masses, of different colours, densities, gravities, and chemical properties." But, as Brown continues, the focus shifts from working over physical matter to the labor of writing:

> In like manner, if we describe the various ranks of organized beings, from man to moss, we describe the earth, and may therefore be considered as geographers. If we view the surface of the earth, as divided horizontally into land and water, and vertically into hill, valley, and plain . . . we are geographers. If we consider man in his social, political, or physical condition, and the surface and products of the earth in relation to the works and subsistence of men; as divided among nations; as checkered by cities, villages, and fields; as ploughed, or pastured, or resigned to the reign of nature, we are still geographers.

20. Charles Brockden Brown, *A System of General Geography* (Philadelphia, 1809), 1–5.

For Brown, geographic writing encompasses fields that we would now identify as geology, botany, natural history, anthropology, political science, sociology, or agricultural science. The "Prospectus" thus reads like a summation of a life's work subsuming everything in the interests of geography. At the same time, it also reads like a repudiation of Brown's early literary career as a fiction writer. The list of fields controlled by Brown as the geographical author comprises scientific disciplines, but not the arts.[21]

Brown gives the prospectus, created shortly before his death, the air of a political manifesto. In light of his literary career, his persona of the geographer seems to sublimate Brown's career as a novelist, editor, and journalist. More specifically, it echoes his rejection by Thomas Jefferson, to whom Brown as an aspiring writer had applied for financial aid and federal patronage. In this context, the "Prospectus" offers a rare literary glimpse of Brown's torturous relationship with the cultural work of literature in the age of Jeffersonian politics of expansion and its proleptic rhetoric of the "republican empire." Having cultivated a Federalist attitude during his novel-writing days, Brown intervened in the public debate over the Louisiana Purchase, publishing four political pamphlets that attacked the republican ideology of Jeffersonian policies. In the first pamphlet, *An Address to the Government of the United States, on the Cession of Louisiana to the French* (1803), Brown not only criticizes the allegedly Francophile Jefferson for stalling negotiations with the French but calls for the immediate annexation of the Louisiana Territory. To illustrate the urgency of this territorial action, Brown mimics the voice of the French ambassador reporting to Napoleon: "[The Americans] are a people of yesterday. Their institutions have just received birth. Hence their characters and views are void of all stability. Their prejudices are all discordant." While the pamphlet's theatricality is geared to rankle Americans into political action, its more subtle critique describes a nation that was hopelessly defenseless because its "scattered members" were incapable of "coalescing into one symmetrical and useful body." Annexing the Louisiana Territory, as demanded by the pamphlet's logic, would stabilize the nation. Expansion would bring at once cohesion, symmetry, and utility to the body politic; or, to put it otherwise, annexing the Louisiana Territory would give geographical certainty to the otherwise spatially uncertain aggregate called the United States.[22]

21. Ibid., 4.

22. Charles Brockden Brown, *An Address to the Government of the United States, on the Cession of Louisiana to the French* ... (Philadelphia, 1803), 63. These pamphlets have been

When reading the "Prospectus" in the context of Brown's political ambitions, the narrative persona of the geographer simultaneously reconciles two opposite perceptions of authorship. Through the voice of the geographer, Brown is able to maintain his original fictional persona of the solitary author who works through the trauma of post-Revolutionary cultural upheavals. At the same time, however, Brown's geographic ambitions ground him inside the contested space of territorial politics and the ongoing debate over the form and function of the modern nation-state. But, even if the authorial figure of the geographer allowed Brown to locate his last literary efforts somewhere between that of the Romantic genius and the Jeffersonian realpolitiker, then the discourse of geography had the last word. It served as Brown's metanarrative: "Geographical systems are, in general, collections of miscellaneous knowledge, in which that particular branch of information will predominate, in which the writer is most conversant, or to which he is most addicted." At the end of his literary career, Brown confesses in not so many words that geography had become his own literary addiction. Brown explores social and affective consequences of this addiction through his unlikely analogue, the young lovelorn heroine Jane Talbot.[23]

Jane Talbot

Jane Talbot was Brown's last published novel. For many literary historians, the fact that Brown ceased publishing novels signals literary failure; critics blame this failure on the author, the publishing industry, and an unappreciative readership. In studies of the early American novel, *Jane Talbot* often serves to demonstrate the genre's technical and the author's personal limitations. Yet, Brown's final novel appears less disruptive to

discussed by Christopher Looby, *Voicing America: Language, Literary Form, and the Origins of the United States* (Chicago, 1996), 194–202. On Jefferson's rejection of Brown, see David Lee Clark, *Charles Brockden Brown, Pioneer Voice of America* (Durham, N.C., 1952), 163–164. This rejection hovers in the background of many influential readings: for example, Looby, *Voicing America,* 146; it also informs Warner, *Letters of the Republic,* 118–150.

Jefferson's theory of the "republican empire" became the operative concept through which he and many postcolonial Americans imagined the modern nation-state as a proliferation of republican ministates that could easily exist outside the original national territory and thus set the stage for the invasion of those continental spaces that were not yet under American rule. On the debates and concepts surrounding his imperial vision, see Peter S. Onuf, *Jefferson's Empire: The Language of American Nationhood* (Charlottesville, Va., 2000), 1–17, 45, 53–79.

23. Brown, *System of General Geography,* 2.

the story of American literary history once it is no longer viewed through the narrow context of Brown's work as a novelist, but viewed through his lifelong commitment to the representation of geographic knowledge.[24]

The love story of *Jane Talbot* revolves around geographic distances. Jane falls in love with Henry Colden, who is described as "contemplative and bookish," "somewhat visionary and romantic." Jane's guardian, Mrs. Fielder, opposes the match and forces her to break off the relationship. Jane and Henry leave each other on unpleasant terms, and a distraught Henry takes to the seas. Jane, of course, is still in love with Henry and is able to track his movements via correspondence that Henry's sister receives from a mutual acquaintance. In order to preserve a sense of connection between them, Jane takes up the habit of tracing Henry's journey through maps and geography books. But what begins as an activity to keep her occupied as she awaits, Penelope-like, the return of the seafaring lover soon becomes an object of affection unto itself.[25]

Jane Talbot is written in epistolary form. In Letter 62, Brown (whom one senses is desperately seeking to end the plot) hazards Jane's love of geographic knowledge as the literary solution through which to settle both the heroine's romantic affair and the novel's survey of liberal conceptions regarding free will, communal mores, and individual happiness. Hoping to learn more about the fate of her missing suitor, Jane writes to Henry's sister, confessing a radical change of heart as to how she now defines happiness.

> When I found that my *happiness* was embarked . . . in a tedious and perilous voyage, was it possible to forbear collecting all the informa-

24. Instead of reading *Jane Talbot* as the exit work of a novelist who is conflicted about the function of the novel in early American culture, I see it as only one of several experiments Brown was pursuing simultaneously. Brown's novels are closely spaced, thus defying a specific interpretive value that could be attributed to their periodization. Rather, *Jane Talbot* must be seen within the context and range of Brown's literary lifework, which included more nonfictional than fictional projects, in particular projects on geographical and statistical discourse. For a survey of the largely negative reception of *Jane Talbot,* see Donald A. Ringe, "Historical Essay," in Charles Brockden Brown, *Jane Talbot, A Novel,* ed. Sydney Krause et al. (Kent, Ohio, 1986), 459–471. My argument is inspired by the constructive readings of Paul Witherington, "Brockden Brown's Other Novels: *Clara Howard* and *Jane Talbot,*" *Nineteenth-Century Fiction,* XXIX (1974), 257–263; and Sydney J. Krause, "*Clara Howard* and *Jane Talbot:* Godwin on Trial," in Bernard Rosenthal, ed., *Critical Essays on Charles Brockden Brown* (Boston, 1981), 184–211.

25. Brown, *Jane Talbot,* 225.

tion attainable respecting his route, and the incidents likely to attend it? I got maps and charts and books of voyages, and found a melancholy enjoyment in connecting the incidents and objects which they presented, with the destiny of my friend.

Jane shifts her desire from her lost love to the discourse of geography as a new constitution of her "happiness." Through reading geographic texts, Jane is transformed from a woman whose idea of happiness revolves around idealistic, sentimental definitions of love into one who finds fulfillment in geographic knowledge.[26]

That the engagement with geographic information enables Jane to convert her grief over the loss of Henry into a substitute embodiment of happiness gives her cause for concern. When Jane writes to Henry's sister, "Repeated meditation on displays of Shoal, Sand-bank and Water, has created a sort of attachment to Geography for its own sake," she is not merely advertising her own knowledge but offering a confession. As "a sort of attachment," her relationship to geography assumes amorous overtones. While she began reading with the honorable intent of maintaining a connection with her lover, Henry has now been displaced in her thoughts by the geographic information that Jane is pursuing irrespective of Henry's plight.[27]

Jane's intense affective response to geography is the sort of guilty pleasure usually associated with novels: Jane transposes the contemporary critique of novel reading onto the unlikely genre of geography books. Just as critics warned that young, impressionable girls could be seduced by novels into a habit of compulsive reading and inhabiting fictional worlds, so too Jane has entered a mental world dominated by geography and geographic fantasies. "The map of the world exists in my fancy in a most vivid and accurate manner," she confesses coyly. Jane is self-conscious about the troublesome implications of her geographic addiction:

How freakish and perverse are the rovings of human curiosity! The surprise which Miss Betterton betrayed, when, in answer to her inquiries as to what study and what book I prized the most, you told her that I thought of little else than of the art of moving from shore to shore across the water, and that I pored over Cook's voyages so much that I had gotten the best part of them by rote, was very natural. She must

26. Ibid., 411.
27. Ibid., 412.

have been puzzled to conjecture what charms one of my sex could find in the study of maps and voyages. *Once* I should have been just as puzzled myself.

If Miss Betterton's surprise is considered as "natural," Jane implies that her own study of geography, a study which in fact adheres to the pedagogic protocols of geography textbooks (learning facts "by rote"), is construed as unnatural. What is perhaps freakish is not so much that Jane studies geography but the degree to which she now studies it "for its own sake." The goal of geographic instruction, as constructed within innumerable geography textbooks, was pragmatic, whether achieving a better understanding of one's own property, tracing the journey of friends, or becoming a better citizen. Jane's naughty pleasure is not simply that geographic reading has replaced her amorous devotion to Henry but that this reading has, in effect, become autoerotic.[28]

Jane's guilty reading pleasures, however, are in some ways precisely the response demanded by the geographic textbooks themselves. Seeking to mold the ideal republican citizen, Noah Webster and Jedidiah Morse deliberately worked to instill an affective relationship between the reader and the nation's geography as the starting point of civic virtue. They sought to broker, in their own words, an "attachment" between reader and nation. Thus, when Jane discovers that "repeated meditation . . . has created a sort of attachment to Geography," far from committing a literary sin she epitomizes the idealized virtuous geographic reader.

In sending the bookish and Romantic Colden off to sea, Brown in essence replaces the (European) form of the novel with the (American) geography book. In so doing Brown displaces the modes through which the novel creates affective responses; the sentimental novel evokes emotion and empathy through the vehicle of carefully limned fictional characters. The geography book, by contrast, creates affect through the process and pleasure of memorization. Jane clearly enjoys relating "that [she] pored over Cook's voyages so much that [she] had gotten the best part of them by rote." Jane's memory, however, here exceeds the national bounds; if she is guilty of too much geographical feeling, her pleasure is derived from experiencing the geography of the world (or rather South Sea) and becomes affiliated less with the habit structures of a national than a transnational, planetary consciousness. Likewise, Dunlap's account of young Brown's domestic examination is a scene that demon-

28. Ibid.

strates the pleasures of geographic memorization as a totalizing global system (remember, Brown purportedly could generally give some account of almost any part of the world).[29]

This privileging of geographic and potentially imperialistic enjoyment raises two problems. First, it makes evident an inherent flaw in the affective logic of geography textbooks. While the intended object of affection in these books is the land and nation, the abstract nature of these concepts makes them elusive targets for developing an emotional bond. This difficulty is to be overcome by memorization, which gives flesh and form to the abstract idea of nation. However, through rote memorization the reader, far from becoming empathetic with another, turns inward. It is the properties and abilities of one's own mind that become the object of fascination. With Jane, this internalization is given graphic expression. She says, "I have always found an unaccountable pleasure in dissecting, as it were, my heart; uncovering, one by one its many folds, and laying it before you, as a country is shown in a map." Here the art of reading a map engenders, not a republican civic sensibility, but an intellectual and affective narcissism. Jane seems to be acting upon this narcissism when, at the end of the novel, having come into money, she leaves the city of Philadelphia, refuses to relocate to New York City, and buys instead a profitable farm on "the Banks of the Delaware" in southern New Jersey. There, unmarried, she divides her time between writing self-reflexive letters, studying maps and geography, and conversing with the occasional houseguest.[30]

Jane Talbot creates a literary impasse for Brown as a novelist. The book does not respond to the contemporary antinovel rhetoric by defending the virtues of the novel. Rather, this novel appears to disavow the affective strength of the genre itself. Jane's obsession with geographic materials threatens *Jane Talbot*'s structural integrity and argument, causing the failure of the novel's controlled romance while also undoing the novel's breathtaking debate over how men and women could achieve personal happiness in a modern society that was governed by competing moral and social philosophies. Just as romance fiction was criticized for distracting young women from their duties (marital or national), maps and voyages are here presented as seducing Jane into a life of mundane leisure and planetary reflection. Such a life could destabilize the existing patriarchal order and its implied traffic in women. A more subtle reading, however,

29. Ibid.
30. Ibid., 255.

shows that it undermines the Jeffersonian order proposed by his Republican administration in 1800.

On the surface, Jane's retreat to the country repeats Jefferson's fantastic scheme of the republican imperial landscape. Jefferson envisioned a uniform landscape, consisting of Anglo-American farmsteads spread evenly across the North American continent in accordance with the Land Ordinance Act of 1785 and the Northwest Ordinance Act of 1787. Sponsored by Jefferson himself, these ordinances were designed to regulate the present and future territory of the American nation-state. Beginning at the western frontiers of the original thirteen states, the ordinances imposed a rectilinear land-survey system, thus implementing the geodetic grid as the dominant frame of reference that would come to determine "the spatial organization of two-thirds of the present United States."[31]

Around 1800, the geometric organization of the land was just beginning to affect the representation of the country's western physical landscape (Figure 49). In the East, the rectangular land survey had made regional impressions on the landscape, as the gridded survey pattern had been a part of the British colonial mapping system. What is more significant is the extent to which the grid survey was first and foremost a paper construct that postcolonial politicians transformed into a "national" standard of geographical representation. The geometric lines of the grid on the map—and not the neatly subdivided townships sections on the land itself—functioned as the textual scaffold fostering "a strong common culture of reference" through which citizens could imagine the nation's geography and the domestication of the nation's unsurveyed and undeveloped hinterlands, not to mention the economic transformation of land into salable lots or the political management of both the land and its occupants. In order to implement the larger geopolitical design, both acts decreed a six-mile-square grid as the most basic unit of representa-

31. John R. Stilgoe, *Common Landscape of America, 1580 to 1845* (New Haven, Conn., 1982), 99. The literature on the land ordinances is extensive. I have benefited the most from Peter S. Onuf, *Statehood and Union: A History of the Northwest Ordinance* (Bloomington, Ind., 1987); Hildegard Binder Johnson, *Order upon the Land: The U.S. Rectangular Land Survey and the Upper Mississippi Country* (New York, 1976); Norman J. W. Thrower, *Original Survey and Land Subdivision: A Comparative Study of the Form and Effect of Contrasting Cadastral Surveys* (Chicago, 1966); Douglas R. McManis, *The Initial Evaluation and Utilization of the Illinois Prairies, 1815–1840,* University of Chicago, Department of Geography, Research Paper no. 94 (Chicago, 1964). On the British colonial origins of the grid, see Edward T. Price, *Dividing the Land: Early American Beginnings of Our Private Property Mosaic* (Chicago, 1995).

Figure 49. Map of Albany. *By A. Johnson. 1818.* John Johnson Papers,
Courtesy of Special Collections, University of Vermont Library

tion. Accordingly, they instructed that "the surveyors shall proceed to
divide the said territory into townships of six miles square, by lines running due north and south, and others crossing these at right angles."[32]

At its base, the new system reflected a strong wish for political order

32. Philip Fisher, "Democratic Social Space: Whitman, Melville, and the Promise of
American Transparency," *Representations,* no. 24 (Fall 1988), 62; *An Ordinance for Ascertaining the Mode of Disposing of Lands in the Western Territory* [Philadelphia, 1785], sect. 4.
The rectilinear appearance of the western American landscape did not elicit comments in
the popular press and creative writings until the middle to late nineteenth century, when,
for example, a traveler like Ralph Waldo Emerson reported from a trip to Milwaukee that
"the world there was done up in large lots" (cited in Alfred Kazin, *A Writer's America:
Landscape in Literature* [New York, 1988], 57). The geographer J. B. Jackson, examining the
writings of settlers and travelers, traces the earliest comments on the country's geometric
landscape to 1817. See "The Order of a Landscape: Reason and Religion in Newtonian
America," in D. W. Meinig, ed., *The Interpretation of Ordinary Landscapes: Geographical
Essays* (New York, 1979), 159.

and transparency; for many, its design promised "egalitarianism through geometry," thus putting an end to the political battles over the ownership, distribution, and management of the nation's lands. On the one hand, the system projected the fantasy that land would become accessible to the common man as a legitimate commodity, allowing characters like Jane Talbot to own and settle a piece of land (which, as the ordinance system conveniently failed to acknowledge, might still be occupied by its original and rightful owners, the Native Americans). On the other hand—and this is where Brown's novel enters the political arena and critique of the new land system—the grid layout would create an undifferentiated landscape of isolated homesteads with artificially defined distances separating the settlers.[33]

Jane's life on her isolated estate imitates the isolation predicted by the ordinances for the future citizens of the nation-state. In this context, her compulsive reading of geographies ceases to be a debilitating obsession. Rather, it emerges as the communicative tool that binds this geometrically compartmentalized American community. Following the logic of the six-mile township system, the ordinances unwittingly forced the citizen into a space whose design by default separated the nuclear republican unit, the farming family or landowner, ultimately forcing individuals into an anti-social life. In view of Jane's reading habits, geographies (and not histories or novels) provide the literary site in which the new citizens can convene and socialize, in addition to becoming socialized. Through geographies, Jane not only keeps in touch with Colden, but she is able to entertain company. Geography books protect Jane from isolation, daydreaming, and the general collapse into an unproductive state of reverie and fantasy that was usually attributed to the habit of novel reading. Instead, by reading geography Jane remains sociable and well socialized; like the news media of the early decades, the genre of geography keeps this early American subject integrated in the web of economic and political discourse.[34]

33. Hildegard Binder Johnson, "The United States Land Survey as a Principle of Order," in Ralph E. Ehrenberg, ed., *Pattern and Process: Research in Historical Geography* (Washington, D.C., 1975), 116.

34. Interestingly, the communal and communicative function of geography books, or for that matter also maps, has been largely overlooked in histories of early national print culture. On the media and types of information circulating in the early Republic, see Richard D. Brown, *Knowledge Is Power: The Diffusion of Information in Early America, 1700–1865* (Oxford, 1989); Thomas C. Leonard, *News for All: America's Coming-of-Age with the Press* (Oxford, 1995).

Edgar Huntly

If *Jane Talbot* addresses the narcissistic and social consequences of an intense emotional relationship to geography books, *Edgar Huntly* explores an opposite phenomenon, the unmaking of the self by entering a world that is uncharted and therefore uncontrolled by geographic writing systems. While the book's sense of space is at first highly demarcated, it gradually descends into the aesthetic realm of European Romantic landscapes before settling on the representational world of the American wilderness. Ultimately, the novel reveals the psychological consequences of the geographically trained, republican-minded citizen who by wandering off the pages of the geographic narrative moves outside the nation and its controlled spatial system.

Edgar Huntly; or, Memoirs of a Sleep-Walker (1799) opens by explicitly declaring its intent to enter into a different affective mode. Seeking to call "forth the passions and engaging sympathy of the reader, by means hitherto unemployed by preceding authors," Brown's novel is calculated to evoke "the incidents of Indian hostility, and the perils of the western wilderness" in order to arrive at a more "suitable" depiction of "our own country." Built around the solitary voice of the somnambulistic narrator, the novel subsequently offers a unique realization of the novel form. *Edgar Huntly* aims to capture the audience's "sympathy" through the odd (and unsympathetic) central character of Edgar, a figure who commits gruesome murders in the course of the tale; rather than create the nationalistic passions for "our own country" through geographic description, *Edgar Huntly* takes the reader off the map, into the dangerously uncharted territory of undescribed space.[35]

The uncanny aura of the book is mostly developed through the surreal element of Edgar's "memoirs" as a sleepwalker, in which space by definition loses its social and psychological fixity. However, the spatial disorientation experienced by the novel's characters (and readers) is not so much the direct product of sleepwalking as it is the result of the novel's systematic subversion of a seemingly conventional geographical setting. Edgar Huntly's description of the political township of Solebury plays upon the reader's familiarity with both the colonial and the postcolonial land surveys and their cartographic as well as geographic reading protocols. Writing to his fiancee, Edgar describes his local setting thus:

35. Charles Brockden Brown, *Edgar Huntly; or, Memoirs of a Sleep-Walker* (1799) (New York, 1988), 3.

It would not be easy to describe the face of this district, in a few words. Half of Solebury, thou knowest, admits neither of plough nor spade. The cultivable space lies along the river, and the desert, lying on the north, has gained, by some means, the appellation of Norwalk. Canst thou imagine a space, somewhat circular, about six miles in diameter, and exhibiting a perpetual and intricate variety of craggy eminences and deep dells?

Edgar recalls the more recent national and distant colonial rhetoric of land classification schemes. The description of Norwalk cannily reproduces the descriptive nomenclature of land use patterns, dividing land into "cultivable" and "desert" wasteland. The geometric specificity that accompanies the description invokes the "six miles" grid design that was recently passed into law by the Land Ordinance Act. Retreating further into history, Edgar seems to recall the six-mile circular pattern that determined the establishment of townships in the northeastern parts of the country. The description thus draws and depends upon the reader's inherent sense of geographical constructions of the early Anglo-American community; more specifically, it prepares the reader for viewing the novel's landscape as a geographical sensorium by tapping into his or her familiarity with community maps, map-reading skills, and overall competence as a geographically literate member of society.[36]

But whatever comfort the reader might take in this familiar scene of geographical orientation is quickly undermined by the corresponding narrative description. Despite adhering to the formal protocols of land measurement, Norwalk remains eerily resistant to description ("it would not be easy to describe"). Edgar recounts how every time he enters Norwalk it is shrouded in "utter darkness" or becomes an amorphous "maze." Indeed, contrary to the reader's expectation of methodical transparency— both raised by textbook lessons and in particular by the national surveying project—the landscape of Norwalk becomes an antigeographical exercise in which Edgar exposes the discursive limits of a geographically constructed society.[37]

36. Brown, *Edgar Huntly*, 91. The six-mile ratio for ordering land goes back to an anonymous tract called "The Ordering of Towns" (1638), which suggested that the ideal New England township "ought to be a square six miles on a side." Cited in Stilgoe, *Common Landscape*, 99.

37. Brown, *Edgar Huntly*, 23, 97. Traditional readings look at these terms through the lens of psychoanalysis, interpreting Edgar's clouded vision as an expression of his con-

Edgar's inability to describe Norwalk in succinct, geographic terms may be a shortcoming, not of the township, but of our narrator's own liberal education. We might imagine an ideal reader (such as Dunlap's vision of the young Brown himself), schooled in the geography textbooks of Morse, Guthrie, and others, would be prepared to organize the township in both spatial and descriptive terms. Edgar, however, suffers from a Romantic European education. The reader learns that, before his adventures in Norwalk, Edgar had already toured the greater district of Solebury under the guidance of his mentor and teacher, the English émigré Sarsefield. As "his favorite scholar and the companion of all his pedestrian excursions," Edgar had a unique educational experience, for Sarsefield

> was fond of penetrating into these recesses, partly from the love of picturesque scenes, partly to investigate its botanical and mineral productions, and, partly to carry out more effectually that species of instruction which he had adopted with regard to me, and which chiefly consisted in moralizing narratives or synthetical reasonings.

While Edgar's education carries a thin veneer of the scientific in its attention to botany and geology, these studies are subordinate to the study of narrative and the picturesque. (His failure to designate that these scientific "investigations" revolve around the careful analysis of specimens and taxonomic organization suggests that the examination of botany and minerals becomes code for appreciating the sentimental or sublime emotions evoked by flora and craggy cliffs.) Thus when Edgar asks his reader, "Canst thou imagine a space, somewhat circular, about six miles in diameter, and exhibiting a perpetual and intricate variety of craggy eminences and deep dells," the cartographic imagining deemed proper according to the predominant geographic pedagogy (understanding the importance of the six-mile pattern) is quickly superseded by the Romantic vision of "craggy eminences and deep dells." Edgar has learned to read the world, not geographically, but novelistically or poetically.[38]

As suggested by his preface to *Edgar Huntly,* in order to convey the American landscape Brown appropriates the dominant European novelis-

---

flicted emotional response to frontier violence, immigration, and patriarchal authority; to this I want to add the metaphorical dimension referring to Enlightenment technologies of visual reception and representation, ranging from the surveyor's optical instruments to the image of the map.

38. Ibid., 92–93.

tic mode of representing landscapes that consist of "gothic castles and chimeras." Whereas in the European novel such architectural ruins symbolized the last vestiges of an old, feudal, and archetypal order, in an effort to Americanize his novel Brown turns to a new type of cultural ruin, the American environment. Instead of presenting gothic castles, Edgar Huntly presents a gothic "western wilderness" as the possible vestige of an old American order that casts its looming shadow upon the contemporary reader. Writing in compliance with the descriptive convention of the gothic mode, Brown subsequently locates Edgar Huntly inside a chaotic, labyrinthine, and monumental landscape.[39]

As he moves into the wilderness of Norwalk, Edgar enters a space that becomes increasingly unmappable, either in cartographic or narrative terms. This space functions as something of a proving ground for exploring the consequences of the unlanded individual. Indeed, *Edgar Huntly* has persistently been viewed as a formal expression of a general sense of psychopolitical disorientation. While this disorientation has numerous causes and manifestations, a key source of confusion, as critics have argued, stems from the issue of land and landownership. In a culture that had traditionally hinged upon a landed identity, a man's sense of self increasingly came under great pressure in the new American political landscape when, like Edgar, he was left landless. Without land to back up economic status, individuals were left politically unrepresented and socially displaced. Indeed, as land was becoming scarce in the East, we might suppose that there emerged a pathological condition that refracted the individual's sense of self. If literary productions such as Brown's *Edgar Huntly* are a guide to a culture's fears, the sense of disorientation and misrepresentation takes on a haunting quality, always prohibiting individual characters from settling down.[40]

39. Ibid., 3.

40. Here I invoke studies such as William Hedges, "Charles Brockden Brown and the Culture of Contradictions," *Early American Literature,* IX (1974), 107–142; Norman S. Grabo, *The Coincidental Art of Charles Brockden Brown* (Chapel Hill, N.C., 1981); Sidney J. Krause, "Historical Essay," in Charles Brockden Brown, *Edgar Huntly,* ed. Krause and S. W. Reid (Kent, Ohio, 1984); Roland Hagenbüchle, "American Literature and the Nineteenth-Century Crisis in Epistemology: The Example of Charles Brockden Brown," *Early Am. Lit.,* XXIII (1988), 121–151; Beverly R. Voloshin, *"Edgar Huntly* and the Coherence of the Self," *Early Am. Lit.,* XXIII (1988), 262–280.

On land as the source of disorientation, see Smith-Rosenberg, "Subject Female," *Am. Lit. Hist.,* V (1993), 481–511. See also Richard Slotkin, *Regeneration through Violence: The Mythology of the American Frontier, 1600–1860* (Middletown, Conn., 1971).

The formation of an American subject was compromised by the unrelenting acts of violence that were committed against the original landowners, the Native American population. In order for Euroamericans to maintain a landed identity, both land and geographic identity needed to be stripped from the indigenous population. *Edgar Huntly* graphically dramatizes the bloody process of annihilating the Indian population, as we witness the novel's hero brutally kill a Delaware. Edgar describes the Indian as a figure that first "moved upon all fours" and then bore all the "indubitable indications of a savage"; after being shot, the Indian "rolled upon the ground, uttering doleful shrieks" until Edgar finally bludgeoned him to death.[41]

The extermination of the Native American here depends as much on his actual execution as on his loss of voice. The incident finds a parallel in a moment when Edgar tomahawks a panther. He again describes how, having spotted "a post where a savage was lurking," the tomahawk "penetrated the skull and the animal fell, struggling and shrieking, on the ground." The dying shrieks of Indian and animal thus become indistinguishable, as human and nonhuman are rendered equally voiceless. This violent loss of voice is also a function of the loss of geographic orientation. In *Edgar Huntly,* the descent into the geographically disorderly wilderness—away from the space so rigorously described, delineated, and defined in American maps and geography books—does not simply demonstrate Edgar's fallibility as an American reader but indicates a process whereby spatial disorientation leads to the elimination of the speaking subject. The danger of losing self and voice is not limited to the native population. Covered with the blood of his Delaware victim, Edgar himself is mistaken for an Indian by his own teacher Sarsefield, who attempts to kill him. At the book's climax, the ominous, ungeographic space of Norwalk has transformed Edgar into an inarticulate being on the verge of being assassinated by the English purveyor of knowledge and aesthetics.[42]

In the novel's contrived American setting, unmoored from geographic conventions, the English language seems to have lost its function as an effective tool of communication and ultimately no longer offers a means

41. Brown, *Edgar Huntly,* 191–192.

42. Ibid., 159. For a different geographic reading of why Brown's characters fall silent, see Hsuan L. Hsu, "Democratic Expansionism in 'Memoirs of Carwin,' " *Early Am. Lit.,* XXXV (2000), 144–149; Looby, *Voicing America,* 168–170.

for writing an American novel. By the same token that the novel's American landscape turns all languages into a monoglot howling and shrieking, in short, into sheer voice, it ultimately creates a contact zone in which the native living languages, the Delaware dialect and Edgar's American English, become virtually dead languages. Upon his return to Solebury, even his former teacher has difficulties understanding Edgar; meeting Sarsefield for the first time after the shooting incident, Edgar remembers that "the sound of my voice made him start," and he recounts that Sarsefield's first response is: "Am I alive? am I awake? Speak again I beseech you, and convince me that I am not dreaming or delirious." Edgar's voice has become that of the returning dead rather than the sleeping, for it seems to have lost the power to identify him as a member of his native linguistic community. His English seems to have become altered to the point that neither his speech nor his person is well received by those whose life and identity depended upon being competent English-speakers and cohabitants of a geographically delineated space. Indeed, those characters who are invested most in the English language (and the English tradition of the novel), like Sarsefield and his aristocratic English wife, in the end flee the American subject and setting, avoiding Edgar and the township of Norwalk by returning to England. Language without a geographical frame of reference alone is proven to be an insufficient means of self-identification in Brown's America.[43]

Edgar's experience of Norwalk has traditionally been understood as a critique of Anglo-American relations with Native Americans. The space of Norwalk becomes the archetypal killing field in which at once colonial and federal Indian removal policies become reenacted. Edgar, who overtly doubles as a native when he is covered in "savage" blood, gets caught in the crossfire of the Solebury militia's war against the last remnants of the township's original population. However, underlying this critique is a more subtle, geographic one aimed at the land management model proposed by the federal government. The novel's implication that the experience of a geographically unsystematized American landscape hinders

43. Brown, *Edgar Huntly,* 232–233. I am not forgetting Edgar's double, the Irish immigrant Clithero, who, having also survived the tour of Norwalk, has completely lost his capacity for conventional, that is, rational speech; considered to be mad (even by Edgar himself), he is eventually locked up in a "place of confinement for lunatics" (283), the last sociological institution listed by geographers.

In my discussion of language, I expand and depart from Jared Gardner's astute reading of the function of language in *Edgar Huntly* (*Master Plots,* 74).

Edgar from becoming a fully recognizable American subject becomes in fact a commentary on the Land Ordinance Act of 1785.

As Norwalk develops into a geographic sensorium in which Edgar learns his lesson in an open-air classroom fashion, it also becomes a pedagogic space that echoes a specific territorial provision. Norwalk is similar to "Lot No. 16," which, according to the Land Ordinance Act, was reserved "for the maintenance of public schools." Within each township ("six miles square") that the United States government hoped to appropriate from western Native American tribes, 640 acres would be set aside for the purpose of supporting the township's educational system. Brown's novel complicates the analogy between Solebury and the act's projected townships even further. According to section 13, lots number 8, 11, 26, and 29 were reserved by the United States for undefined special purposes. By the 1790s, these lots were almost exclusively used as a form of payment for veterans of the Revolutionary war or the military in general. Thus, Brown's novel has its protagonist move through a space that was specifically earmarked both for educating the American citizenry and for rewarding the American patriot. As Edgar roams the larger township of Solebury, his geographic education is disrupted by each of these spaces, thereby undercutting the federal fantasy that a systematized landscape could become the discursive basis for creating a disciplined national American identity.[44]

As much as Charles Brockden Brown was a geographile, his novels display a complex and even tortured relationship to geography as its own narrative form. By allowing geographic textualities to intrude upon his literary texts, Brown forces a character like Jane Talbot to deviate from her proper generic role as a romantic heroine, turning her instead into a solipsistic reader of geography textbooks. On the other hand, it is the lack of proper geography books, and a properly codified and textualized national space, that strips Edgar Huntly not only of his national identity but of his very identity as a rational subject. Both novels, in radically different forms, thus illustrate the dangerous consequences of a nation that had come to base its identity in large part on geographic text.

---

44. *An Ordinance for Ascertaining the Mode of Disposing of Lands in the Western Territory*, sects. 4, 13. The Land Ordinance Act conferred "grants of land to the officers and soldiers who had engaged or should engage in the service of the United States during the war, and continue therein to the close of the same, or until discharged by Congress, and to the representatives of such officers and soldiers as should be slain by the enemy, in the following proportions, to wit: To a major general 1100 acres, to a brigadier 850, to a colonel 500, . . . to an ensign 150, and to a non-commissioned officer and soldier 100" (sect. 13).

chapter six

NATIVE AMERICAN
GEOGRAPHIES AND
THE JOURNALS OF
LEWIS AND CLARK

On February 19, 1806, a hostile congressional inquiry challenged President Thomas Jefferson about the progress of the Lewis and Clark expedition. Jefferson responded by delivering a message in which he presented to the American public the first official report of the expedition leaders. Seeking to mitigate antiexpansionist sentiments, Jefferson reminded his audience, "In pursuance of a measure proposed to Congress . . . Captain Meriwether Lewis . . . was appointed with a party of men, to explore the river Missouri . . . to seek the best water communication thence to the Pacific ocean." Moreover, "they were to enter into conference with the Indian nations on their route, with a view to the establishment of commerce with them." As evidence that the expedition was acting in compliance with these general instructions, Jefferson produced a letter by Lewis, dated April 7, 1805, which he paraphrased to speculate on the expedition's otherwise unknown whereabouts: "They entered the Missouri May 14. 1804. and on the 1st of Nov. took up their winter quarters near the Mandan towns, 1609 miles above the mouth of the river, in Lat. 47° 21′ 47″ N. and Long. 99° 24′ 45″ W. from Greenwich." In the absence of other concrete news about the expedition's status, Jefferson then referred his skeptical audience to a copy of the map Lewis had submitted with his report (Figure 50). Continuing to cite from his distant and possibly even lost correspondents, Jefferson read the note written by William Clark, the mapmaker: "During his stay among the Mandans, he had been able to lay down the Missouri according to courses and distances taken on his passage up it, corrected by frequent observations of longitude and latitude; and to add to the actual survey of this portion of the river, a general map of the country between the Missisipi and Pacific, from the 34th to the 54th degrees of Latitude." And he concluded his speech by making the

Figure 50.
A Map of Part of the Continent of North America. *By Nicholas King. 1805.* Courtesy, The Library of Congress

formal announcement, "Copies of this map are now presented to both houses of Congress."[1]

Thus begins the literary history of the Lewis and Clark journals—as a quotation and a manuscript map presented to the public in the rhetorical space of a presidential message. From the start, Lewis and Clark's writings were appropriated by the rituals surrounding political authority and statesmanship: in quoting geographical coordinates, the cartographic grid, and the map, the American president took possession of the expedition's narrative not only as a state-funded project but also as the basis of political capital. "Taking possession of the land means integrating new territories into the living processes of the appropriating state." By submitting the still-incomplete expedition map to Congress, Jefferson presented the textuality of geographical writings—as British and other colonial officials had since the sixteenth century—as the primary evidence for defending a politically ambitious decision. In his presentation, the Lewis and Clark map became the bureaucratic blueprint for what would follow: other expeditions, more detailed accounts, the Indian removal policy, the Homestead Acts, the violent encounter with and erasure of the Native American population. In short, through Lewis and Clark's letter and map, Jefferson as the head of state began the story of the federal project of territorial enclosure and western colonization, the national plot of an American continental empire.[2]

1. Donald Jackson, ed., *Letters of the Lewis and Clark Expedition, with Related Documents, 1783–1854* (Urbana, Ill., 1962), 298–299 (cited hereafter as *LLC*). The map used by Jefferson was Nicholas King's copy, *A Map of Part of the Continent of North America . . . Compiled from the Authorities of the Best Informed Travelers by M. Lewis* (1805) (Figure 50). King used Lewis's original map, *A Map of Part of the Continent*, which is reproduced in Gary E. Moulton and Thomas Dunlay, eds., *The Journals of the Lewis and Clark Expedition* (Lincoln, Nebr., 1983–2001), I (hereafter cited as *Journals*).

2. Myra Jehlen, "The Literature of Colonization," in Sacvan Bercovitch, ed., *The Cambridge History of American Literature,* I, *1590–1820* (Cambridge, 1994), 156. Scholarship tends to be inconclusive about determining the journals' entry into the public imagination. For a detailed publication history, see Paul Russell Cutright, *A History of the Lewis and Clark Journals* (Norman, Okla., 1976). The first authorized account, the *History of the Expedition under the Command of Captains Lewis and Clark* (Philadelphia, 1814), was edited and published by Nicholas Biddle, who selected and organized materials from the actual Lewis and Clark journals. Popular interest in the expedition's narrative was not revived until the turn of the twentieth century—at the same time as Frederick Jackson Turner was popularizing the rhetoric of the closing of the frontier—when Elliot Coues published an expanded version of Biddle's *History* (New York, 1893) and Reuben Gold Thwaites undertook to edit the seven volumes of the *Original Journals of the Lewis and Clark Expedition*

It is an overstatement to argue that the expedition's first public report authored historical events. But, when read in terms of the nation's profound investment in geographical literacy, the first installment of the Lewis and Clark journals becomes a cultural index measuring the extent to which geographical writings not only reflected the discourse of politics but shaped more broadly the public's cultural attitudes toward western expansion. The journal and map were instances of what have been called "texts as events." Through Jefferson's politically strategic and theatrical deposition, the expedition map instantaneously advanced to the position of the official textual "matrix or holding pattern within which a series of widely differing events can and do occur." In view of its historical moment, the map reflected the ambitions of a political leader and faction interested in territorial expansion; it furthermore held a personal, sentimental meaning, for it contained a lifetime's research and study by the citizen Thomas Jefferson; and, finally, it was the material text and evidence of the expedition's progress, a text inscribed with the marks and observations collected by the designated reporters, Lewis and Clark. To speak more specifically to the map's significance, because it provided a view of the western territories at a politically crucial moment in February 1806, the Lewis and Clark map enabled Jefferson to appease his critics and thus continue to lay the political groundwork that would be the ideological and bureaucratic foundations for the next generation's aggressive territorial politics and the belief that the nation had a manifest destiny to occupy the whole continent.[3]

However, the map's integration of political interests, land management objectives, and the multitude of individual and institutional voices answers only half of the definition of a textual event. Such a text was also open to constant linguistic and textual alterations, as it provided a

---

(New York, 1904–1905). Bernard DeVoto popularized the expedition's writings in a condensed edition, *The Journals of Lewis and Clark* (Boston, 1953), now supplanted by Gary Moulton's complete and definitive edition.

The Lewis and Clark expedition has become a fixture in accounts of western expansionism. See, for example, Reginald Horsman, *Race and Manifest Destiny: The Origins of American Racial Anglo-Saxonism* (Cambridge, Mass., 1981); Jack Ericson Eblen, *The First and Second United States Empires: Governors and Territorial Government, 1784–1912* (Pittsburgh, Pa., 1968).

3. See J. G. A. Pocock, "Texts as Events: Reflections on the History of Political Thought," in Kevin Sharpe and Steven N. Zwicker, eds., *Politics of Discourse: The Literature and History of Seventeenth-Century England* (Berkeley, Calif., 1987), 21.

glimpse of "a history of languages and *mentalités* that do not consist of texts but into which texts . . . do seem to enter and produce profound modifications." In the case of the Lewis and Clark records, two kinds of geographic languages modified the map and the expedition journals. The first and most obvious language shaping their map was the Euroamerican geographic archive, initially controlled by Jefferson and thus implicitly also by the United States government. The second and less visible language entering the map was that of the Mandan and Hidatsa people who provided much of the information so eagerly anticipated by the expedition's official sponsor.[4]

What is remarkable about his presidential address is the way in which Jefferson managed to explain away his and the audience's uncertainty over the map's and subsequently the report's reliability. Speaking before Congress in 1806, Jefferson distributed copies of a map that he had helped design before the expedition's departure and into which Lewis and Clark had entered their findings while spending a winter among the Mandans. Used as the expedition's blueprint and recording device, this initial map represented the known course of the Missouri River and displayed the contours of the western half of the North American continent. When compared to the map Jefferson showed to Congress, the original differed from the now publicly circulated copy in that the latter contained new local inscriptions, such as place-names and water routes written along the Missouri River and leading up to the already known location of the Mandan villages. For Jefferson, the most important aspect of the returned copy of his original map was that it now revealed an array of topographical signs marking mountains, plains, and especially waterways between the Upper Missouri and the Pacific Ocean, which promised the discovery of the much-desired and so far elusive transcontinental passageway.[5]

Yet—and this is the truly remarkable aspect of Jefferson's performance—the very map upon which Congress was supposed to trace the fate of the expedition as well as the future of the nation was in large part the product of the authorial collaboration between the two expedition leaders and a host of Native American mapmakers. In 1806, President Jefferson and the American public were reading a map of North America that, as far

4. Ibid., 22.

5. *LLC,* 28. On the differences between the Lewis and the King maps, see John Logan Allen, *Passage through the Garden: Lewis and Clark and the Image of the American Northwest* (Urbana, Ill., 1975), 227–233.

as the Euroamerican archive of geographic knowledge was concerned, ended at the Mandan towns on the Upper Missouri. The geography projected by the map west of this point was the product of Lewis and Clark's translations of Native American maps provided by the leaders of the Mandan and Hidatsa tribes. Jefferson hinted at the indigenous geographic archive briefly when he explained to Congress that the very map before them contained "additions . . . from information collected from Indians with whom [Lewis] had opportunities of communicating during his journey and residence with them." This was the official paraphrase of Lewis's report to the president: "The map, which has been forwarded to the Secretary at War, will give you the idea we entertain of the connection of these rivers, which has been formed from the corresponding testimony of a number of Indians who have visited that country, and who have been seperately and carefully examined on that subject, and we therefore think it entitled to some degree of confidence."[6]

The Lewis and Clark map and, to a certain degree, also their journals are thus the product of authorial collaboration, the combined product of Jefferson's map and expedition orders, Native American testimonies, and Lewis and Clark's geographical transcriptions and observations. Once understood in the terms of multiple authorship, the journals no longer can be viewed simply as an expedition account representing the western continent. Rather, they become the textual record delineating the confrontation between two epistemologically divergent modes of geographic representation. The Lewis and Clark journals, on the one hand, were scripted narratives reflecting the nation's expansionist agenda of geopolitical organization. On the other hand, in their application of these instructions to Native American geographies, Lewis and Clark navigated the world according to an alternative, non-European mode of structuring geographic space. As a consequence of their efforts in transcription and translation, the expedition leaders became spatially and textually disoriented. Losing their place in the constructed space of the map, they not only struggled for the expedition's basic survival but suffered personally from a fundamental crisis of representation. Unable to reconcile the European mode of geographic representation with that of Native Americans, they discovered the limits of geographical literacy. But, while their original journals reveal the compromised agency of early American self-imaginings, this confusion over geographical discourse and identity was

6. *LLC,* 233, 299.

never made public and was more or less negated by the rapid publication of unofficial and infinitely more Romantic expedition accounts.

Published for the first time in the form of a presidential address, the Lewis and Clark records were used not only to confer political authority upon the expedition's sponsor and patron. They also demonstrated the extent to which the discourse of geography provided Jefferson and his American audience with a strategic tool through which to prescribe and control the nation's literary basis. In Jefferson's account before Congress—which was soon to be published as the "Message from the President of the United States, communicating Discoveries made in exploring the Missouri, Red River, and Washita, by Captains Lewis and Clarke, . . . Read in Congress, February 19, 1806"—his almost excessive use of geographic coordinates was significant because they were indexes of the way in which he privileged the geographic record over Lewis and Clark's written reports. Inherent in this message was the rhetorical expectation that the map was the expedition's documentary narrative. The repetition of geographic coordinates and distance markers not only reasserted the map image but declared the map as the literary container controlling both the expedition's movement in physical space and the narrative space of the written report. While this allowed Jefferson technically to maintain long-distance control over the expedition, the geographic recitations transferred literary authority from the map's actual authors thousands of miles away to the map's official patron and the reader. Indeed, the act of geographic reading made the expedition's political sponsors—not just Jefferson himself but also his advisers, the nation's geographer general, and a cohort of fellow academics and cultural leaders—into the expedition's coauthors. While Lewis and Clark were the primary authors of their journals day by day, it was their training by a collective of American citizens and their combined geographical knowledge that monitored the expedition leaders, their actions, and, ultimately, the subject matter of the expedition itself, the imagined setting of the western passage.

Indeed, the Lewis and Clark journals in all their textual variety, consisting of descriptive narratives, survey maps, and drawings, were written as an exercise in geographic prescription. They constituted a document written as much in response to an unknown geography as in service of geographical literary conventions and the bibliographic order of Jefferson's library. The process of geographic prescription began decades before the actual expedition took place. As early as 1783, Jefferson had planned a journey across the continent. Writing a letter to George Rogers Clark, William's elder brother, he invoked the rumors that the English were raising "a very large sum . . . for exploring the country from the Missisipi to California." "They pretend it is only to promote knolege. I am afraid they have thoughts of colonising into that quarter."[7]

Although the money never materialized for an American expedition, Jefferson privately continued to build up one of the nation's most comprehensive geographic archives delineating the western continent. Jefferson collected European travel narratives and maps modeled on Native American sources. A year before the passage of the Land Ordinance Act of 1785, Jefferson circulated a document planning the government of unsettled western territories lying within the national border. His attached map, while not yet laid out according to the rectangular grid pattern, graphically anticipates the foundation of states, listed from north to south as "Sylvania," "Michigania," "Assenisipia," "Illinoia," "Polypotamia," and so forth. The combined passage of the Land Ordinance of 1785 and the Northwest Ordinance of 1787 reflected not only Jefferson's but also the country's general imperial perspective. It implemented a writing system that, by its universal portrayal of land as subject to the national grid, already represented on paper the possible inclusion of territories far beyond the existing national borders, two decades before the French offered to sell the Louisiana Territory.[8]

By the time he wagered the congressional proposal that would finally grant him financial support for the western explorations by Lewis and Clark, Jefferson had embraced the English conceit and camouflaged the

7. *LLC*, 654.

8. Thomas Jefferson, "Report of a Plan of Government for the Western Territory, 1784," in Merrill D. Peterson, ed., *The Portable Thomas Jefferson* (New York, 1977), 254–258. On Jefferson's collection on the American Northwest, see Allen, *Passage through the Garden*, 60–72. See also Moulton, "Introduction," in *Journals*, II, 1–48.

On the residual and emergent territorial appetites of eighteenth-century Anglo-Americans, see Marc Egnal, *A Mighty Empire: The Origins of the American Revolution* (Ithaca, N.Y., 1988). On imperial attitudes inspired by the two ordinances, see Robert David Sack, *Human Territoriality: Its Theory and History* (Cambridge, 1986); William Boelhower, *Through a Glass Darkly: Ethnic Semiosis in American Literature* (Venice, 1984).

expedition's inherently imperial agenda by making the conventions of literature the key to advertising and selling the project. In his correspondence with the members of the various congressional factions, Jefferson emphasized that in order to mollify the international contenders for the western territories—France, Spain, and Russia—the expedition had to maintain the appearances of a "literary pursuit."[9]

While this diplomatic conceit failed to convince some of the imperial powers—the Spanish, for example, saw through Jefferson's ruse and, fearing American "thoughts of colonising," refused permission for the government-sponsored expedition to "explore the course of the Missouri River"—it described the practical strategies that determined the geographical education of the individual expedition members. Jefferson arranged for Lewis and Clark to go through a crash course in modern scientific theories and related literary practices. They were thus not only trained in land surveying, astronomical observation, and navigation but were introduced to the nomenclature of botany, geology, and medicine, the narrative structure of natural history, and the art of mapmaking. Thus, before Lewis and Clark put either pen or pencil to paper, Jefferson had imposed a certain authorial control over all aspects of the expedition's literary productions: in order to facilitate the expedition's successful geographical narrative—the proof of a water route to the Pacific—he dictated everything from the choice of writing utensils to the secret writing codes required for the transmission of classified information.[10]

Thus overseeing the literary education of the expedition party, Jefferson ultimately made geography the expedition's master narrative. In addition to providing a map showing the most recent information regarding the Missouri River and the western half of the North American continent, Jefferson gave Lewis and Clark shortly before their departure a letter containing his personal instructions for recording the alien lands and peoples. Prefaced with the directive, "You will . . . endeavor to make yourself acquainted, as far as a diligent pursuit of your journey shall admit, with the names of the [Indian] nations and their numbers," Jefferson's instructions were written in the form of a questionnaire:

9. LLC, 13.

10. Jehlen, "Literature of Colonization," in Bercovitch, ed., Cambridge History of American Literature, I, 150; LLC, 18. On Jefferson's training of Lewis and Clark, see Silvio A. Bedini, Thomas Jefferson: Statesman of Science (London, 1990), 339–350; William H. Goetzmann, New Lands, New Men: America and the Second Great Age of Discovery (New York, 1986), 112.

the extent and limits of their possessions;

their relations with other tribes of nations;

their language, traditions, monuments;

their ordinary occupations in agriculture, fishing, hunting, war, arts, and the implements for these;

. . . .

Other objects worthy of notice will be

the soil and face of the country, it's growth and vegetable productions, especially those not of the U.S.

the animals of the country generally, and especially those not known in the U.S.

the remains or accounts of any which may be deemed rare or extinct;

the mineral productions of every kind . . . ;

volcanic appearances;

climate, as characterised by the thermometer, by the proportion of rainy, cloudy, and clear days, by lightning, hail, snow, ice, by the access and recess of frost.

This list, which imitates the questionnaire Jefferson had answered for his *Notes on the State of Virginia,* dictates, in the vein of the school geographer's catechism, the categories and the priorities of geographic information. Lewis and Clark are to begin their records by drawing the territorial boundaries of Native American nations. This was to be appended with both empirical and descriptive observations, so that in the end the official narrative not only provided a comprehensive description of the traversed territories but afforded that kind of geographic information that Jefferson deemed vital to administering the territorial annexation and cultural alignment of the western lands with the national domain.[11]

In case there was any doubt about the mission's literary goal, Jefferson's letter spelled out for the future journal its thesis and opening lines. The thesis statement was clear: find "the most direct and practicable water communication across this continent for the purposes of commerce." For the opening lines of the journals Jefferson suggested the following script: "Beginning at the mouth of the Missouri, you will take observations of latitude and longitude, at all remarkeable points on the river, and especially at the mouths of rivers, at rapids, at islands, and other places and objects distinguished by such natural marks and characters of a durable kind, as that they may with certainty be recognised here-

11. *LLC,* 28, 61–63.

after." In practice, this meant that mapping the expedition's route and geographical observations were to become the expedition leaders' daily authorial duty.[12]

Jefferson's concern for finding "durable" places and objects echoes the general cultural attitude toward maps and geographic representations as material and inherently stable texts. Thus understood, the Lewis and Clark map, consisting of figures, words, and the all-encompassing grid, would simultaneously transfix the unknown western lands and stabilize the untold course of the expedition. The concern for durability allows Jefferson to assign the map, and subsequently all of Lewis and Clark's literary records, two functions. First, by invoking the geographic records as stable texts, he confers upon the expedition's narrative the status of a scientific experiment; with each mapping of a geographic datum, the expedition's course (and narrative) becomes a predictable event, an event that not only can be traced locally but, like a mathematical proof, can be repeated indefinitely. Second, with the implication that geography is a durable text comes the implication that it is also a durable object, a consumer good. Indeed, Jefferson shows an obsessive concern for the preservation of all records, and "his instructions to Lewis suggest that the written records themselves constitute the major find or commodity to be brought back." Or, as Jefferson informed Lewis:

> Your observations are to be taken with great pains and accuracy, to be entered distinctly and intelligibly for others as well as yourself, to comprehend all the elements necessary, with the aid of the usual tables, to fix the latitude and longitude of the places at which they were taken, and are to be rendered to the war-office, for the purpose of having the calculations made concurrently by proper persons within the U.S. Several copies of these as well as of your other notes should be made at leisure times, and put into the care of the most trust-worthy of your attendants, to guard, by multiplying them, against the accidental losses to which they will be exposed.

Writing the expedition's journal was thus made a group effort. It was the concern not just of the two leaders but of almost half of the expedition's company.[13]

12. *LLC*, 61–62.

13. Jehlen, "Literature of Colonization," in Bercovitch, ed., *Cambridge History of American Literature*, I, 157; *LLC*, 62

At least eight members of the expedition took up the task of writing and rewriting the daily occurrences and observations. The journals kept by Sergeants Patrick Gass, John Ordway, and Charles Floyd were strikingly similar. Indeed, this mixed assembly of authors produced a surprisingly static, homogenous account. With personal anecdote only occasionally breaking up the journals' narrative structure, it appeared that Jefferson's geographic writing instructions were a successful tool in making multiple authors produce and reproduce one uniform narrative. By abiding the process of geographic writing, the expedition company worked at the bidding of the writing master; from a distance, Jefferson controlled many moments of leisure as his instructions transformed a band of military men into a modern scriptorium, a semimechanical copy shop.[14]

THE GEOGRAPHICAL APPRENTICES AND THEIR RECORDS

Writing the journals, Lewis and Clark also adhered obediently to Jefferson's instructions. For the outbound journey to the Pacific Ocean, the story of their journals can be divided chronologically and geographically into two parts. The first presents the journey up the Missouri River to Fort Mandan between May 1804 and April 1805. On the way, Lewis and Clark rigorously trained their crew, at the same time surveying and recording the course of the river and the lay of the land. At Fort Mandan, they diligently wrote up their own observations as well as those taken from interviews with Mandan and Hidatsa Indians, producing a narrative report, an ethnographic table, and a topographic map—the very materials prescribed by Jefferson and then cited in his message to the American people. For the second half of the expedition, between April and November 1805, the story encompasses the outbound expedition crossing the unknown lands from the Mandan villages to the Pacific Ocean.[15]

For most of the first part of the outbound journey, the entries of Lewis and Clark create a parallel and complementary narrative. On September 17, 1804, for example, Lewis enters into his journal:

14. Cutright, *History of the Lewis and Clark Journals,* 8–11.

15. Here I want to acknowledge the essays compiled by William F. Willingham and Leonoor Swets Ingraham, eds., *Enlightenment Science in the Pacific Northwest: The Lewis and Clark Expedition* (Portland, Oreg., 1984), where scholars discuss the documents produced during the expedition's first leg. For example, James Ronda discusses Lewis and Clark's ethnographic writings, Gary Moulton their maps, and John Logan Allen the reception history of the journals but with conclusions that are different from mine.

On the Lard. shore, one mile and a haf above the mouth of Corvus Creek observed equal Altitudes of ☉ with Sextant.—

	h	m	s		h	m	s
A.M.	7	46	49	P.M.	2	59	50
"		47	25		3	1	30
"		49	12	"		3	3

Altd. by sextant at the time of Observatn. 53° 17′ 45″
Observed meridian Altitude of ☉'s L.L. with Octant by the back Observation 87° 31′ 00″.

As the expedition's appointed prose writer, natural historian, and ethnographer, Lewis generally added to the cartographic reduction of places a topographic description, particularizing the land. Thus, he enters for the same day:

> Having for many days past confined myself to the boat, I determined to devote this day to amuse myself on shore with my gun and view the interior of the country lying between the river and the Corvus Creek . . . passed a grove of plumb trees loaded with fruit and now ripe. observed but little difference between this fruit and that of a similar kind common to the Atlantic States . . . found the country in every direction for about three miles intersected with deep revenes and steep irregular hills of 100 to 200 ft high . . . this senery already rich pleasing and beatiful, was still farther hightened by immence herds of Buffaloe deer Elk and Antelopes.

Lewis here cleaves to Jefferson's writing instructions. As demanded by the letter, Lewis uses quantitative measurements to catalog local samples of flora and fauna, comparing these with those species familiar to the eastern audience. However, when analyzing the country's geography—what Jefferson called the "soil and face of the country"—Lewis indulges in poetic license, applying the aesthetic measurement of the picturesque. Instead of using size and weight, Lewis invokes the categories of the "pleasing" and the "beautiful" as well as the category of "s[c]enery." This category mediates between the aesthetic and the economic. As he discusses the country's geographical properties in economic terms, the value of beauty is "hightened" because the "immence herds" suggested fertile soil and hunting grounds for the prospective colonist.[16]

By comparison, Clark, as the designated cartographer, keeps his jour-

16. *Journals*, III, 80–81, 85.

nal entries focused on the questionnaire's geodetic rationale. On September 18, 1804, he wrote:

> I Killed a prarie wolf to day about the Sise of a Gray fox with a bushey
> tail   the head and ears like a Fox wolf, and barks like a Small Dog—
>   The annimale which we have taken for the Fox is this wolf, we have
> seen no Foxes.
>   . . . Set out early   wind from the N W. Modrt.   our boat being
> much litened goes much better than usial

Course N. 45° E.	1	m[il]e. to the lower point of a Island (1)
N. 25° E.	3	me. to a pt. on the L.S. passed the Isd. at me. & Some Sand bars makeing from it a Creek opsd on S. S.
N. 14° E.	1½	mes. to a poi[n]t of willows on the L.S.
N. 10 W.	1½	mes. to a point of wood on the L.S. hard wind
N. 22 W.	1	me. to a pt. of wood on the L.S. and came to at 5 oClock to jurke the meat killed to day and what was
	8	collected from what was Killed yesterday, I e 10 Deer to Day 4 & a Elk yesterday a Cole night for the Season

The hunting scene aside, in which the "prarie wolf" becomes subject of a comparative natural history lesson, Clark uses his words sparingly. Instead, his journal consistently subordinates the daily narrative to geographic figures; distance markers tally the recorded events while geographic coordinates structure the written signs on the page.[17]

I present this lengthy comparison to illustrate the extent to which the journals fulfilled Jefferson's logic of geographic authorship. Regardless of their personal cravings for diversion, their recordings of the fauna and flora, or their efforts in delineating the environment according to either an aesthetic or a scientific mode of representation, Lewis and Clark's journal entries were fundamentally subject to the narrative grammar and vocabulary of modern geography books. Whereas the narrative form of the journal invited a linear and inherently open-ended historical narrative, when considered as a practical extension of Jefferson's working map and ques-

17. *Journals*, III, 86.

tionnaire, the Lewis and Clark journal entries emerged as a closed—or, rather, territorially enclosed—text. As a contained text, the journal, the daily mappings, and the overall compressed mode of selective representation create the illusion that the world is to be recorded in a set of finite homologies and with corresponding structures. Just as local places were fixed by coordinates, so too the narrative entries describing local animal life and the cultural habits of the newly encountered Native American peoples appeared immutable. In their overall narrative technique, the journals suggest that whatever special textual format was used—whether the diary, taxonomic table, map, or poetic description—it was always an expression of a universal geography.

But the narrative was not quite universal enough. Though written outside the national domain, the journals illustrate in principle the textual manifestation of "the association between power and *locales*" in the organization of modern nation-states. The expression of power is best imagined as a locale: "Locales refer to the settings of interaction, including the physical aspects of setting—their 'architecture'—within which systemic aspects of interaction and social relations are concentrated." As Lewis and Clark's journals were written in relative obedience to Jefferson's instructions, they were not only unable to transcend the prescriptive structural form of Jefferson's original map but with every journal entry reified the monitorial function of the government-sponsored "literary pursuit." Indeed, Jefferson's textual apparatus often clouded Lewis and Clark's response to what they actually saw; their records and manuscript maps persistently registered imaginary geographic features, projecting a continuous transcontinental fluvial morphology that resembled Jefferson's speculative geographic model of a northwest passage.[18]

THE TWO-WAY RECORD

And yet, for a brief period, the official narrative fell into profound disarray. In contrast to the care previously given to the mapping of the land, the Lewis and Clark journals become increasingly discontinuous after leaving Fort Mandan. For the distance of three hundred miles, between

18. Anthony Giddens, *A Contemporary Critique of Historical Materialism*, II, *The Nation-State and Violence* (Berkeley, Calif., 1985), 12–13; Allen, *Passage through the Garden,* 367–369.

the Great Falls of the Missouri and Traveler's Rest in the Montana Rocky Mountains, their otherwise meticulous geographic records show a large gap. Lewis writes in sporadic effusive bursts, before he stops recording daily events in his journal altogether. At the same time, Clark's log becomes even sparser and shows gaps despite his daily routine of recording geographic observations in journal maps. In doing so, both Lewis and Clark effectively disobey the president's charge to provide an exact transcript of the land and the expedition's activities. They interrupt the continuity of their documentary narrative. By not keeping their journals and geodetic log as well as cartographic drafts, both Lewis and Clark sever themselves from the authorial supervision of their patron. And, more significantly, for the duration of their narrative silence they disrupt the structural unity of Jefferson's prescribed geographic textuality, thereby suspending the formulated conception of a familiar, controlled western landscape.[19]

In critical discussions, this gap is explained as the result of Lewis and Clark's contact with the concrete reality of the American continent. According to literary historians, the physical hardship of journeying in a rugged terrain sapped the men's energies. Hunger, exhaustion, and illness prevented Clark, the better-skilled mapmaker of the two, from drawing out his geodetic and geographic observations. This interpretation also serves to explain Lewis's prolonged narrative silences. Viewed in such physiological terms, critical discussions engender historical-fictional accounts of their own, celebrating the fitful and uneven narrative of the journals as a tale of both masculine and narrative endurance, as the raw and muscular material prefiguring the national form of the great American literary epic. Expanding from the physiological analysis are psychological interpretations that divide the journal's authorship according to the analytical predilection for explaining the individual in terms of either rationality or emotionality. Scholars persistently identify Clark as the rational, objective, and, in short, ideal scientific recorder. By contrast,

19. Moulton divides the "Expedition maps" into two categories: atlas maps (laid down on separate sheets of paper) and journal maps (those drawn on the pages of the journals). Moulton concedes that "Clark's mapping strategy is not clear." Despite an unbroken series of atlas maps, the dwindling and final lack of journal maps after Fort Mandan remains unexplained—"another mystery . . . in the number of suspected losses of maps and journals." See his essay "Lewis and Clark: Pioneering Cartographers on the Columbia River," in Willingham and Ingraham, eds., *Enlightenment Science,* 19–26.

Lewis is identified in terms of Romantic authorship, as sensitive and subjective—that is, as the literary voice of the journals.[20]

After leaving the Mandan villages Lewis and Clark did more than travel through the vast, mountainous, and largely unpopulated landscape of what today are the states of Montana and Idaho. They also made contact with the natural and the sublime, experienced their terrors, and subsequently got lost in space. Possibly coping with bouts of agoraphobia and cultural alienation, they lost their common discursive sense of orientation. Without recourse to such mollifying frames of reference as the picturesque, they switched their narrative code. Having so far relied upon the narrative demands of a documentary geographic report, both journalists responded with what amounts to writer's block. While Clark continues to write perfunctorily, like an automaton he merely records the basic observations necessary for tracking the course. Lewis, on the other hand, responds to the novel terrain by turning from the everyday journalistic to a more effusive poetic mode of writing. When arriving at the Great Missouri Falls, he produces several narrative sketches that show the attributes of a spontaneous overflow of emotion as well as the coded language of the Romantic imagination; these outpourings were then followed by months of relative silence.[21]

The narrative gap may be attributed to both a literal and a figurative crisis of orientation. This disorientation, however, I suggest originates less in heroic or Romantic conceptions of the modern self than in the daily practice of applying the literary conventions of geographic discourse. In the weeks after leaving the Mandan villages, Lewis and Clark not only traveled through alien landscapes; they also navigated the novel terrain

20. For scholarly discussions in this vein, see Bernard DeVoto, *The Course of Empire* (Boston, 1952); Goetzmann, *New Lands, New Men,* 97–126. More popular presentations of this kind can be found in Stephen E. Ambrose, *Undaunted Courage: Meriwether Lewis, Thomas Jefferson, and the Opening of the American West* (New York, 1996); Dayton Duncan, *Lewis and Clark: An Illustrated History* (New York, 1997). For a more critical analysis of both the nationalistic overtones and process of masculinization at work in the Lewis and Clark expedition, see Jehlen, "Literature of Colonization," in Bercovitch, ed., *Cambridge History of American Literature,* I, 152–153; Dana D. Nelson, *National Manhood: Capitalist Citizenship and the Imagined Fraternity of White Men* (Durham, N.C., 1998), 74–75.

21. See Jehlen, "Literature of Colonization," in Bercovitch, ed., *Cambridge History of American Literature,* I, 158–161. See also Albert Furtwangler, *Acts of Discovery: Visions of America in the Lewis and Clark Journals* (Urbana, Ill., 1993), 25–27; Larzer Ziff, *Writing in the New Nation: Prose, Print, and Politics in the Early United States* (New Haven, Conn., 1991), 159–160.

depending on an alien, non-Western mode of geographic representation. For the second part of the outbound journey, Lewis and Clark used Native American sources extensively for plotting the expedition's course. Having spent the previous winter among the Mandan and Hidatsa tribes, they undertook the bibliographic task of collecting, comparing, and transcribing Native American geographic accounts and documents into the expedition's official map. Mandan and Hidatsa maps and narrative mappings of the western lands here entered into the Jeffersonian cartographic blueprint for future American social engineering. In this context, the narrative gap in the journals is more than a moment of practical disorientation. It is the product of making literary contact with Native American authorship and in fact becomes a transcript of the discursive collision between two incompatible modes of recording the geography of the land.

For Lewis and Clark, making contact with Mandan and Hidatsa geographers became principally a literary transaction, involving authors and translators working as editors as well as various scripts and transcripts. Clark's journal entry for January 7, 1805, illustrates one of many recurring entries in which the Anglo-American geographer prepared the geographic record:

> A verry Cold clear Day, the Themtr Stood at 22 d below o wind N W., the river fell 1 inch   Several indians returned from hunting, one of them the Big White Chef of the Lower Mandan Village, Dined with us, and gave me a Scetch of the Countrey as far as the high mountains, and on the South Side of the River Rejone, he Says that the river rejone recves 6 Small rivers on the S. Side, and that the Countrey is verry hilley and the greater part Covered with timber, Great numbers of beaver etc.— the 3 men returned from hunting, they kill'd 4 Deer and 2 wolves, Saw Buffalow a long ways off, I continue to Draw a connected plote from the information of Traders, Indians and my own observation and idea—from the best information, the Great falls is about [800?] miles nearly west.

Clark's entry illustrates the ways in which Native American mapmakers injected their geographic knowledge and epistemology into the expedition's narrative. Upon invitation, usually conducted at moments of conviviality, Clark or Lewis asked the tribal chiefs or elders to produce a sketch of the land. These sketches were usually written with sticks or charcoal in ashes, sand, or on skins. On one occasion, the sketch consisted of a three-dimensional model of the land, using objects laid out on the ground. Throughout the expedition, geographic writings like these functioned as metatextual vehicles capable of mediating between vastly different linguistic cultures. The graphic nature of both Native American and Anglo-American topographic sketches repeatedly facilitated communication between the expedition and native populations, despite the fact that the process of direct translation between the various European and Amerindian languages had already failed.[22]

Once they recognized Native American maps as a communicative intertext, Lewis and Clark almost immediately began to seek control over the native geographic archive. Acting in continuation of Jefferson's questionnaire, they in turn would question the native mapmaker's role of authorship and the authenticity of the text. As Lewis explained in his first letter report to Jefferson, the map that was included in the packet had undergone extensive authentication: the map was not only "formed from the corresponding testimony of a number of Indians who have visited the country" but was also the result of Lewis and Clark's having "seperately and carefully examined [them] on that subject." Only after going through this interview did Lewis feel comfortable approving the contents of the map, stating, "We therefore think it entitled to some degree of confidence." Lewis's letter suggests that much of their authorial labors consisted of the kind of legalistic detective work that usually accompanies the evaluation of eyewitness reports or, in this case, the textual scholarship involved when documenting the provenance of literary editions. In their interviews, Lewis and Clark thus went so far as to assign Native American mapmakers the Foucaultian "author-function" as a means for both classifying and transcribing their geographic writings.[23]

For example, when working on their first official report while wintering among the Mandan people on the Upper Missouri River, it was only after Lewis and Clark named "Big White" as the individual author and subjected him to a cross-examination that they felt secure enough to register the Mandan "testimony," the tribal elder's sketch map, as an authentic document. The same principle applied when the Mandan chief Sheheke gave Clark a "Scetch of the Countrey as far as the high Mountains and on the South Side of the River Rejone." The "Scetch" was incorporated into the expedition's geographical archive, where it was filed for future reference under the name of the author. By treating Native American geo-

22. *Journals,* III, 269, V, 88, VII, 54, 86, 92.
23. *LLC,* 233.

graphic texts as literary artifacts, Lewis and Clark translated the Mandan sketches into "scientific" texts; in Foucaultian terms such texts "dealing with cosmology and the heavens, medicine and illnesses, natural sciences and geography were accepted [since] the Middle Ages, and accepted as 'true,' only when marked with the name of their author." Once the native reports were classified as scientific texts, Lewis and Clark were able to align the Mandan map with Jefferson's "instructions" to expand the geographic archive of the United States government "with the names of the nations and their numbers; the extent and limits of their possessions; their relations with other tribes of nations; their language, traditions, monuments."[24]

An examination of Clark's copy of Big White's maps shows the similarity between the geographic records derived from European cartographers and those assembled by Native American geographers. Crafted in the tradition of picture writing, Big White's sketches resembled outwardly the kind of pictorial map used for pilgrimages in medieval Europe, Renaissance topographies, and eighteenth-century travel maps of America. The Mandan line map was familiar to the trained eyes of Clark in particular because it resembled his own journal maps of the country's geography: lines stand for rivers, dots for places and mountains, and spatial relations imply scale and distance. This, at least, was the way in which Clark interpreted the graphic systems used by the Mandan mapmaker. In transcribing the maps offered by Big White and others, he assumed the Mandan and Hidatsa maps were part of a universal writing system shared by both the native population and Anglo-American geographers. Writing with the conviction that he recognizes the chief's description as the land lying between Fort Mandan and the "high" Rocky Mountains, Clark unhesitatingly transcribed and assimilated Big White's sketch into the "connected plote" of the small-scale map that he and Lewis would not only send to Jefferson but would use to navigate a terrain that so far no European mapmaker had visited.[25]

24. *Journals,* III, 269; *LLC,* 62; Michel Foucault, "What is an Author?" in Josué Harari, ed., *Textual Strategies: Perspectives in Post-Structuralist Criticism* (Ithaca, N.Y., 1979), 148–149. James P. Ronda makes the important suggestion that the sketches collected by Lewis and Clark might also have consisted of verbal descriptions, which would emphasize the extent to which the rules of literature informed the expedition's mode of collecting information. See *Lewis and Clark among the Indians* (Lincoln, Nebr., 1984), 128.

25. Big White's maps were the foundation of Clark's map sent to Jefferson and the secretary of war. See *Journals,* I, maps 31a, 31b.

Lewis and Clark were neither particularly naive nor the first to read Native American drawings as cartographic records. An illustrious group of Anglo-American writers ranging from Captain John Smith to Thomas Jefferson had commented on the uncanny similarity between native maps and Western cartographic representation. However, throughout the Anglo-American history of cartographic encounters, Native American symbol or line maps were either viewed dismissively, as primitive pictures, or they were read transculturally, as evolutionary precursors to and illustrations of the technological advances made by European mapmakers and geographers. Both of these attitudes prevented Anglo-American writers, including Lewis and Clark, from realizing how comparatively ungeographic the Native American maps were in relation to modern textbook definitions of geography and its modes of representation. Native American maps were conceived in the oral tradition; stored in the memories of chiefs and elders, they were only supplements to an orally performed "picture." The map's graphic appearance, so familiar to the geoliterate eye, easily misleads because it represents the experience of the land and landscape without using a common writing system like the geographic grid. As Barbara Belyea explains, "Amerindian maps rely not on fixed positions in space but on a pattern of interconnected lines. Spacing and directions of north/south/east/west are simplified, even ignored, since the key to reading the map is not to locate points in space but to trace a continuous path from one geographic feature to another."[26]

26. Barbara Belyea, "Inland Journeys, Native Maps," *Cartographica,* XXXIII, no. 2 (Summer 1996), 6. Her essay is one of a growing number of studies concentrating on the process and politics surrounding the translation of Native American maps. See also Matthew Sparke, "Between Demythologizing and Deconstructing the Map: Shawnadithit's Newfound-land and the Alienation of Canada," *Cartographica,* XXXII, no. 1 (Spring 1995), 1–21.

For a survey and discussion of Native American mapmaking and its intertextual relation to colonial British writings, see the essays in G. Malcolm Lewis, ed., *Cartographic Encounters: Perspectives on Native American Mapmaking and Map Use* (Chicago, 1998); also see Mark Warhus, *Another America: Native American Maps and the History of Our Land* (New York, 1997); Louis De Vorsey, Jr., "Silent Witnesses: Native American Maps," *Georgia Review,* XLVI (1992), 709–726; Rainer Vollmar, *Indianische Karten Nordamerikas: Beiträge zur historischen Kartographie vom 16. bis zum 19. Jahrhundert* (Berlin, 1981); Lewis, "Indicators of Unacknowledged Assimilations from Amerindian Maps on Euro-American Maps of North America," *Imago Mundi,* XXXVIII (1986), 9–34; Lewis, "Indian Maps: Their Place in the History of Plains Cartography," *Great Plains Quarterly,* IV (1984), 91–108; Lewis, "Indigenous Maps and Mapping of North American Indians," *Map Collector,* IX (1979), 25–35.

Reading Native American maps with the goal of translating them into the code of European scientific geography, then, inevitably became an exercise in misreading. The apparent graphic similarity between Native American maps and Lewis and Clark's geographic map was fortuitous at best, for native maps did not distinguish exclusively between river courses, portages, and trails; nor did they require the explicit representation of scale or direction. To make matters even more complicated for Lewis and Clark, Big White's maps not only marked geographic features but were graphic representations charting geographical spaces and tribal histories. Routes, landmarks, sacred sites, and historical events all appear at once in the Native American map. "When copied by explorers who had little knowledge of these characteristics . . . such patterns often appear to us, in the light of our knowledge of the geography, as so erroneous as to have been based on little more than myth." The Native American map image functioned as a documentary narrative weaving together geography, history, and mythology.[27]

The above analysis describes Lewis and Clark's efforts of translating Amerindian records in the emerging terms of Romantic literary history; it separates geography from mythology precisely at the cultural moment when the early American student of literature was supposed to distinguish between history and myth. Such a distinction would have been more than alien to the Mandan and Hidatsa Indians. They used maps in their various material incarnations (birch bark, leather, sand, and rock) in order to keep track of both present and past migrations, of migrations that were undertaken by the living as well as the dead. For the Native American geographer, ultimately the land itself constituted a three-dimensional, deep text marked by the accretions of sameness, and not the kind of two-dimensional text by which Western geographers sought to negotiate the differences in space only. In the pictographic maps that Mandan or Hidatsa elders offered to Lewis and Clark, lines delineated crossings between the sacred and the physical world, dots traced the tribal settlements as well as those of their gods, and spatial relations negotiated the distance between time and eternity.[28]

Finally, what made these seemingly "written" maps virtually untrans-

27. Lewis, "Indian Maps," *Great Plains Quarterly*, IV (1984), 104.

28. For a conceptual discussion of "deep space" representations of land among non-European cultures, see D. F. McKenzie, *Bibliography and the Sociology of Texts* (London, 1986), 31–35; Yi-Fu Tuan, *Space and Place: The Perspective of Experience* (Minneapolis, Minn., 1977). For map examples linking time and place, see Warhus, *Another America*, 7–9.

latable for Lewis and Clark was the fact that they were part of ritual cere-
monies in which maps were produced in response to specific situations
and requests, such as a hunt, a seasonal migration, or an intertribal meeting. Native American maps were made from memory, not from a specific
textual archive; it was "the act of making them that was important, the
recapitulation of environmental features, not the material objects themselves." The Mandan and Hidatsa texts were produced for the benefit of
Lewis and Clark at the performative moment when the tribal elders were
demonstrating their hospitality by offering to educate the cultural strangers. Conversely, throughout the ritual of asking for and receiving directions, the expedition leaders were put on the spot in that they had to
navigate the elders' political and social authority while seeking to decipher which parts of the ritual acts carried the pedagogical, performative,
or informational function. Following the interviews, as they were describing the country by using the Native American maps, Lewis and Clark
experienced, at least briefly, the unfamiliar position of discursive sub-
ordination. The ritual's symbolic density compromised their individual
authorial agency, relegating them to a "liminal minority position." In
the case of their interview with Big White, the Mandan chief unwittingly
anticipated and inverted the expedition's rhetorical subject position.
Wielding a technology that looked almost interchangeable with the European geoliterary apparatuses of conquest and subjugation, this Native
American mapmaker here unwittingly invaded and colonized the Anglo-
American geographical writing habits and at least briefly shaped the expedition's documentary narrative.[29]

LOST IN SPACE

It was no wonder, then, that Lewis and Clark got lost in space. Having
meshed Native American geographic texts with those prepared by the
American government, their literary pursuit fell into complete disarray.
Once the expedition started its second leg toward the Pacific by following
the neatly transcribed native instructions, Lewis and Clark quickly realized that they were traveling, in Western conceptions of space, a road to
nowhere. Rivers didn't show up where they were supposed to be; dis-

29. Robert A. Rundstrom, "A Cultural Interpretation of Inuit Map Accuracy," *Geographical Review*, LXXX (1990), 165. Here I invoke the work on postcolonial and national subjectivity by Homi K. Bhabha, "DissemiNation: Time, Narrative, and the Margins of the Modern Nation," in Bhabha, ed., *Nation and Narration* (New York, 1990), 291–322.

tances were off by hundreds of miles; projected villages were regularly missing because they had long since ceased to exist. The expedition's progress and its literary project were fundamentally disrupted from the moment when Lewis realized not only that he had misread the Native American maps but that he and his fellow note takers had no recourse to a geographical lexicon or mode of representation by which to decipher the Mandans' and Hidatsas' thick description of the land, a land constructed in terms of time as well as space.

The extent of their disorientation becomes explicit in the journal's literary rather than geographical mode of writing, in particular when Lewis describes his encounter with the Great Missouri Falls on June 13, 1805. There he scaled the bluff opposite the falls, thus assuming the scopic position of both the geographic author and modern Romantic subject. For several pages, Lewis indulges in an elaborate description of the "grandest sight I ever beheld": "From the reflection of the sun on the spray or mist which arrises from these falls there is a beatifull rainbow produced which adds not a little to the beauty of this majestically grand scenery." Although engaging the various writing strategies that had been at his disposal since his training in Philadelphia, Lewis grapples with uncertainty. "After wrighting this imperfect discription," he continues:

> I again viewed the falls and was so much disgusted with the imperfect idea which it conveyed of the scene that I determined to draw my pen across it and begin agin, but then reflected that I could not perhaps succeed better than pening the first impressions of the mind; I wished for the pencil of Salvator Rosa or the pen of Thompson, that I might be enabled to give to the enlightened world some just idea of this truly magnifficent and sublimely grand object, which has from the commencement of time been concealed from the view of civilized man; but this was fruitless and vain. I most sincerely regreted that I had not brought a crimee [camera] obscura with me by the assistance of which even I could have hoped to have done better but alas this was also out of my reach.

Lewis marshals in rapid succession the literary strategies and technological instruments that were available to the American citizens for representing the land. First, he tries the word; taking his cues from belles lettres, he imagines himself in the place of the popular nature poet James Thomson, author of *The Seasons* (1730). To this he adds the medium of the image, and becomes the Romantic quasi-realistic painter Salvator Rosa.

As if remembering his scientific training in physics and optics, he assumes the perspective of the visual artist and prototypical future photographer, viewing the world upside down as if from inside the camera obscura.[30]

However, after invoking these various technologies to capture the terrific experience of the moment, Lewis realizes that none of the conventional practices of the Western "literary pursuit" was capable of recording the physical as well as spiritual depth that the falls' apparition was evincing in his mind. In a final effort to grasp the meaning of the Missouri Falls (and the country he had traveled so far) in relation to himself, Lewis returns to what he knows best, the mapping project. Instead of "pening" the country, he turns to charting "some of the stronger features" of the land in map form. But to Lewis's surprise his efforts were frustrated again: even the cartographic mode of representation does not enable him to transfix and locate the country's emotive source of beauty and personal significance, or what Lewis calls the "object which at this moment fills me with such pleasure and astonishment."[31]

Indeed, after this episode Lewis assumed a profoundly antiauthorial posture. Lewis leaves off his description in the hope that perhaps one day "some able pencil" will come along to map and write his experience, at once observing and expressing the unfamiliar combination of viewing an alien landscape and lived-in space. In the weeks that followed—and here we must put this episode in the context of the overall narrative trajectory of the expedition—the representational uncertainty that was unveiled by the Missouri Falls marked the beginning of an extended period during which Lewis more or less withdrew from his authorial task. For the space of several weeks the journals record mostly Clark's laconic entries, detailing the expedition's geographic position in the global grid, the traveling distances, and memorable landmarks. But Lewis will not be heard from again until the expedition approaches the Pacific Coast.

Lewis's silence has been explained in terms of his role as the expedition leader who, distracted by the loss of geographical direction, lost his personal sense of compass. Another way of explaining his silence would be to argue that Lewis as the representative Anglo-American subject confronted the extent to which a Western geographical consciousness abstracted, and thus possibly erased, not so much the local land but the individual sub-

30. *Journals,* IV, 285.
31. Ibid.

ject's sense of self. When using the native sketches, Lewis discovered that the expedition's descriptive technologies—including maps and narrative—were operating inside a textual matrix whose primary function was to represent space as an inherently empty and emptiable construct. Moving inside such an unfamiliar and unmarked space, any geoliterate Anglo-American citizen would have had great difficulty in embedding and sustaining his or her personal identity. Being stranded in the expansive space of the western continent, Lewis discovers that in comparison to the Native American mapmaker he was suddenly occupying a textually inscribed subject position that fails to relate the depth of the outside world to the inside of one's personal imaginings.

Or it may be said that Lewis deconstructs the Western and Anglo-American discourse of geographic writing. His inability to use a map or a geographical writing protocol in order to locate his emotional sense of subjectivity points to an epistemological crisis surrounding the discourse of modern geography. In this technology-driven discourse, the designation of the personal and the emotive was by definition either completely deferred or became transferred to group identities like the nation. As the location of the modern subject as such was not the intention of either school or official geographies, the internalized writing practices of geography prevented Lewis from perceiving the land through the eyes of the individual and ultimately alienated him from the geographic writing project.[32]

The silence and the experience of utter disorientation were a relatively brief episode in the overall structure of the journals. A close reading of the journal entries written during the descent of the Columbia River suggests that Lewis had recovered his sense of authorial duty as well as his footing in Anglo-American modes of writing about the land. Indeed, he even seems to have become reconciled to the geographic writing project. During the journey back, it is interesting to note, it was Lewis, the prose writer, and not Clark, the mapmaker, who frequently assumed the role of

32. In this context it is important to point out the work of Alexander von Humboldt, who tackled this epistemological dilemma by linking traditional geography to the function of biophysical processes. While Humboldt actually met Jefferson and many of the American scientific elite, his writings would not become influential until the mid-nineteenth century. For an overview of Humboldt's geography and its reception, see David N. Livingstone, *The Geographical Tradition: Episodes in the History of a Contested Enterprise* (Oxford, 1992); Margarita Bowen, *Empiricism and Geographical Thought: From Francis Bacon to Alexander von Humboldt* (Cambridge, 1981).

the master geographer, co-opting the pedagogic function of geographic writing in a way that is reminiscent of the Mandan mapping ritual. Moving back east and toward the Rocky Mountains, Lewis utilized maps and geographic sketches with the specific purpose to educate the Shoshone and Nez Percé tribes about the proper lay of the land. The ritual of geographic education here became reversed; it was no longer the tribal chiefs passing on knowledge to the American soldier-travelers, but Lewis who explained the continental geography. As the expedition backtracked many of its original trails, it became apparent that the two leaders assumed the authorial position similar to the one created by the expedition's sponsor, Thomas Jefferson. As they conversed with the various tribes, they discussed local geography no longer in native terms, but through the now-amended map that had originally been given to them by the president.

Lewis and Clark here fulfilled more than Jefferson's literary objective; they incorporated the native mode of geographical representation into the expedition's basic blueprint: the overextended continental image of the national map. Writing in the place of the absent writing master, they no longer used Native American geographies in order to compile a comprehensive transcript of the continent's geography. Rather, they used the Western geographical archive for training Amerindian group elders how to conceptualize the land properly, that is, as a textually defined container holding up for scrutiny land and people like so many literary objects. It is in view of this pedagogic zeal to simultaneously override and rewrite Native American geographies that the journals reveal a rare authorial investment and cultural judgment that was otherwise noticeably absent from the Lewis and Clark records. This decision provided the textual evidence confirming the suspicions held by the fellow imperial powers interested in the American Northwest, namely that American literary pursuits meant nothing less than "colonising into that quarter." By teaching the Western mode of geographic representation to Native Americans, Lewis and Clark invariably contributed to the project of continental colonization. As the expedition's dominant literary code, geographic writing thus not only controlled the journalistic agency of the writers but emerged as the basic literary and conceptual tool underwriting the national project of the "literary annihiliation" of the Native American.[33]

33. Ziff, *Writing in the New Nation,* 172. The geographic training sessions complicate the journals' widely celebrated "neutral scientific standard," as is frequently argued in discussions about Anglo-American military explorers and their exchange with Native Americans of the trans-Missouri West. For celebratory or uncritical discussions of the journals'

Indeed, when looking at the literary landscape of early-nineteenth-century America, popular poets as different as Henry Wadsworth Longfellow and Lydia Sigourney, and best-selling novelists like James Fenimore Cooper and Catharine Maria Sedgwick continued to work through the same cultural and pathological practices that reflect the type of geographic negotiation that Lewis and Clark encountered when trying to locate themselves and their Anglo-American culture on Native American maps. Cooper, for example, still finds it necessary to open his epic fiction *The Last of the Mohicans* with a lesson in geography. As if Native American geographies must be placed into the open before being displaced permanently, Cooper details for the audience, first, the disparate modes of geographic representation that underpin both native and Anglo-American cosmologies before asserting, much like Jefferson in his presidential message, the authority and two-dimensional framework of the traditional Western geographic discourse. It was not until nearly two centuries later that Native American authors such as Scott Momaday, Louise Erdrich, and William Least-Heat Moon began to demystify and replace the literary strategies of the nation's geographic master narrative. Least-Heat Moon's novel *PrairyErth: A Deep Map* (1991) offers the kind of local representation that Lewis and Clark's narrative strove for but failed to accomplish, namely a thick description of the land *and* the people, a description in which maps and personal anecdote, official documents and individual journals, history and faith are interwoven into a text of everyday geography.[34]

RECEPTION HISTORY AND NATIONAL (SELF-) INTEREST

I started this chapter with the observation that national interest facilitated the publication of the Lewis and Clark journals. The map and

---

"objective" style, see, for example, the essays in Willingham and Ingraham, eds., *Enlightenment Science;* also Ambrose, *Undaunted Courage,* 284, 337; Goetzmann, *New Lands, New Men,* 112. For a critical reassessment, see Jehlen, "The Literature of Colonization," in Bercovitch, ed., *Cambridge History of American Literature,* I, 153–154. The way in which the scientific fallacy informed travel writers has been the focus of critical attention, for example, in Mary Louise Pratt, *Imperial Eyes: Travel Writing and Transculturation* (London, 1992); James Clifford and George E. Marcus, eds., *Writing Culture: The Poetics and Politics of Ethnography* (Berkeley, Calif., 1986).

34. See James Fenimore Cooper, *The Last of the Mohicans* (1826) (New York, 1986), 31–32.

their letters were made public in order to ensure and legitimate the nation-state's investment in the recently acquired Louisiana Territory. Geographic writings—that is, the method of mapping the earth through coordinate points, the pattern of superinscribing new names over existing ones, and the subsequent geographic narrativization of cultures as spatial forms—provided the virtual means for the public to imagine the investment's returns: land and more land. The act of imagination, however, hinged not only on the way in which Jefferson or the United States government fantasized about gaining access to land and natural resources. It also turned on the way in which the habits of geographical literacy had already prepared the American public for the incorporation of the new territories. The stakes were immensely high because the Louisiana Territory would change the spatial and political integrity of the American nation-state. A whole new set of territorial boundaries would be required to present the state's external order. Such a reconfiguration of the nation's cartographic image inherently bore the potential to rewrite the existing political order and thereby destabilize the precarious balance of power among the members of the Republic.

The discipline of geographic discourse provided Jefferson with the strategic tool through which to prescribe and control the expedition members' individual narratives. When examining the publication history of the journals, this argument needs to be expanded to include the American reading public. While Jefferson used the bully pulpit to convey his vision of a transcontinental "republican empire," it was the nation's self-disciplined application of geographical literacy that set the stage for incorporating the new territories into the spatial figure of the nation-state. Within a year of Jefferson's presidential message, and shortly after the expedition's safe return was made public, at least two unauthorized accounts entered the literary marketplace, in which publishers, claiming popular demand, issued both the map and Lewis's letter, thus creating the first complete story of the expedition.

Among the first expedition narratives to be published were the anonymous British version *Travels of Capts. Lewis and Clarke* (1807) and its American counterpart *A Journal of the Voyages and Travels of a Corps of Discovery* (1807), written by the expedition member Patrick Gass. These narratives and their textual apparatus shaped much of the public response to the expedition and overshadowed the belated appearance of the first authorized account, Nicholas Biddle's *History of the Expedition under the*

Command of Captains Lewis and Clark (1814), which contained the first complete map showing the full journey (Figure 51).[35]

The map text was central to the success of the unofficial narratives. When American readers received copies of *The Travels of Capts. Lewis and Clarke,* one of its selling points was the fact that it was *"Illustrated* with a Map of the Country, Inhabited by the Western Tribes." This British account admitted to depending on the incomplete map Jefferson had shown Congress and on Lewis's first letter report, as neither Biddle's narrative nor the completed map was in circulation yet. The British account furthermore commented on the cartographic encounter between Lewis and Clark and Native Americans. It also observed the similarity between the latter's sketches and the expedition map and by presupposing a universal geographic code ended by subordinating the non-Western geographies to the dominant Western one. The book's map, reflecting the political climate, presented the British point of view: the space Americans called "California" now bore the name "New Albion" (Figure 52).[36]

National differences aside, the unofficial, incomplete, but widely reprinted map functioned to control at once the construction of the travelers and the travel narrative. Like the Jefferson map, it too contained its beginning and end while directing the reader's response with dotted lines and symbols. But whereas in Jefferson's message the map served to circumvent the individual voices of the reporter, in the popular narrative developed by the commercial press the map became the palimpsest on which readers could trace and identify the imaginary voices of Lewis and Clark. Throughout the *Travels of Capts. Lewis and Clarke,* the map

35. Unauthorized and, according to Cutright, "apocryphal" accounts such as the popular *Travels of Capts. Lewis and Clarke* ... (1807; London, 1809), set the tone of the journals' reception history. A more popular reception of the official Lewis and Clark journals probably was stymied by the fact that fellow members of the expedition published their accounts much sooner; see Patrick Gass, *A Journal of the Voyages and Travels of a Corps of Discovery* ... (Pittsburgh, 1807).

Biddle's British counterpart was a revised edition of the earlier anonymously published *Travels of Capts. Lewis and Clarke,* now called *Travels to the Source of the Missouri River and across the American Continent to the Pacific Ocean* (London, 1814) and supposedly written by Meriwether Lewis. This latter edition claimed to be the previously published "Lewis and Clarke's Travels." This work is not, however, what it pretended to be, for it contained no additional narratives but what had been presented in the presidential message. See the preface of *Travels to the Source of the Missouri,* xiv.

36. *Travels of Capts. Lewis and Clarke,* iv, 16, 51.

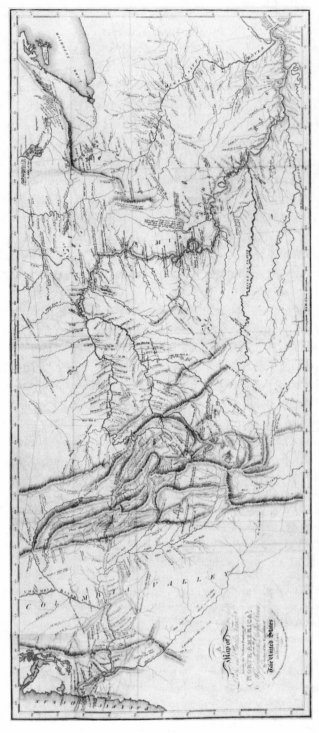

Figure 51. A Map of Lewis and Clark's Track across the Western Portion of North America. *Frontispiece to* Travels to the Source of the Missouri River and across the American Continent to the Pacific Ocean, *by Meriwether Lewis. 1814.* Courtesy, The Library Company of Philadelphia

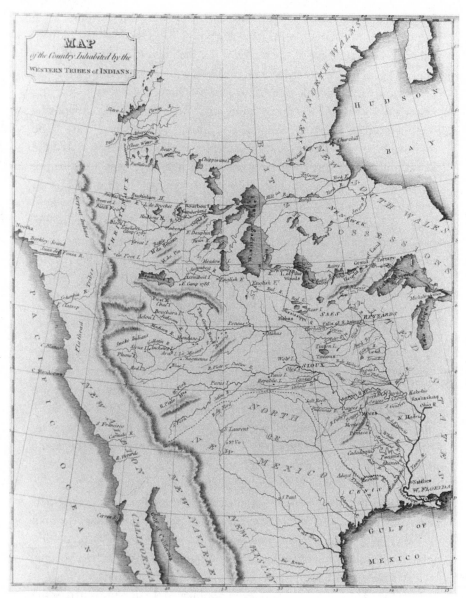

Figure 52. Map of the Country Inhabited by the Western Tribes of Indians. *From* Travels of Capts. Lewis and Clarke. . . . *1809.* Courtesy, Rare Books and Special Collections, Thomas Cooper Library, University of South Carolina

functioned to pinpoint the exact location of the narrative's agents; it became the figurative plot delineating in graphic form the locale of individual actions. In the case of Gass's *Journal,* which was published without a map, the geographic record was reconstituted in narrative form; throughout his journal, Gass linked the daily survey of places to events identifying Lewis and Clark individually by name while referring to the activities he was involved in using the collective pronoun "we." In both cases, the unofficial narratives' representation of geography effectively scripted the Lewis and Clark story in the way in which it has become fixed in the American popular imagination: how it was the great adventure of a diverse band of white military men, including a Native American woman and an African male slave, who embarked upon an epic journey to find the passage to Cathay. According to this narrative, the members of the expedition are no longer exclusively subject to presidential patronage, nor are they subordinates to a calculated government project. They are instead fully individuated agents, who, enabled by the textuality of geographic writing, in particular the map, take possession of the continent, nature, Indians, and, ultimately, the American self.[37]

In the end, the popular press created for the American audience a narrative in which the daily activities of geographical literacy became a function and embodiment of the new Romantic ethos. More specifically, the unofficial version of the Lewis and Clark journals subverted the expedition's initial working definition of authorial character. Jefferson's writing instructions to Lewis and Clark presupposed an ideal republican subjectivity that, conditioned by print culture and the rituals of the public sphere, imagined itself ideally to be white, male, concerned with the common good, and ultimately as being predicated on the effacement of the personal and the body. In the context of the journals, this meant that the map and their geographic records were the primary locale and horizon behind which individual concerns would have to fade away rather than become asserted. As we have seen in the unabridged original journals, the various textual forms of a state-sponsored geographical excursion proved to be the strategic control behind which individual desires or opinion receded.[38]

---

37. For example, in Gass's *Journal:* June 24, 1805, "In the morning Capt. Lewis came up to our camp, We found it very difficult to procure stuff for the boat." Modern studies have emphasized other individual members of the expedition; for example, Elaine Raphael and Don Bolognese, *Sacajawea: The Journey West* (New York, 1994); Robert B. Betts, *In Search of York: The Slave Who Went to the Pacific with Lewis and Clark* (Boulder, Colo., 1985).

38. This definition is in a way an academic conceit hiding the fact that, as the republi-

During the early nineteenth century, however, this traditional definition of republican identity was becoming redefined by a culture in which
power relations were increasingly individualized. Rather than focusing on
the rational heroics of republican action, many writers were now beginning to concentrate on the affective activities of the romantically conceived heroic actions of the national individual. Read in this context, the
fictionalized characters of Lewis and Clark thus walked in the literary
footsteps of established national geographic types, such as the figure of
Daniel Boone. The *Travels of Capts. Lewis and Clarke* now populated the
uncharted terrain west of the Appalachian Mountains with additional
incarnations of situated types, the ever-resourceful and brawny traveler,
frontiersman, and soldier. Already capitalizing on the public's interest in
the continent's western geography, the unofficial journals continued the
established pattern of character typing that the educated reader already
had memorized from Jedidiah Morse's geography books. Furthermore,
once again it was the textual artifact of the map that provided the material
site of character formation. Each of the heroic figures became connected
to administrative boundaries; just as Boone was associated with Kentucky, so too Lewis and Clark became the representative names for the
Louisiana Territory (Jefferson appointed Lewis as governor, and Clark as
the Indian agent and general of the Louisiana militia). In this figuration of
the expedition members, the unofficial journals adumbrated Jefferson's
geographical writing instructions; by fusing the geoliterary characters to a
specifically geopolitical setting, they prenationalized the territories, making their incorporation into the nation-state seem at once natural and
legitimate.[39]

can self is supremely localized because it is invested in landed property, it can also afford
to be disinterested. Yet, for now I follow the prevailing line of interpretation of American
republicanism made by Bernard Bailyn, *The Ideological Origins of the American Revolution*
(Cambridge, Mass., 1967); Gordon S. Wood, *The Creation of the American Republic, 1776–
1787* (Chapel Hill, N.C., 1969). For a revisionist reading, see Michael Warner's influential
work, *The Letters of the Republic: Publication and the Public Sphere in Eighteenth-Century
America* (Cambridge, Mass., 1990).

39. See the studies by Henry Nash Smith, *Virgin Land: The American West as Symbol and
Myth* (Cambridge, Mass., 1950); Richard Slotkin, *Regeneration through Violence: The Mythology of the American Frontier, 1600–1860* (Middletown, Conn., 1971).

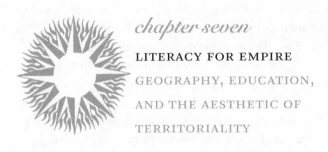

chapter seven

LITERACY FOR EMPIRE

GEOGRAPHY, EDUCATION,

AND THE AESTHETIC OF

TERRITORIALITY

In the decades immediately following the Revolution, Americans used geography to define their own voice and sense of national place. Once this identity had been established, however, geography was no longer used exclusively for the purpose of national consolidation but was employed to sanction and legitimate the expansion of the national domain. This imperialist project achieved popular support, even as it was widely understood that any form of western movement necessitated the removal of the indigenous native population, in part through Americans' internalization of the principles and practices surrounding geographical literacy. To a literate population that had been educated in a geographic vein, the incompleteness of the North American geography on maps and in textbook entries was construed as an eyesore and a source of national embarrassment. The map-logo that had once worked to provide a shorthand for national unity and identity was now viewed as truncated and thwarted. The geographically literate eye desired to see the map extending neatly across the entire continent, achieving not only a political imperative but an aesthetic one.

We find evidence of an explicitly geoliterary aesthetic in the contemporary popular press. After the frontier wars against the Cherokee, Choctaw, and Chickasaw nations, the American *Literary and Scientific Repository* ran a series of editorials in 1821 responding to British accusations of American imperialism. Closing ranks with other popular magazines, the *Repository* attacked a British study, *America and Her Resources,* in which the author castigated "the American rulers . . . endeavouring to direct the whole national mind and inclination of the United States towards their aggrandizement by conquest." In the opinion of the American reviewer, this critique was outrageous—not for its allegation of imperial practices, but for its gross misattribution of political agency. Far from denying the reports of the use of force in the western territories, this author contended that it was, not the elected politicians, but the will of the American people that mandated imperial actions.[1]

The realities of conquest were the direct expression of the American people's newly developed geographic sensibility. In the reviewer's analysis, territorial violence was accepted in the United States because its citizens engaged with maps "ten times more frequent[ly] than is found among any other people." This surplus of geographic texts led to the belief that the individual "American has vastly more *geographical* feeling than the European." This heightened sense of geographic "feeling" (which here seems to indicate something between or including intuition, aesthetic, emotion, sense, and sensibility) virtually demanded territorial action. "The Americans are far from being pleased with the irregular figure which the Republic exhibits upon the map," the author argued. "This and that corner of the continent must be *bought* (or conquered if it cannot be bought) in order to give a more handsome sweep to their periphery. . . . In fact, their boundary line is never so exactly *round* to satisfy the nice eye of an ambitious people; the jagged polygon still needs here and there some trimming; but this perfecting of the figure is to be effected always by increments,—never by retrenchments." The "figure" of the continent is here not anthropomorphized (as it had been to earlier generations who cast the continent as a dramatic persona), but perceived in geometric terms, the basic language of a modern cartographic consciousness. The continental geometry ("line," "exactly round," "polygon[al]") becomes subject to an aesthetic sensibility, valued for its quality as "handsome" and "perfect[ed]."[2]

1. Cited in "Art. X.—*America and Her Resources*. . . . by John Bristed [London, 1818]," *Literary and Scientific Repository,* II (1821), 209. The review appeared initially in the *Eclectic Review* and was reprinted in magazines such as the *North American Review.*

2. Ibid., 209, 211. The 1820s were the decade when the grid and federal surveying project, initiated by the Land Ordinances of 1785 and 1787, was beginning to make itself felt—that is, become visible—in the American landscape and evoke comments in the media. In 1819, for example, discussing the state of "Public Lands" in the United States the surveyor general Josiah Meigs writes: "A few geographical positions on the map of the public surveys, being accurately determined by astronomical observations, it is obvious that, with very little difficulty, the longitude and latitude of every *farm,* and of every *log-hut* and *court house,* may be ascertained . . . so wise, beautiful and perfect a system was never before adopted by any government or nation on earth." *Niles' Weekly Register,* XVI (1819), 363.

On the aesthetic and ideological repercussion of the geometricization of American

Claiming the nation's mass geographical literacy as the foundation of a territorial aesthetic experience, magazine editors and newspaper publishers contrived more than an unrepentant defense of American political practices. They self-consciously defended the early-nineteenth-century realization that, in the words of William Appleman Williams, "empire as a way of life" was rapidly shaping the cultural habits of the American citizenry. For the United States to become an empire, American citizens had to participate candidly in a "process of reification—of transforming the realities of expansion, conquest, and intervention into pious rhetoric about virtue, wealth, and democracy." That process revolved around two definitions of empire: first, that the "meaning of empire concerns the forcible subjugation of formerly independent peoples by a wholly external power," and, second, that "a way of life is the combination of patterns of thought and action that, as it becomes habitual and institutionalized, defines the thrust and character of a culture and society." Through their defense of imperialism in 1821, American authors demonstrated not only how deeply their political attitude was informed by geographical literacy but also the extent to which the rhetoric of empire was the result of the programmatic diffusion of geographical knowledge in American schools and the widespread implementation of territorializing habits into the canon of national education.[3]

The public endorsement of western expansion in the 1820s took place in the context of a larger cultural debate that interrogated how literacy instruction shaped personal development and public mores, as intellectuals considered what kind of literacy was compatible with the Republic's ideals of citizenship and self-government. Modern scholars who have examined the contextual premises of literacy in the early United States have addressed literacy in terms of an ideological confrontation that pitted a dominant republicanism against an emergent nationalism. The logic of consolidated statehood is seen to have dovetailed with the antebellum promotion of universal literacy: spellers, grammars, and novels aligned the theory of language acquisition with the politics of domesticity and

space and its representation, see Philip Fisher, "Democratic Social Space: Whitman, Melville, and the Promise of American Transparency," *Representations,* no. 24 (Fall 1988), 60–101. On the first aesthetic responses to the country's geometric landscape, see J. B. Jackson, "The Order of a Landscape," in D. W. Meinig, ed., *The Interpretation of Ordinary Landscapes: Geographical Essays* (New York, 1979), 159; John R. Stilgoe, *Common Landscape of America, 1580 to 1845* (New Haven, Conn., 1982), 99.

3. William Appleman Williams, *Empire as a Way of Life . . .* (New York, 1980), ix, 4, 6.

capitalism. The evaluation of literacy has thus undergone significant revisions. Once considered the touchstone of the country's cultural revolution and the proud source of American exceptionalism, literacy has become revaluated as the site of domestic discrimination, racial confrontation, and cultural creolization.[4]

Many of these revisionist discussions, however, assume an existing national framework. Studies of signature rates, institutional spelling bees, and personal reading histories are positioned and interpreted as cultural phenomena that were predicated on the nation's seemingly stable, established geopolitical boundaries. Within the context of the early nineteenth century, however, the boundaries of the United States were amorphous and contested, subject to the geopolitics of, for example, the Monroe Doctrine and the Indian Removal Act. Rather than taking place within a determined national space, literacy training was itself *about* the taking of space: the country's literary education, including its emerging public school movement and mass-produced schoolbooks, shaped and was shaped by a nascent imperial literacy.[5]

4. Studies delineating this debate tend to cut across the academic disciplines; see, for example, Linda K. Kerber, *Women of the Republic: Intellect and Ideology in Revolutionary America* (Chapel Hill, N.C., 1980); Robert H. Horwitz, ed., *The Moral Foundations of the American Republic* (Charlottesville, Va., 1986); Gordon S. Wood, *The Radicalism of the American Revolution* (New York, 1991); Ronald J. Zboray, *A Fictive People: Antebellum Economic Development and the American Reading Public* (New York, 1993).

Important examinations of literacy in colonial and early antebellum America are Patricia Crain, *The Story of A: The Alphabetization of America from "The New England Primer" to "The Scarlet Letter"* (Stanford, Calif., 2000); Zboray, *A Fictive People;* William J. Gilmore, *Reading Becomes a Necessity of Life: Material and Cultural Life in Rural New England, 1780–1835* (Knoxville, Tenn., 1989); Cathy N. Davidson, ed., *Reading in America: Literature and Social History* (Baltimore, 1989).

Here I generalize for the purpose of summarizing the more complex arguments made by prominent studies on antebellum literacy, such as Lawrence A. Cremin, *American Education: The National Experience, 1783–1876* (New York, 1980); Lee Soltow and Edward Stevens, *The Rise of Literacy and the School Movement in the United States: A Socioeconomic Analysis to 1870* (Chicago, 1981); Harvey J. Graff, *The Legacies of Literacy: Continuities and Contradictions in Western Culture and Society* (Bloomington, Ind., 1987); Carl Kaestle et al., *Literacy in the United States: Readers and Reading since 1800* (New Haven, Conn., 1991); Grey Gundaker, *Signs of Diaspora, Diaspora of Signs: Literacies, Creolization, and Vernacular Practices in African America* (New York, 1998).

5. The function of geography is missing in Kaestle et al., *Literacy in the United States,* which offers one of the better histories of literacy for the early national decades. More strikingly, the imperial dimension (as does early American geoliteracy) escapes Mal-

"The power of literacy results not directly from learning the ABC's," Dana Nelson Salvino has reminded us, "but rather from a powerful set of beliefs that accompanies the act of learning to read and write." For early-nineteenth-century Americans, geographical literacy provided the discursive outlet for a new, calculated belief in the agency of human territoriality. Human territories, as sociologists Erving Goffman and Irwin Altman have shown, are generally conceived as spaces controlled by a person, family, or other face-to-face collectivity. Control is reflected in actual or potential possession of a space rather than through the evidence of physical combat or aggression; acts of signification rather than acts of physical violence are the hallmark of human territoriality. In this context, the geographer Robert D. Sack has called attention to the complex interrelation of spatial forms of organization and linguistic modes of interaction, arguing that the habits of territoriality become the "geographical bonding agent" that structures, authorizes, and is informed by social relations. According to the *Repository* author cited above, geographical literacy was more than his society's bonding agent. Its signs, symbols, and grammar became the mode of signification by which American citizens not only learned to redraw domestic boundaries by incorporating those of neighboring territories but, having internalized geographical practices, were shifting the national conception of identity toward a more imperial subjectivity.[6]

---

colm P. Douglass's study, *The History, Psychology, and Pedagogy of Geographic Literacy* (Westport, Conn., 1998), where territoriality is still read in behaviorist terms.

In my discussion of boundaries, I expand from Amy Kaplan's observation that the concept (and habit structure) of national discourse in the United States was always already contingent upon the spatial formation of American borders. See her introduction to Kaplan and Donald E. Pease, eds., *Cultures of United States Imperialism* (Durham, N.C., 1993), 14–17. Many of the collected essays explore the material and discursive struggles that unfolded along a variety of border conflicts—from actual military invasion to discursive cross-fertilization.

6. Dana Nelson Salvino, "The Word in Black and White," in Davidson, ed., *Reading in America*, 141–142; Robert D. Sack, *Human Territoriality: Its Theory and History* (Cambridge, 1986), 26. Sack explores the theoretical implications of spatial information on linguistic habits, including a constructionist (as opposed to behaviorist) definition of "territoriality," in *Human Territoriality* and *Homo Geographicus: A Framework for Action, Awareness, and Moral Concern* (Baltimore, 1997), esp. chap. 4. Also see Erving Goffman, *Asylums: Essays on the Social Situation of Mental Patients and Other Inmates* (Garden City, N.Y., 1961); Irwin Altman, *The Environment and Social Behavior: Privacy, Personal Space, Territory, Crowding* (Monterey, Calif., 1975); Stanford M. Lyman and Marvin B. Scott, "Territoriality:

In the effort to further historicize the identity work of geographical literacy, I am thus concerned with the ways in which the early-nineteenth-century geography lessons were instituted as the aesthetic frontier along which citizens continued to fold literacy instruction into geographical definitions of identity. One aspect is how geography became institutionalized in public education, particularly through the newly emerging pedagogic theories of Johann Pestalozzi and Joseph Lancaster, and how these affected traditional geographical instructions. Another, which focuses on geographies published after the War of 1812, compares the first-generation classics of Jedidiah Morse with a series of newly produced textbooks by authors such as Emma Willard and William Woodbridge in order to explore how pedagogic changes in geography lessons influenced the territorial socialization of readers. Finally, how did Americans transform the design of geographic writings into a consensual tool mediating between national and imperial signification, a tool that simultaneously prepared and justified the territorial violence that was occurring on the margins of the national domain?

MASSES, CLASSES, AND THE GENRE OF GEOGRAPHY

During the early decades of the nineteenth century, the literary function of geography was undergoing a critical metamorphosis from stabilizing the union to mobilizing the desire for empire. By about 1800, the new

---

A Neglected Sociological Dimension," *Social Problems,* XV (1967), 236–249; Robert Sommer, *Personal Space: The Behavioral Basis of Design* (Englewood Cliffs, N.J., 1969).

On the different conceptions of "imperial self" as discussed in relation to American literature and culture, see Quentin Anderson, Sacvan Bercovitch, and Wai Chee Dimock. The former considers the construction of American imperial selfhood as the product of a biographic-cultural history that documents the alienation and self-preoccupation of the heroic figures in American literature, such as Emerson, Whitman, and James. In the case of Bercovitch, the self-enclosed imperial self is the product of dialectic mediation in which "the imperial claims [are] implicit in the concentricity of self, text, and interpretation." Dimock has offered cautionary remarks about localizing such a historical identity, arguing instead that it is a metonymic construct and predicated upon "the genetic alignment or interpretive concentricity between text and history." See Quentin Anderson, *The Imperial Self: An Essay in American Literary and Cultural History* (New York, 1971), vii–xiii; Sacvan Bercovitch, *The Rites of Assent: Transformations in the Symbolic Construction of America* (New York, 1993), 270; Wai Chee Dimock, "Class, Gender, and a History of Metonymy," in Dimock and Michael T. Gilmore, eds., *Rethinking Class: Literary Studies and Social Formations* (New York, 1994), 90–91.

citizens had flocked to national maps and geography books because these confirmed recent historical events. The map was the ideal vehicle for visualizing the material form of the abstract nation-state; in conjunction with natural histories and travelogues, the genre of geography propagated new narrative forms by which the citizens anatomized in great detail the parts and properties of the body politic. In true postcolonial fashion, maps underpinned many of the institutional and creative processes by which Americans invented traditional customs and nationalized literary productions. Twenty years later, however, as both the producers and the consumers of geographic writings internalized the political and aesthetic possibilities of geographic writings, the function of geography changed from a constant national form to one encouraging territorial changes.

In the years following the War of 1812, mapmakers and readers directed the political gaze away from sites of domestic interest and toward the country's margins and neighboring territories. Spurred by popular narratives such as the Lewis and Clark journals, American citizens became obsessed with the materials of an emerging imperial geography. They collected maps and statistical accounts of the nation's domestic borderlands, the regions east and west of the Mississippi River. They copied out charts of battlefields, burial grounds, and trading routes; and they avidly subscribed to domestically produced topographies and guidebooks that explained in maps and atlases the country's fledgling infrastructure. The citizens' investment in maps and other geographic writings corresponded with the domestic policy of President James Monroe and his stated goal of creating a continental "home market." Beginning in 1816, Monroe's politics forcibly opened to white appropriation the land of the Cherokees, Choctaws, and Chickasaws—the vast territory extending from central Georgia to the Mississippi.[7]

As ordinary citizens became involved in the fantasy and process of colonization and western expansion, their desire for geographical knowledge elicited calls for the general dissemination of geographic education.

7. On the burgeoning distribution of maps and other cartographic materials in American print culture of the early nineteenth century, see John Rennie Short, *Representing the Republic: Mapping the United States, 1600–1900* (London, 2001); Walter W. Ristow, *American Maps and Map-Makers: Commercial Cartography in the Nineteenth Century* (Detroit, Mich., 1985); Seymour I. Schwartz and Ralph E. Ehrenberg, *The Mapping of America* (New York, 1980); J. B. Harley, Barbara Bartz Petchenik, and Lawrence W. Towner, eds., *Mapping the American Revolutionary War* (Chicago, 1978). On Monroe's land policies, see Charles Sellers, *The Market Revolution: Jacksonian America, 1815–1846* (New York, 1991), chap. 1.

This call was quickly met by the various sectors of the country's emerging culture industry, and several organizations of the new social reform movements took up the cause of promoting the study of geography. In a campaign that eventually resulted in the democratization and professionalization of public education, a medley of teachers, religious leaders, and middle-class patrons—for reasons ranging from cultural nationalism to labor concerns to missionary agendas—lobbied successfully for the introduction of geography and mapmaking into the nation's primary and secondary school curricula. This change was indirectly propelled by higher education as well: between 1810 and 1820 American colleges eliminated geography from their own curricula but retained geographic literacy as part of their entrance examinations, thus pushing geographic instruction into the lower and more popular educational levels. Students attending common schools and private academies participated in mandatory geography lessons. The memoirs of antebellum students give us a glimpse of rote memorization and graphic exercises; they were dominated by the recital of place-names, map drawing, and learning about the Mercator projection (the "grid"). The typical job description for public school teachers even emphasized geography over the conventional three R's. When the state of Massachusetts advertised new teaching positions, it emphasized, *"A person who is not qualified to teach geography, grammar, and geometry,* and not well recommended for *his morals,* etc. is forbid, under heavy penalties by law, to take charge of a school."[8]

Seizing the opportunity to capitalize on this public demand for geographical literacy instruction, the American book industry collectively channeled its energies into the production of school geographies. After

8. Advertisement cited in "Massachusetts' Schools," *Niles' Weekly Register,* XX (1821), 108. On the promotion of geographic education in the early Republic, see the comprehensive study by Daniel H. Calhoun, "Eyes for the Jacksonian World: William C. Woodbridge and Emma Willard," *Journal of the Early Republic,* IV (1984), 1–26; also Nina Baym, "Women and the Republic: Emma Willard's Rhetoric of History," *American Quarterly,* XLIII (1991), 1–23; Kerber, *Women of the Republic,* 214–231; Nancy F. Cott, *Bonds of Womanhood: "Woman's Sphere" in New England, 1780–1835* (New Haven, Conn., 1977), 115–125. On geography and college curricula, see William Warntz, *Geography Now and Then: Some Notes on the History of Academic Geography in the United States* (New York, 1964).

In 1810 Catharine Beecher studied geography and map-drawing at Miss Pierce's school in Litchfield, Connecticut; see Cott, *Bonds of Womanhood,* 115. Beecher's pupil Fanny Fern, who attended the Hartford Seminary in 1828, satirizes antebellum geography lessons in her 1854 novel *Ruth Hall,* in Joyce W. Warren, ed., *Ruth Hall and Other Writings* (New Brunswick, N.J., 1986), 101–103.

1815, many publishing houses and booksellers started marketing under the rubric "geographical" everything from writing manuals and copybooks, to flash cards and dictionaries, to atlases and pocket globes. Paramount in the publishers' lineup was once again the geography textbook. Teachers and students regularly could choose from more than twenty perennial editions. Among these were the country's original geographies, such as Jedidiah Morse's *Geography Made Easy* (1784) and Joseph Goldsmith's *Easy Grammar of Geography* (1804). Largely modernized for republication during the 1810s, these didactic classics competed with a new generation of popular textbooks like Daniel Adams's *Geography; or, A Description of the World* (1814) and William Woodbridge and Emma Willard's best-selling *Rudiments of Geography* (1822) and its republished version *System of Universal Geography* (1824).[9]

THREE KINDS OF PEDAGOGY

Geographers, like most educators of the time, engaged in a highly specialized pedagogic debate about proper reading instructions—a debate that also opens a rare window for reviewing the cognitive and ideological changes that were affecting the definition of literacy and public education. The didactic issue at stake in the geographers' debate was how to construct a durable geographic memory. The debate pitted the residual teaching philosophy of John Locke against the recently devised methodology by the Swiss pedagogue Johann Pestalozzi. The point of contention was whether students ought to learn the ABC by rote, using oral performances, or by written words and visual stimulation. The conflict between these schools of thought informed many of the competing school geographies. Textbook authors of two different intellectual generations such as Morse and Willard endorsed the principles of a Lockean psychology, assuming the mind was a blank slate and destined to be inscribed with

9. This list represents a survey of early American geographic literature held by the American Antiquarian Society, the American Philosophical Society, and the Library Company of Philadelphia, where I was able to compare late-eighteenth- and early-nineteenth-century genres, including local and national maps, atlases, school geographies. For a bibliographic overview of geographic teaching materials, see also Warntz, *Geography Now and Then;* John A. Nietz, *Old Textbooks* . . . (Pittsburgh, Pa., 1961). Writing geography textbooks became a lucrative business for early antebellum authors, supporting many of the country's creative writers, including Harriet Beecher Stowe, William Gilmore Simms, and Walt Whitman.

permanent impressions bearing linguistic or semiotic properties. In this context, authors of two different generations agreed upon the necessity of developing a geographic writing system—including abstract symbols, complex maps, and geographic narratives—by which the "real lines of geography" become transposed into "abiding," "durable," and "deep and distinct impressions."[10]

But they fundamentally differed about how geography lessons were to achieve an abiding durability and depth. For Morse, the geography lessons of the 1810s and 1820s were still those of the 1780s and 1790s; geography was a matter of literary discipline in which national feeling became bound to the reader through the oral memorization of textbook knowledge. As late as 1818 he maintained that his *Geography Made Easy* was "a reading-book, that our youth of both sexes, at the same time that they are learning to read, might imbibe the acquaintance with their country and an attachment to its interests." On a different occasion he wrote: "In the best maps, especially in those on a small scale, errors are so numerous, that the mind cannot rest with confidence in their testimony. We want the confirmation of the book." In the name of nationalism, geographic instruction was continually tied to one of the nation's self-constituting mechanisms, the spoken and written word. Furthermore, if we consider that Morse's geography lesson was linked to a strict pedagogic code, his reading exercises served a primarily disciplinary function in that the mistaken spelling of a place-name or the faulty drawing of a map allowed teachers to cudgel the young in order to build their national character.[11]

By contrast, Willard and Woodbridge eschewed this punitive model of geographic learning. Their teaching methods used the nonauthoritarian

10. Jedidiah Morse, *Geography Made Easy* (Boston, 1820), iii; Morse, *Modern Atlas Adapted to Morse's New School Geography* (Boston, 1822), i; and Emma Willard in her coauthored work with William C. Woodbridge, *Rudiments of Geography, on a New Plan, Designed to Assist the Memory by Comparison and Classification* . . . (Hartford, Conn., 1822), viii. I attribute the authorship of *Rudiments* in equal parts to Willard and Woodbridge, because, as Willard explains her share of authorial labor in the book's second and retitled edition, "The arrangement entered into between Mr. Woodbridge and myself, was predicated solely on my having compiled and taught a system of modern geography similar to his: whereas my writing the ancient, was merely an accidental consequence of my becoming a partner in the concern." A new edition appeared as *A System of Universal Geography: On the Principles of Comparison and Classification* (Hartford, Conn., 1824), xx. On the pedagogical debates over literacy in the early nineteenth century, see Soltow and Stevens, *Rise of Literacy,* 16–102.

11. Morse, *Geography Made Easy* (Boston, 1818), iv; *Geography Made Easy* (1820), v.

principles of internalized perception proposed by Pestalozzi. In particular they sought to address the old-style curriculum's slavish adherence to rote learning; they perceived the failure of this pedagogic method was rooted in the memorization of words outside a meaningful frame of reference. Or, as the journal *Academician* stated in 1819:

> Our youth are made to languish over books of *words,* accompanied only by the midnight lamp, without explanation or oral instruction, and compelled to recite these words, not understood, *verbatim,* on entering school the next morning. This, although a popular method, is one of the most inconsistent and absurd requisitions that was ever enforced on human beings. We demand of them *ideas,* but they have none to give; we demand the *words,* they repeat them; but they only know that the letters are *black.* Is this knowledge? will this make a rational being? will it not leave the mind inactive? will not the learner depend wholly on the bare *letters,* and not the meaning of the author he is reading?

Expanding from Pestalozzi's method of whole-word and object-learning, Willard and Woodbridge argued in their *Rudiments of Geography* that in geography lessons the map must come before geographic description, the visual before the verbal: *"No language can impress ideas so deeply on the mind as information addressed to the eye. . . .* A description cannot give so distinct views of the geography of a country as a *map,* and no words can so fully convey the idea of a remarkable custom or curiosity as a *drawing* or *engraving."* Instead of relying on the written book, the authors prescribe a set of exercises that forces the students to engage through slate and pencil with their immediate geographic surroundings. By mapping out their environs, the student is meant to experience the medium of transcription—here the map, the scale, and pictographic symbols—as a form of individualistic instruction and self-improvement. The pupil is no longer the passive vessel for receiving and reciting geographic information (the model fostered by rote memorization), instead achieving a cartographic, and even artistic, competence to view, draw, and record the world in his or her own way. The world is mastered through individual perception rather than through absorbing facts; students are trained to see the world, not to memorize it.[12]

12. "On Teaching Geography," *Academician,* I (1819), 245; Woodbridge, *Rudiments of Geography* (Hartford, Conn., 1825), ix. The impact of the Pestalozzian pedagogy was duly noted by magazines such as *Niles' Weekly Register,* XV (1819), and by one of the nation's

Caught between the opposing schools of hard verbalism and soft visualism, geography teachers turned to a third kind of pedagogy, the monitorial, or Lancastrian, system. Beginning in 1805, Joseph Lancaster proposed a schooling system in which a single teacher could operate a school of five hundred pupils. This system, emphasizing recitation and classroom competition, used student monitors and a standardized routine of quasi-mechanical exercises intended to replace corporal punishment (Figure 53). In order to demonstrate the efficiency of the monitorial system, American commentators turned to the Lancastrian method of geographic instruction. "Let a school of ninety-six pupils be divided into twelve classes of eight in each," the *Academician* writes, "the eight classes formed into semicircles, round a map, holding books in their hands, and each pupil taught by his class leader who requires each pupil to point out the places named, or answer such questions as relate to the situation, bearing, relative distance of places and their latitudes and longitudes, and they will acquire a practical facility and precision in geography." The construction of geographic literacy here becomes the subject of mass literary production. Students study geography in a pedagogic climate of alienation and detachment; as group recitation replaces previous demands of local or national geographic memory, they learn, under time pressure, to reproduce geographical knowledge from rapid readings, or rather viewings, "holding books in their hands."[13]

Not coincidentally, these pedagogic debates over how to construct the nation's geographic memory rehearsed some of the same debates that were raging over the role of public education in the westward expansion of the United States. With discussions clashing over the appropriate use of brute force and endeavors to control the discipline and organization of a vast number of students or spaces with the remote figure of the teacher or government, the fundamental question raised by geographers was a familiar and urgent one: how can a people reconcile the nationalizing function of geographical literacy with an imperial agenda? How can the

first teaching journals, the *Academician,* published by yet another geographer, Albert Picket. The role of Pestalozzi in American education has been discussed by Carl F. Kaestle, *Pillars of the Republic: Common Schools and American Society, 1780–1860* (New York, 1983), 67; Soltow and Stevens, *Rise of Literacy,* 96–97; Cremin, *American Education,* 77–79.

13. "The New School; or, Lancasterian System," *Academician,* I (1818), 100–101. See also Joseph Lancaster, *The British System of Education* . . . (London, 1812). On Lancaster's pedagogy, see Kaestle, *Pillars of the Republic,* chaps. 1, 2. Here I would like to thank Patricia Crain for sharing her work on Lancaster.

Figure 53. British System of Education. *By Joseph Lancaster. 1812.*
Courtesy, University of Delaware Library

geographer reconcile his or her self-stipulated demand for stabilizing the nation in view of ever-shifting boundaries following the various territorial conquests? In more practical terms, the question posed by geographers was, If indeed the nation has established itself as a durable and abiding impression, how do geographers change this geographic memory without sacrificing its claim to durability?

PICTURES OF A PLASTIC NATION

Joseph Lancaster offers a glimpse of how many second-generation geographers would solve this didactic dilemma. In "National Education" for *Niles' Weekly Register,* he assumes the position of the geoliterate citizen:

> I was looking at the map of NORTH COLUMBIA, from the Atlantic to the Pacific ocean . . . [and] contrasted the first settlements at *Jamestown* and *Plymouth,* with the present States and their ramifications. . . . I was ready to exclaim, here is an ample footing for another *Atlas,* not merely to stand, but to *travel,* from one immense ocean to another. . . . What an unparalleled national capacity for extension and power. With a destiny so grand, how momentous the importance of forming the national character, while YET plastic, to its eminent prospect and future grandeur!

Lancaster here makes an eloquent pitch for a geographic pedagogy grounded in aesthetic principles. Using an overstated prophetic (and mythic) language, Lancaster promotes the replacement of the national atlases from the 1790s. These old atlases were preoccupied with historical geography, that is, with the detailed and accurate representation of the colonial past and settlements *("Jamestown* and *Plymouth")*. By contrast, and in view of the "present States and their ramifications," Americans now needed a new kind of atlas containing a more flexible ("plastic") mode of geographic representation, a mode that involved not only the reinterpretation of American maps to reflect "a national capacity for ex-tension" but a new artistic style for shaping and visualizing ("prospect") the nation's projected continental reach.[14]

Within the classroom, many geography textbooks and atlases were al-ready putting into practice Lancaster's comments, training the citizens of the young Republic to picture the geography of the world and the nation in terms of a grandiose territorial plasticity. The perhaps most crucial and, in many ways, also most basic picture preparing the student for a world that was for the taking was the global geodetic grid. Like most contempo-rary textbooks, Joseph Worcester's *Elements of Geography* (1819) includes a chapter "Construction of Maps," which relies on the skeletal outline of the Mercator map and its distorted representation of the Northern Hemi-sphere (Figure 54). Unlike associative word and literary maps, the Mer-cator map served as an abstract storage system, urging the geographic reader to compartmentalize the world before writing it. Only after the grid had taken control over the blank page did the textbook allow the novice mapmaker to inscribe other carto-literary elements, such as con-tour lines, pictographic signs, and place symbols.[15]

The completed Mercator map not only collapsed and contained spatial differences inside the totalizing framework of geometrical lines, but it also anticipated a new hemispheric world order. Worcester's lesson en-tailed sketching out the territorial markers of the competing empires of the United States and the United Kingdom, using Philadelphia and Cape Horn as the endpoints of a trans-American empire and London and the

14. Joseph Lancaster, "National Education," *Niles' Weekly Register,* XVII (1820), 323.

15. J[oseph] E[merson] Worcester, *Elements of Geography, Ancient and Modern . . .* (Boston, 1819), 320. On the range of signification engendered by nonverbal writings and discussions on cartography, see Roy Harris, *Signs of Writing* (London, 1995); Edward R. Tufte, *Envisioning Information* (Cheshire, Conn., 1990).

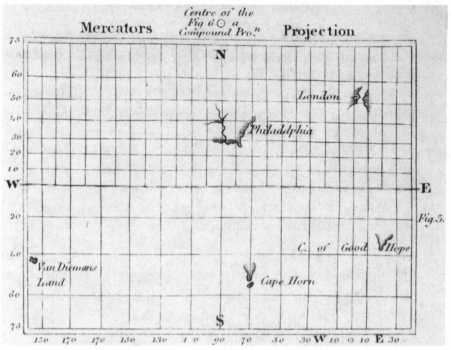

Figure 54. Mercator Projection. From Elements of Geography, Ancient and Modern, *by J[oseph] E[merson] Worcester. 1819.* Courtesy, American Antiquarian Society

Cape of Good Hope as markers for the British Empire. Antebellum students thus literally sketched out what would become the basic tenet of United States imperial policy; as if he were putting into practice the lessons in Worcester's textbook, in 1823 President Monroe laid claim to all of the Western Hemisphere in the name of the American people's interest. For a generation of students who had already performed this territorial exercise in their own books, the move must have seemed perfunctory and matter-of-fact rather than daring and (literally) outlandish.

Compared to the global map lesson of the grid, Emma Willard and William Woodbridge encouraged a more localized system of representing territories. In their *System of Universal Geography* they domesticated the overtly abstract and defamiliarizing appearance of the grid map by urging the student to "draw simple maps, beginning with a plan of his table, or the room in which he is, proceeding to delineate successively a plan of the house, garden, neighborhood, and town, until he has represented with tolerable correctness, the relative situation and outlines of the principal objects within his view." Willard and Woodbridge designed lessons in "home geography" that not only emphasized the visual perception of the world but transformed the reading subject into an explicitly local object. This geographic writing process now redefined the individual reader in relational terms; using spatial proportions and material similarities as territorial markers, this lesson in home geography simultaneously binds the reader to the visually concrete environment of the local neighborhood while also lodging his or her geographic sense of selfhood inside the more abstract geographic frameworks.[16]

For the sake of practice, the authors introduced a separately published *Outline and Skeleton Maps,* also called a "Geographical Copy Book." There the student wrote himself and his domestic environs into the confines of the emerging imperial map of the United States; first "inserting only the cities on the Outline Map; he then copies the outlines on the Skeleton Map; and is thus easily led on, until he can draw the map [of America] from *memory alone.*" The cartographic grid serves as a type of textual superstructure that students use to cognitively organize their world and their lives; the map works as a mnemonic device similar to the graphic form of the nation's map logo. This action of geographical inscription, moving from the immediate surroundings to the expanse of the continent, domesticates the nation, naturalizing it as an inhabited, familiar, and proprietary space.[17]

If this domestic mode of mapping evoked the cultural agenda of national domesticity, the atlases that Woodbridge compiled to accompany the textbook soon gave playful cartographic charting a harder, more pragmatic edge. Woodbridge incorporated the method of cartographic representation developed by Alexander von Humboldt, using isomorphic lines to designate characteristics of the land such as altitude, temperature zones, patterns of vegetation, and agricultural products. Isomorphic maps depict not simply geopolitical territorial boundaries but the various qualities of the land itself. Woodbridge supplemented his companion atlas for the textbook with two such thematic maps: the "Isothermal Chart; or, View of Climates and Production" and the "Moral and Political Chart of the Inhabited World" (Figures 55, 56). Examining the value schemes used in the latter map, we discover that Woodbridge mixed principles of geographic description with cultural hierarchies. Both the textbook and the atlas map instructed students to trace out the properties of

16. Woodbridge [and Willard], *System of Universal Geography,* xvi.
17. Ibid.

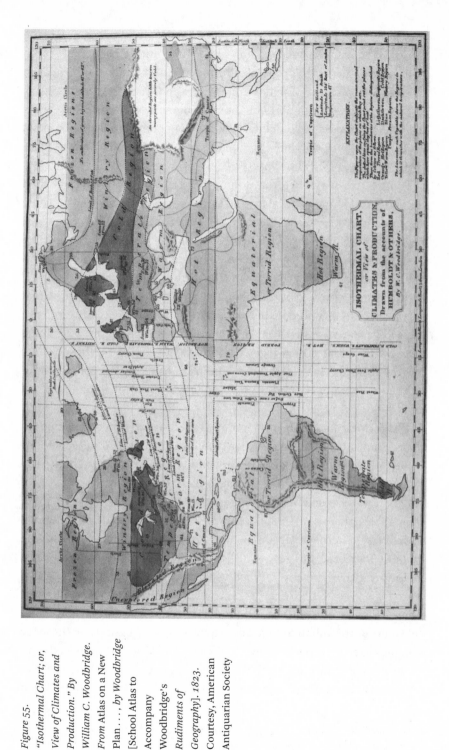

Figure 55.
"Isothermal Chart; or,
View of Climates and
Production." By
William C. Woodbridge.
From Atlas on a New
Plan . . . , by Woodbridge
[School Atlas to
Accompany
Woodbridge's
Rudiments of
Geography]. 1823.
Courtesy, American
Antiquarian Society

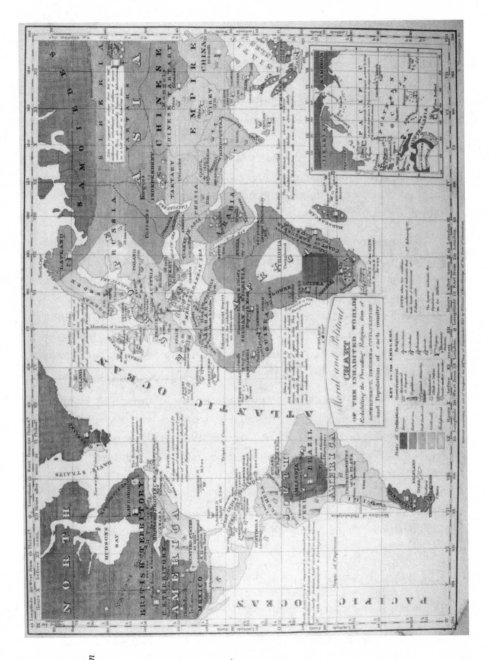

Figure 56. "Moral and Political Chart of the Inhabited World." By William C. Woodbridge. From Atlas on a New Plan . . . , by Woodbridge [School Atlas to Accompany Woodbridge's Rudiments of Geography], 1823. Courtesy, American Antiquarian Society

sameness, linking climate zones *and* the civilized world (defined by religion and government, with Christianity and democracy on top, paganism and tribal culture at the bottom). While the map echoes the environmental determinism of the eighteenth century, the hierarchical representation of territories was made possible through the application of a simple evaluative color code (areas deemed civilized are colored light, barbarian areas dark).[18]

This agenda is also at the heart of *Butler's Geographical and Map Exercises: Designed for the Use of Young Ladies and Gentlemen* (1813). He too promotes the pedagogic function of geographic instruction through isomorphic mapping exercises:

> To provide an easy and familiar elementary tract coinciding with this idea, which, without fatiguing the attention by a prolix catalogue of hard names in the letter-press, or maps crowded with a multiplicity of unimportant places, should initiate the pupil in the first principles of this pleasing science. . . . By maps of this kind, having the outlines carefully coloured, the young scholar is enabled to distinguish at a glance the whole extent of countries and provinces, with their boundaries, their figures, and their relative situations.

The cartographic color-coding might have begun innocently enough with efforts to demarcate transregional temperature patterns, vegetation zones, or distribution of land use. Yet, as Woodbridge's practice map reveals, his cartographic reading exercise trained the student to chart more than the territorial dimensions of the country: it taught the newly minted geoliterate citizen how to stake out a claim to a latitudinal slice of global territory.[19]

Thus, the mode of displaying large spaces quickly assumed an overtly

18. William Woodbridge, *Atlas on a New Plan . . . Woodbridge's Larger Atlas* (Hartford, Conn., 1822), *Atlas on a New Plan, Exhibiting . . . School Atlas to Accompany Woodbridge's Rudiments of Geography* (Hartford, Conn., 1825). On the impact of isodynamic maps and Humboldt, see Margarita Bowen, *Empiricism and Geographical Thought: From Francis Bacon to Alexander von Humboldt* (Cambridge, 1981); D. R. Stoddart, *On Geography and Its History* (New York, 1986); David N. Livingstone, *The Geographical Tradition: Episodes in the History of a Contested Enterprise* (Oxford, 1992).

19. Samuel Butler, *Butler's Geographical and Map Exercises: Designed for the Use of Young Ladies and Gentlemen* (1809; Philadelphia, 1813), iii. The Woodbridge maps and Butler's exercises reflect the rise of and interest in thematic maps. For a general history, see Arthur H. Robinson, *Early Thematic Mapping in the History of Cartography* (Chicago, 1982).

ideological function. In the American context of expansionist ideologies, this is illustrated in John Melish's *Geographical Description of the United States* (1816), in which the author relied on decorative coloring in order to lay claim to territories bordering on the country's political domain. As Melish explained, the color green signified United States lands, red the British possessions, and yellow the Spanish territories. Between the advancing color red and the receding yellow, the choice of green portrayed more than an innocuous landscape of fertile pastures. Similar to the rhetoric of manifest destiny, which depended on a racial color code—placing white over red, brown, and black—the territorial work of Melish's maps and atlases turned upon a chromatographic differential derived from international mapmaking conventions. It coincided with the color-coding of French and Prussian military maps that used the color green to signify lowlands under two hundred meters. Read in these terms, the map's use of green for the western territories indicated that more than two-thirds of the North American continent spread out horizontally, on the level, and visibly unencumbered by any topographic obstacles, from the Atlantic to the Pacific. Having clearly marked the property of the United States and emphasizing the graphic space of the map over geopolitical inscriptions, Melish thus effectively created a territorial horizon that was uniform and, by virtue of its uniformity, obviated the foreign chromatic interference of the British or Spanish territories.[20]

What on first sight appeared to be a strategic marketing device for packaging geography as if it were a children's coloring book, then, in fact served a larger political process by which Native American land claims were nullified. The colored map, in conjunction with map-reading lessons, demonstrated to students in vivid terms how to perform the work of empire, for example, in the "State of Ohio" by erasing the present "Indian boundary line," "where the Indian title is not yet extinguished, and of which the United States hold the pre-emption right." The process of era-

20. John Melish, *A Geographical Description of the United States, with the Contiguous British and Spanish Possessions: Intended as an Accompaniment to Melish's Map of These Countries* (Philadelphia, 1816), 3. For the racial base of American land claims in the nineteenth century, see Reginald Horsman, *Race and Manifest Destiny: The Origins of American Racial Anglo-Saxonism* (Cambridge, Mass., 1981); the classic study by Albert K. Weinberg, *Manifest Destiny: A Study of Nationalist Expansionism in American History* (Chicago, 1935). On color-coding of military maps, see Ulla Ehrensvärd, "Color in Cartography: A Historical Survey," in David Woodward, ed., *Art and Cartography: Six Historical Essays* (Chicago, 1987), 144.

sure is made explicit in a striking passage from *A Geographical Description of the United States* in which Melish prepares the student for the removal of the western native population by intermingling and equating expansionist rhetoric with an aesthetic imperative:

> Part of this [western] territory unquestioningly belongs to the United States. To present a picture of it was desirable in every point of view. The map so constructed, shows at a glance the whole extent of the United States territory from sea to sea; and, in tracing the probable expansion of the human race from east to west, the mind finds an agreeable resting place on its western limits. The view is complete, and leaves nothing to be wished for. It also adds to the beauty and symmetry of the map.

Training the young reader in this geographic aesthetic, Melish elides the fact that the western territories were already inhabited by human beings. Instead, the map is rendered as a geometric drawing one might view in a gallery ("view," in fact, appearing twice). A work of beauty and classical symmetry, this completed transcontinental map produces mental pleasure and satisfaction. The viewing pleasure is augmented by the pleasant contemplation of the promise of "the probable expansion of the human race" across the entire continent. The judgment of the viewer is thus directed toward the aesthetic symmetry of the map and its political parallel, seeking to achieve a balanced view of a nation evenly divided according to the federally mandated distribution of townships and individual homesteads.[21]

Turning to actual geography lessons, American children learned to appropriate the space of the North American continent through the use of color and drawing exercises. In early-nineteenth-century academies, boys and girls continued to produce ornamental maps as their mothers did two decades earlier. In an exercise that today would be more at home in an art class than in geography, these pupils used pen, ink, and thread to draw, paint, and stitch geographical outlines and political boundaries on paper and silk. In so doing they also learned to view the map and its territorial work in aesthetic rather than political terms. Melish himself emphasized the aesthetic goals of the mapmaking project, urging students to ensure that "the form and general features of the map would present a very *beautiful picture*." And this picture could not be complete or beautiful

21. Melish, *Geographical Description*, 4, 51–52.

without the western territories. He argued it was simply bad geographic taste to have the map of the United States "end with the Rocky Mountains." He considered it a matter of "propriety of adding the two western sheets, so as to carry it to the Pacific Ocean."[22]

GEOGRAPHIC AGENCY AND THE FANTASIES OF EMPIRE

By about 1820, the various practices of literacy training were thus fundamentally located in a political culture of territoriality. Through learning to read, draw, and write the pupil was obliquely and directly trained to link the internalization of geographical knowledge with external expressions of territorial aggression. Exercises in geographic competence suggested that literacy and territorial action were being considered as correlative activities, dispensed and advocated by educators with coy propriety according to students' age and ability. Working to fulfill the logic of modern literacy—becoming a civic virtue and a ground of basic and universal competence—geography textbooks instilled the idea that acts of territorialism were everyday expressions of basic literary competence. Just as the letters of the alphabet are in and of themselves meaningless and would not call attention to the meaning of a word or the identity of the author, maps protected their meaning and their makers from accusations of participation in the continuing expansion of the national borders. Thus, the emphasis on geographical principles of literacy—including the grid and the "beautiful picture"—at once disguised and facilitated the extent to which the letters of geography had become aligned with a general will that was increasingly shifting the basis of its territorial claims from the ritual of making a rational or affective argument to one that hinged merely on intuitive reflex.

For the idea of expansion to become an intuition rather than an official action or memory, the territorial aesthetic of geography must work outside the geographer's immediate textual environment. If the idea of expansion was naturalized, it had to be pervasive and universally applicable, becoming the bonding agent that fused the new, imperial geographic instruction to the fully disciplined, that is, educated national subject. Three textual examples demonstrate how geographical exercises empha-

---

22. Ibid., 4 (emphasis added). On the creation of maps in schools, see Kerber, *Women of the Republic,* 215–217; Betty Ring, *Girlhood Embroidery: American Samplers and Pictorial Needlework, 1650–1850* (New York, 1993).

sized the student's bodily participation in the emerging imperial ideology: the spelling book, the writing manual, and the pages of the popular press.

For a first example, I must invoke Noah Webster and his ubiquitous *American Spelling Book*. In its 1817 edition, Webster continued to introduce geographic elements into the textbook sections on ciphering and pronunciation. Still writing after nearly four decades of his plan to establish a national reading standard, Webster presents the student with a geographic reading table. While this table arranged the nation's constitutive parts under the header *"United States,"* unlike the list of previous editions the reader now witnessed the addition of new, western place-names and geographic identities ("Lou-is-ian'-a," "New Or'-leans," "Lou-is-ia'-ni-ans"). Webster's speller continues to organize place-names according to the by now customary geographical grammar, conjugating a list of locations by their geographic coordinates (north to south), to which he now adds in a separate table their respective distances and territorial size. By demanding that students recite this geographic vocabulary, Webster's instructions thus follow his original linguistic reform design; the spelling lesson maintains the logic of the national geography, as the vocalization of these place-names reproduced the cartographic outline of the nation-state.[23]

However, this recital of geographic referents also created a soundscape containing an outwardly colonizing potential. On the one hand, as Webster explained, his exercise intended "in a copious list of names of places, rivers, lakes, mountains . . . to exhibit their just orthography and pronunciation, according to the analogies of our language." On the other hand, however, he conceded that "the orthography ought to be conformed to the practice of speaking." "The true pronunciation of the name of a place, is that which prevails *in and near* the place." Webster here offered an early example of a linguistic practice that demonstrated how the agenda of Americanizing the English language now hinged on a territorializing ideology. By having place-names operate in a more flexible fashion ("in and near"), the spelling exercise allows for place-names to make a general spatial demand, intrinsically taking possession of areas lying outside the confines of the political boundaries of, say, the western states or even the United States. Indeed, as the orally conducted spelling lesson rehearsed its lines of geographic location and affiliation in this later edition of the

23. Noah Webster, *American Spelling Book* . . . (Hartford, Conn., 1817), 121.

American Spelling Book, its tonal scale subordinated regional differences to the largest common territorial denominator: following the differential order of moving from the general to the particular, pupils voiced the name of the North American continent before other geographic regions, the United States before Canada or Spanish Florida. The collective mantra of a unified American geography had triangulated the nation's political geography into a symphonic performance whose boundaries expanded or contracted depending on the volume and proper pronunciation of the student's geographical alphabet. In this new geographical spelling exercise, students learned more than how to noisily claim a common geopolitical identity; they also practiced how the geographically inflected American English language extended territorial rights.[24]

The second example illustrating the aesthetic logic of a new, imperial geography is much more obvious and can be found in the paleographic exercises of the early-nineteenth-century writing handbook. In Abner Reed's manual, *A New Plain and Easy Set of Geographical Running Hand* (1801), students begin with copying out the alphabet in lower and upper cases ("a, b, c, etc."; "A, B, C, etc.") before moving into the actual geographical exercise ("Boston, the capital of Massachusetts and of N. England"). The apparent banality or perfunctory nature of these writing exercises is shattered, however, when Reed has his students practice their hand with a bracing list of words: "and, band, bind, mind, hill, kill, brood, blood." Buried inside the letters of the alphabet and the geographic longhand style was an ideological exercise that, through free association and phonemic minimal pairing, generated the fantasy of direct chirographic control over the spaces touched by the pen ("bind"). The act of putting a pen to paper was likened to violently taking possession of territories ("brood, kill, blood"). To the inquisitive writing apprentice who was trying to make sense of the written lines, the message constantly pointed to a similar outcome ("band . . . kill . . . brood" or "bind . . . hill . . . blood"). The geographical running hand connected the manual task of writing to the blood-and-soil rhetoric of modern expansionist ideologies.[25]

That the new imperial geographical literacy was becoming not only a repetitive mechanical assertion but a dominant visual attitude is made abundantly clear in a brief propagandistic commentary on all things

24. Ibid., v (emphasis added).

25. Abner Reed, *A New Plain and Easy Set of Geographical Running Hand Copies for the Use in Schools* (East Windsor, Conn., 1801), [2–3].

"Geographical" published by *Niles' Weekly Register* in 1823. There the voice of the public declares:

> The wilderness is conquered, and the busy hum of industry has succeeded the whoop of the wild inhabitant of the woods. . . . The Rocky mountains are as if in view at St. Louis; and St. Louis, that seemed as the uttermost point west, now in free communication with Baltimore, has opened a trade with the internal provinces of Mexico! A settlement at the mouth of the *Columbia* has been seriously advocated in congress, and will soon be made under the sanction of government; and, in a few years, we may expect that some persons *there,* feeling themselves too much crowded, like 'Leather Stocking' in the 'Pioneers,' will seek a country more *west*—Japan, perhaps, if good hunting could be expected therein!

The narrator pictures the North American geography like a Melish map. By assuming the subject position of the expansionist mapmaker, all geographical obstacles become leveled so that there is nothing to prevent the total annexation of all land west of the Mississippi River; for it is not just the Rocky Mountains that are "as if in view at St. Louis," but the Pacific Ocean.[26]

In the end, with the ascendance of the mass media, the expansionist policies of the nation-state become the applied expression of the American public's everyday geographical literacy. This literacy enabled the general public to lay claim to any part of the continent. At the same time, while this kind of competence was unchecked and willful, it was perfectly anonymous. The very territorial mobility that was inherent to map and textbook reading created a sense of security, protecting the geographically literate American from the risk of discovery and possible exposure as the territorial aggressor. If indeed mass geographical literacy fostered an imperial attitude among individual citizens, the public will to forcefully expand their national horizon can no longer be exclusively explained through early republican land policies (the Land Ordinance Acts) or the spread of national ideologies (mass print culture). Nor can it be fully explained through the paradoxical Jeffersonian idea of the national citizen's being a member of a "republican empire," or that this will was simply handed down by a powerful centralized state apparatus. Rather, the will to territorial aggrandizement reflects in principle a participatory

26. "Geographical," *Niles' Weekly Register,* XXIV (1823), 71.

process that was structured and propagated by a culture of geographic letters, by American citizens who, by compulsively engaging with the discourse of geography, had collectively internalized the subject's principal logic: if geography meant literally to draw or write the earth, its figurative meaning was to territorialize, to constantly assert and transgress boundaries.[27]

According to the *Literary and Scientific Repository,* the American editorial voice I cited at the beginning of this chapter, this internalization consisted of transforming the realities of expansion and conquest into the least rational form of self-expression. For violent acts of territoriality to be committed unthinkingly and en masse, people must act with passion or out of "geographical feeling." In the author's opinion, it was a modern fallacy to assume geographic literacy did not excite a base passion for conquest. After all, "A map is a seductive article" and "is the mischievous *familiar* of ambition." He even suggested that the habitual viewing of maps induced a somatic "craving for territory," just as bookish knowledge of geography triggered a pathological condition so that the American people "are actually possessed by the mania of encroachment." But, whereas in Europe geographic literacy served tyrannical powers, in America the widespread dissemination of geographic literacy transformed the realities of conquest into a rhetoric of virtue and democracy. In 1821, the fantasy was that "this nefarious passion meets with the most favourable circumstances for its development, when, to an habitual familiarity with geographical ideas, is conjoined a full and direct exercise of political faculties." In reality, the assumption that imperialism could be tamed by a people's self-government was just that, a fantasy of territorial violence.[28]

27. In early-nineteenth-century America, I believe, geographic literacy closed the gap that according to Jürgen Habermas existed between the state and society by linking the individual anonymity afforded by print with the material signifiers of self-made maps and map-writings. See *The Structural Transformation of the Public Sphere: An Inquiry into a Category of Bourgeois Society,* trans. Thomas Burger and Frederick Lawrence (Cambridge, Mass., 1991), 1–56. For similar reasons, my argument at once expands from and complicates Benedict Anderson's claim that "language had never been an issue in the American nationalist movements." See *Imagined Communities: Reflections on the Origin and Spread of Nationalism* (London, 1991), 196–197.

For studies arguing in this vein of a "republican empire," see Peter S. Onuf, *Jefferson's Empire: The Language of American Nationhood* (Charlottesville, Va., 2000); James C. Scott, *Seeing like a State: How Certain Schemes to Improve the Human Condition Have Failed* (New Haven, Conn., 1998).

28. "Art. X," *Literary and Scientific Repository,* II (1821), 210–212.

Education, 10–11, 142–143; and geography, in eighteenth century, 8–12, 90–92, 95, 137–139, 142–143, 149–163; and geography, in seventeenth century, 9–10; and surveying, 26–29; of George Washington, 43; and child psychology, 120; and pictures, 138, 159–161; and writing instruction, 151–153, 253; and word versus image, 155–157, 246–248, 253; and territorialism, 241, 243, 249; and geography, in nineteenth century, 243–250; and monitorial system, 249–250. *See also* Brown, Charles Brockden; Geography textbooks; Language; Literacy; Pedagogy

Elements of Geography (Morse), 147, 155, 157–158

Elements of Geography (Worcester), 251–252

Elements of Geography (Workman), 147

Elites, 8, 11–12, 79, 96, 229n. 32

Elizabeth I, 8

Elocution, 52–53, 65–68. *See also* Rhetoric

Embree, Thomas, 101

Emerson, Ralph Waldo, 195n. 32

Empire: and British America, 8, 21–23, 56, 96; and United States, 188, 194–195, 206, 238, 240, 244, 260–263. *See also* Identity; Republicanism

Emplacement: and surveying, 37–38, 45; and handwriting, 152–153. *See also* Identity

Encyclopedias, geographic, 153–155

Enlightenment: and encyclopedic mentality, 154

Environmental determinism, 5n. 1, 71, 77–78; and geography textbooks, 165–170

Epistemology. *See* Language; Representation

Erdrich, Louise, 231

Estate maps, 20–21

Evans, Lewis, 30, 132

Ewing, James, 101

Expansionism, 204–209; and aesthetics, 15, 238–240, 257–259; and colonial advocates, 96. *See also* Empire; Territorialism

Faden, William, 76n. 22

Federalist Papers, The, 98–99, 130–131, 171

Federalists, 98–101

Ferguson, Robert A., 100

Fern, Fanny, 245n. 8

Fichte, Johann Gottlieb, 119

Filson, John, 144–145

Fisher, George, 107

Floyd, Charles, 215

Fortune's Football (Butler), 179, 181–184

Foucault, Michel, 223

Franklin, Benjamin, 24–25, 57, 96, 146

Franklin, Mary, 138

Frontiers. *See* Borders and boundaries

Gadsden, Christopher, 51, 96

Games, 58, 123, 125, 181–182. *See also* Education

Gass, Patrick, 215, 236

Gender and geography, 40–41. *See also* Material culture; Sentimental objects

Genre of geography, 4, 13, 243–244; and oratory, 15; and textbooks, 15, 145–146, 149–158, 246; and novels, 15, 174–177. *See also* Book history; Geography; Maps; Surveying

Genre paintings, 122–123, 170. *See also* Earl, Ralph; Krimmel, John Lewis; Morse, Samuel F. B.; Portraits

Gentility, 122–123, 158. *See also* Material culture

Geodaesia; or, The Art of Surveying (Love), 27–35; popularity of, 27–28, 45

Geodesy, 17; and language, 18; and writing, 19, 25–29, 43–44; and aesthetics, 32–34, 38, 44–45, 50. *See also* Surveying

Geographical, Historical, Political, Philosophical, and Mechanical Essays (Evans), 30, 132

Geographical Copy Book, The (Woodbridge and Willard), 253

134–141; and literacy, 240. *See also* Geography textbooks

National maps: and linguistics, 100; and orality, 105–106; in the United States, 116–120, 121–129; and meridian, 118; early modern history of, 120; circulation of, 121–124; and material culture, 121–124, 126, 140; and aesthetics, 124–130, 239; and ambiguity, 130; as logo, 134–141; and needlework, 137–139; as sentimental objects, 137–141; and expansionism, 239, 250–251, 257–259. *See also* Atlas; Maps; Morse, Jedidiah

Nation building, 8, 14–15; and geographic aesthetic, 88–89; and language, 98–100, 170–171; and alphabet, in United States, 101–103. *See also* Maps

Nation-state: and planning mentality, 20–22; and maps, 100, 116–118; and United States, 101n. 5; and iconography, 117; and Louisiana Territory, 204–206, 211, 232; plasticity of, 250–251. *See also* Anderson, Benedict; Giddens, Anthony

Native Americans, 208–209, 215, 223, 226, 230, 241; and surveying, 48; and plat, 48, 49n. 35; and mapmaking, 49n. 35, 209, 223–225; allegorical figure of, 55, 61–62; and cartography, 65–73, 211, 223–226; and eloquence, 70–71, 73; and geographic authorship, 209, 222–226; and liminality, 226; and erasure, 257–258

Natural history, genre of, 144–145

Needlework, 137–139

Nelson, Dana D., 242

New Guide to the English Language, A (Dilworth), 104–105

New Map of North America, A (Wells), 82–83

New Plain and Easy Set of Geographical Running Hand, A (Reed), 261

New System of Modern Geography, A (Guthrie), 163

New-York Magazine, 173

Nez Percé, 230

Niles' Weekly Register, 250, 262

Notes on the State of Virginia (Jefferson), 132–134, 144–145, 213

Novelization, 163–170, 181n. 3

Novels, 173–184, 189–203; early American, 173–177; and identity, 173–177; and landscape, 174–176; and spatialization, 175–177; and geographical feeling, 176; and homeland, 176; and characters, 176, 177–184, 189–203; and picaresque, 177–184; and geographic literacy, 177–184, 189–203; and domesticity, 183–184

"On the Education of Youth in America" (Webster), 142–143

Orality, 70–71, 101–107; and print, 74n. 20, 80; and geographic literacy, 104–106, 148–153. *See also* Rhetoric

Oratory, 51–52; and colonial characters, 53; and map talk, 60–61; and class, 79; and geographical knowledge, 90–97. *See also* Blair, Hugh; Elocution; Rhetoric; Rice, John

Ordway, John, 215

Ortelius, Abraham, 120

Otis, James, 54, 76, 79–80, 96

Paine, Thomas, 80, 91–95

Parliament, British: and land charters, 16; and colonial representation, 75

Participatory culture, 141, 237, 263

Patriotism. *See* Sensibility

Pedagogy: and geography, 85, 124–125, 135–139, 155–156, 243, 246–250, 252–256; and orality, 101–107; and pronouncing form method, 102, 260; and nationalism, 103–105, 247; visual, 107–110; and object-learning, 248. *See also* Education; Locke, John; Morse, Jedidiah

Penmanship. *See* Handwriting; Washington, George

Pennsylvania Magazine, 27, 124, 162–163

Performance, 67, 79

Personification, 55; and North American continent, 92–97. *See also* Characters; National character

Typing, 170. *See also* Characters; Genre paintings; Regionalism

Uncle's Present, The (anon.), 113
United States according to the Definitive Treaty of Peace, The (McMurray), 135–136
Universal languages, 66, 108, 223; and hand signs, 66–67; and revolutions, 108

Vico, Giambattista, 168
Vindication of the British Colonies, A (Otis), 79–80
Visible World; or, A Picture and Nomenclature (Comenius), 108–110
Voice: of Americans, 52–55, 62; and silence, 63, 68, 228–229; and distance, 78–79, 92; and unity, 79; of America, 80; and sovereignty, 94–96

Wallis, John, 141n. 42
Wall maps, 57, 65, 123, 135. *See also* Material culture
Ward, John, 93n. 37
Washington, George, 19, 42–45
Watts, Isaac, 88–90
Webster, Noah, 102–107, 142–143, 169, 171, 176, 260–261

Weed, Enos, 107
Weekly Magazine (Brown), 185
Wells, Edward, 82–83
Wells, Richard, 54, 92
Willard, Emma, 243, 246, 247n. 10, 252–253
Williams, Samuel, 90–91
Williams, Stephen, 26
Williams, William Appleman, 240
Winthrop, James, 131–132
Witherspoon, John, 102
Wittgenstein, Ludwig, 12
Women: role of, in literacy instruction, 112, 161–162. *See also* Brown, Charles Brockden; Education; Gender and geography; Geographic literacy; Ripley, Sally; Rowson, Susanna; Willard, Emma
Woodbridge, William, 243, 246, 248, 252–256
Worcester, Joseph, 251
Word maps, 114–116, 130–131. *See also* Geography textbooks; Morse, Jedidiah
Workman, Benjamin, 147
Writing. *See* Cartography; Education; Geography; Literacy; Surveying

Zubly, John, 78n. 26, 90